Blessed Christmas — and '07

Dear Larry Dear Joyce —

Memories of past with dear
Norman Rockwell

Marie Archie

Thank You for Your Friendship

Simple Acts of Faith

Heartwarming Stories of One Life Touching Another

NORMAN ROCKWELL

Text by Margaret Feinberg

HARVEST HOUSE™ PUBLISHERS

EUGENE, OREGON

Simple Acts of Faith
Text Copyright © 2003 by Margaret Feinberg
Published by Harvest House Publishers
Eugene, Oregon 97402

Library of Congress Cataloging-in-Publication Data
    Feinberg, Margaret, 1974–
        Simple acts of faith / paintings by Norman Rockwell ; text by Margaret Feinberg.
           p. cm.
        ISBN 0-7369-1073-5 (alk. paper)
        1. Christian life—Miscellanea. 2. Kindness—Religious aspects—Christianity—Miscellanea.
    I. Rockwell, Norman, 1894–1978. II. Title.
        BV4513.F45 2003
        242—dc21   2003001825

The author, Margaret Feinberg, can be reached at P.O. Box 2981, Sitka, AK 99835 or by emailing mafeinberg@juno.com.

Artwork and Compilation of Artwork Copyright © 2003 by the Norman Rockwell Family Entities. Reproduced by the permission of the Norman Rockwell Family Agency Inc. "Family Grace" and "A Scout Is Helpful" appear courtesy of the Collection of The Norman Rockwell Museum at Stockbridge. All other images appear courtesy of the Curtis Publishing Company.

Design and Production by Koechel Peterson & Associates, Inc., Minneapolis, Minnesota.

Scripture quotations are from: *The Living Bible*, Copyright © 1971. Used by permission of Tyndale House Publishers, Inc., Wheaton, Illinois 60189. All rights reserved; and the Holy Bible: New International Version®. NIV®. Copyright © 1973, 1978, 1984 by the International Bible Society. Used by permission of Zondervan Publishing House.

Printed in Hong Kong.

05 06 07 08 09 10 11 12 / NG / 10 9 8 7 6

●

Life is made up not of great sacrifices or duties,

but of little things,

in which smiles and kindness and small obligations,

given habitually,

are what win and preserve the heart.

SIR HUMPHREY DAVY

●

A Boy and His Bike

No act of kindness, no matter how small, is ever wasted.
AESOP

•

In a suburb of Dallas known as Richardson, a small, bright-eyed gentleman named Jim Hoyt manages his own bike store. The mom-and-pop shop, Richardson Bike Mart, is known throughout the community as a strong sponsor of bike racers, and Hoyt maintains a personal passion to help kids get started in the sport.

Keeping an eye on the street front, Jim noticed a young woman who faithfully took her son to a nearby shop for fresh doughnuts each week. He began talking to the woman, discovered she was a single mom, and instinctively knew she was struggling to get by. Jim took an interest in the small family and decided to give the woman a discount on a bicycle: a Schwinn Mag Scrambler. The mom accepted the offer, and through the kind act of a stranger, seven-year-old Lance Armstrong was introduced to the world of biking. Describing the bike, Armstrong writes, "It was an ugly brown with yellow wheels, but I loved it. Why does any kid love a bike? It's liberation and independence, your first set of wheels."

Armstrong would go on to set an unprecedented record of winning the gruesome Tour de France multiple times, and in 1996 he established the Lance Armstrong Foundation, a charity to aid the fight against cancer.

And whatever you do, do it with kindness and love.
THE BOOK OF FIRST CORINTHIANS

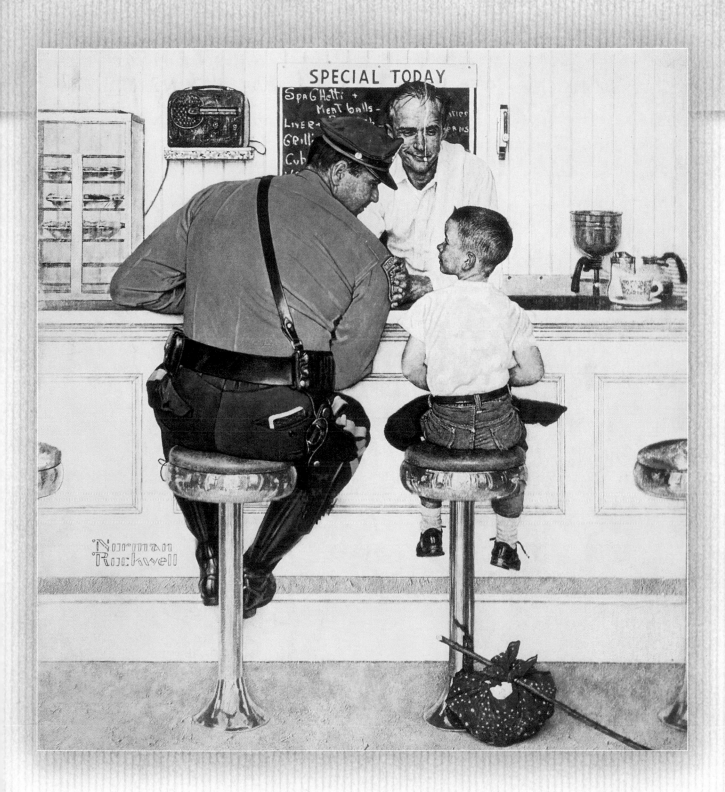

SPECIAL TODAY

SpaGHetti +
MeaT balls
LiveR
GRilli
Cub

Norman
Rockwell

Norman Rockwell

Just Say Hello

It's not the years in your life that count, it's the life in your years.
ABRAHAM LINCOLN

•

More than anything, Sam wanted to become the president of the university's student body. He learned early on that the secret to campus leadership required the simplest act: Speak to those coming down the sidewalk before they speak to you.

Sam did it all the time. Whether he was carrying books, papers, or merely taking a stroll, he would keep one eye on the person coming toward him. If he knew the person's name, he would call it out. If not, he'd still speak to them. Before long, he knew more students than anyone in the university, and many recognized him and considered him a friend.

He not only became president of the student body but president of the senior men's honor society, an officer in his fraternity, and president of the senior class.

An article in his fraternity newspaper described, "Sam is one of those rare people who knows every janitor by name, passes plates in church, and loves to join organizations."

Indeed, his secret weapon was simply being friendly, and it's one that carried Sam Walton far, if not to the top of the business world.

Greet each other warmly in the Lord.
THE BOOK OF SECOND CORINTHIANS

A Reservoir of Love

We make a living by what we get, but we make a life by what we give!
WINSTON CHURCHILL

•

Few roles afford someone the opportunity to shape and impact a human life quite like being a parent. Elizabeth Everest never had that privilege. Born into humble means, Elizabeth became a nurse and nanny rather than a wife and mother. She looked after the small daughter of a clergyman before accepting the role of caring for an infant named Winston. Eventually, a little brother named Jack arrived.

Though she had few material possessions to share with the boys, she gave them a priceless treasure: her love. She poured her gift of storytelling on them. She painted wild imaginary pictures with words and told cliffhanging tales. She cared for the boys during the trials of adolescence and the tribulation of puberty. She continually shared from her reservoir of love, affection, and nurturing grace with wholehearted abandon.

Elizabeth Everest died in 1895. She never knew the impact she inadvertently had on the young man and on the course of history. The child she nurtured eventually grew up to be Winston Churchill, the prime minister of England who bravely led his nation through the turbulent years of World War II. One woman's love helped shape one of the greatest leaders of all time.

My power shows up best in weak people.
THE BOOK OF SECOND CORINTHIANS

Saint Jean

We are cups, constantly and quietly being filled. The trick is knowing how to tip ourselves over and let the Beautiful Stuff out.

RAY BRADBURY

•

Nearly 20 years ago, Jean Webster was heading to work when she saw a man digging through an old dumpster for food. Moved by the scene, she bought the alcoholic a cheeseburger and invited him to her home after work for a full meal. She told the man named John he was welcome to stop by every day for food, and he did. Before long, he wasn't alone. John's friends began tagging along, and before Jean knew it, she had a line of hungry people waiting outside her door.

Each day, Webster made sure everyone—even when the tally reached into the hundreds—had something to eat. She served the downtrodden out of her own pocket, by herself, often sacrificing the money for her own heart medicine to buy food.

After 15 years, the news of Webster's service spread, and the leaders of several area churches founded The Friends of Jean Webster. A commercial kitchen was built in an old church, and countless volunteers were inspired to serve because of one woman's compassion toward the homeless. Today, the 67-year-old African American, known as "Saint Jean" to the community, still serves meals to more than 600 people five mornings a week.

Happy is the generous man, the one who feeds the poor.
THE BOOK OF PROVERBS

An Unexpected Question

*Treat people as if they were what they ought to be, and you help them
to become what they are capable of being.*
JOHANN WOLFGANG VON GOETHE

•

An injury at birth and the medical problems that followed left little Frank with a defect known as cystic hygroma. Complications following surgery left the young child with a tongue that hung out of his mouth oozing a bloody black residue.

On the first day of school, Frank discovered he didn't look like the other kids, and the children never stopped reminding him of this cruel truth. The young boy passed from grade to grade teased, mocked, and tormented by his peers. Though surgeries repaired the disfiguration, they couldn't heal the silent wounds.

One day a gym teacher randomly asked Frank an unexpected question: "How are you doing? You feeling okay?" Something in the tone of the voice told him that this adult actually might care. Instead of answering, Frank chose to write down his experience. He recounted the years of abuse from his peers and described the torment taking place in the school's locker room.

The teacher not only read the letter; he responded. Frank was dismissed from gym class and any further locker room abuse. From that day on, Frank's life was different. He could pursue the activities he enjoyed and discover his talents. One teacher's act of intervention opened a world of opportunity for this youth to learn and grow.

That young man is now older, wiser, and a little more widely known. You may have even read one of his books: *This Present Darkness, Piercing the Darkness* or *The Oath*. Today, Frank Peretti is a bestselling author with more than nine million books in print.

One at a Time

Character may be manifested in the great moments, but it is made in the small ones.
PHILLIP BROOKS

•

Whether from a near or distant coast, I do not know, but there's a tale of a young boy who walked along the beach of his native shore looking for starfish. He slowly approached each one, trapped in the hot sun by receding tides, and carefully pried away its legs from any rocks before tossing it back into the sea. Under his tender, daily care hundreds of starfish returned to the water.

One day an older man walked upon the shore. He watched the young boy's careful, repetitive ritual for some time before approaching him.

"Why do you throw the starfish back into the sea?" the old man inquired.

"Because the starfish will die if left in the hot sun on the shore," the boy explained.

"But there are millions of starfish," the old man contended. "And there are a multitude of shores with countless beaches upon which you will never walk. On each of those beaches are throngs of starfish which you will never save. Why do you bother?"

The boy looked down at the sand beneath his feet. Then he reached down and picked up one of the colorful, pointed creatures.

"Because today, this day, this one will live," the boy replied, throwing the starfish back into the sea.

The man watched in disbelief as the boy continued his rote practice.

The old man reflected for some time, then he reached down, picked up a starfish, and threw it into the sea.

14

Norman Rockwell

The Dictionary Project

If we all did the things we are capable of doing, we would literally astound ourselves.
THOMAS EDISON

•

Nearly eight years ago, Mary French was sitting in her Charleston, South Carolina home reading a newspaper when she stumbled upon a letter to the editor asking for someone to start a dictionary project in the county. Mary responded with a letter saying she was interested in getting involved; she began writing letters to local businesses asking for funds to buy dictionaries for local elementary children.

In her first year, she handed out 6,000 dictionaries. Now Mary French distributes more than 500,000 each year. The Dictionary Project is in the process of distributing a dictionary to every third grade school student in South Carolina for the fourth year in a row, and it has expanded into 35 other states.

The idea for The Dictionary Project began with Annie Plummer, an African American woman who worked as a cleaning lady and crossing guard. She was familiar with the hardships of life due to a limited education. She decided that if somehow she could get a dictionary into the hands of children, it would make an impact in their education and their communities.

Today, the idea of this woman, who never graduated from high school, is a national mission.

The Real Winner

The greatest love is shown when a person lays down his life for his friends.
THE BOOK OF JOHN

•

It was an Olympic moment. Nine competitors lined up on the precisely painted white lines waiting for the start of the race. The gun cracked and the competitors headed toward their destiny. The 100-yard dash is only a flash of a moment in time, but it somehow paused when one of the racers stumbled and fell. His knee felt the crushing pain, and his heart was punctured by disappointment. He couldn't hold back the emotion. Large warm tears rolled down his face. The other competitors could hear his cries. One by one, they stopped, turned around, and ran back to the young competitor.

One of the Special Olympians, a girl with Down's Syndrome, said, "This will make it better," and leaned down and tenderly kissed the boy. The boy returned to his feet, and, linking arms with the rest of the runners, they joyfully walked to the finish together.

As they crossed the finish line, the entire stadium stood to their feet echoing a long ovation, as everyone involved was reminded that helping others win in this life is more important than winning for oneself.

To me it seems that to give happiness is a far nobler goal than to attain it: much more a matter of helping others to heaven than of getting there ourselves.
LEWIS CARROLL

Norman Rockwell

A Small, Furry Gift

Whatever you are, be a good one.
ABRAHAM LINCOLN

•

In the 1920s, a kindergarten teacher told one of her students, "Some day, you are going to be an artist." Her prophecy came true. The boy was Charles Schulz.

As a child, Schulz had a fascination with popular comics including *Popeye* and characters created by Walt Disney. After seeing an ad that asked, "Do you like to draw?" Schulz began studying art and eventually published his panel cartoon *Li'l Folks* in the *St. Paul Pioneer Press*. After multiple rejections, the artist finally sold the strip to the United Feature Syndicate, which renamed the comic strip *Peanuts*.

On October 2, 1950, *Peanuts* debuted in seven news-papers. By 1999, it was syndicated in more than 2,600 newspapers worldwide. Schulz was given the Reuben Award, comic art's highest honor, twice and named International Cartoonist of the Year in 1978.

Though favorite characters from the comic strip are still debated among fans, one of the most loved is Snoopy. Interestingly, the inspiration for this colorful character was from a dog given to the Schulz family when Charles was only a child. The sketch of the dog became the artist's first published drawing and eventually became known to the world as Snoopy. A small, furry gift became the stimulus for one of the most popular cartoon dogs in history.

If I were given the opportunity to present a gift to the next generation, it would be the ability for each individual to learn to laugh at himself.
CHARLES SCHULZ

Share the Light

One of the greatest discoveries a man makes, one of his great surprises,
is to find he can do what he was afraid he couldn't do.
HENRY FORD

•

Edward Kimble couldn't resist the quiet but persistent nudge inside his soul. His mind told him he would look like a fool, but his spirit gently reminded him that something greater was at stake. He walked into the shoe store and struck up a conversation with the salesman. Before they finished talking, Kimble shared his faith and the man became a believer.

The shoe salesman's name: Dwight L. Moody. He became one of the most widespread and popular evangelists of his generation.

Moody's contagious message of faith spread across continents and reached the ears of Frederick B. Meyer, a pastor and author, who was inspired to become an evangelist. Meyer reached large audiences, one of which included a university student named Wilbur Chapman who helped spread the gospel. Chapman eventually employed a baseball player named Billy Sunday to conduct an evangelistic crusade.

Years passed and Sunday was invited to hold his own evangelistic meetings in Charlotte, North Carolina. The meetings went well, and another evangelist, Mordecai Ham, was asked to hold another crusade. A few came forward, including one rather tall, young man. You may have heard of him. His name is Billy Graham.

One man's act of faith started a chain reaction that resulted in the good news being spread around the globe.

And be sure of this—that I am with you always, even to the end of the world.
THE BOOK OF MATTHEW

22

Simple Acts

*When we do the best that we can, we never know what miracle
is wrought in our life, or in the life of another.*
HELEN KELLER

•

Jay Kesler was working at a Youth For Christ Camp when a young woman pulled him aside to share her story. Sitting in the chapel, she began to retell her stories of mistreatment as a child. Her father had sexually abused her several times a week since she was four years old, and a sense of guilt and shame plagued her life.

Looking at the young woman's hands, Jay noticed scars lining each of her wrists.

He decided to press the subject, "Why didn't you do it?"

Her answer surprised him.

She said she had been watching a recently married youth pastor at her church. She noted the ways he tenderly and lovingly responded to his wife. When they were standing in line at church, he would squeeze her right hand. When they were beside each other at service, they would take a moment to hug. One day, when no one was around, she watched the youth pastor open the car door for his wife before getting in.

They were small gestures, hardly noticed by anyone, but they ministered hope and healing to this woman. Through the quiet acts of love between this man and his wife, this peering stranger recognized that not all men were abusive like her father.

That night, she became a Christian.

You are the world's light—a city on a hill, glowing in the night for all to see.
THE BOOK OF MATTHEW

God's Gift

Be completely humble and gentle; be patient, bearing with one another in love.
THE BOOK OF EPHESIANS

•

Walter was one of those people who felt so out of place all the time that he actually made everyone else feel awkward, too. Rather than brighten up a room with his presence, he silently cast a shadow. His appearance was sloppy, dated, and mismatched. He made unnecessary and sometimes downright inappropriate comments. His jokes weren't funny. He even smelled bad. And while his intentions were generally good, he had a knack for delivering blindsided comments that cut you to the core.

Walter was a regular attendee of our prayer group, and quietly every member struggled with his presence.

It became a personal relief when Walter missed a meeting. His odd personality didn't fit into the prayer group except for one factor: He loved Jesus. And that made him part of the body of Christ whether we liked it or not.

Eventually everyone began to pray for Walter. At the end of a year, there was little noticeable change in Walter. The biggest changes came within each of us. We realized Walter was actually a gift from God to help mature each of us. God used a disheveled man to reveal our own unkempt attitudes and call us closer to Himself.

"For I know the plans I have for you," says the Lord. "They are plans for good and not for evil, to give you a future and a hope."
THE BOOK OF JEREMIAH

27

Love Your Enemies

Be gentle and ready to forgive; never hold grudges.
THE BOOK OF COLOSSIANS

•

In 1956, a small group of missionaries, including Nate Saint, Jim Elliot, Roger Youderian, Ed McCully, and Peter Fleming, were part of a historic journey to meet the Aucas or "naked savages" (as the tribe was then known) in the jungles of Ecuador.

The Aucas were renowned for their high homicide rate, so the missionaries spent months preparing for the visit. They flew over the area and dropped gifts and supplies in order to develop a good rapport. They were hopeful their efforts would help connect the isolated group to the outside world that was clashing with them and, more importantly, the gospel.

Upon landing, the five missionaries were killed by the tribesmen. The dramatic story quickly spread through articles appearing in popular magazines, including *Life* and *Reader's Digest*. But the story didn't end on that fateful day almost a half century ago. In fact, it was just the beginning.

Rather than harbor bitterness and resentment, the missionary families offered one of the most powerful acts of faith: forgiveness. Within three years of the killings, Nate Saint's sister Rachel Saint, and Elisabeth Elliot, widow of Jim Elliot, moved to the rain forest to live with the tribe. Slowly, many of the tribesmen in the contact group converted to Christianity—including those who had killed the missionaries.

Today, the Waodani, or "the people" as they call themselves, are known as a peaceful community free of the violent and murderous stigma that plagued them for years.

Never Give Up

Don't be weary in prayer; keep at it; watch for God's answers...
THE BOOK OF COLOSSIANS

•

Most had given up on Aurelius. The rebellious teenager rejected his devoted mother's teachings of faith and thrust himself headfirst into promiscuity. By the age of 18, he was a father, but rather than marry the young woman, he decided to keep her on the side as a mistress.

During his twenties, he wrote a small handful of books but spent his free time in the theater and debating academic issues. Guiltless immorality permeated his life. He was as far away from God as one could imagine, but his godly, praying mother Monica refused to give up hope. She continued praying. Eventually, Aurelius had a revelation of truth. He returned to the faith and dedicated his life to the priesthood.

Due to the residual affects of one mother's prayer, Aurelius not only changed his heart, but he changed history as well. Today, we know Aurelius Augustinus, the bishop of the North African city of Hippo, simply as Saint Augustine, a church father whose book, *The City of God*, proved a powerful defense of the faith, and whose works are among the most widely read in the world.

Now faith is being sure of what we hope for and certain of what we do not see.
THE BOOK OF HEBREWS

Norman Rockwell

The Gift of Mercy

Giving is the secret of a healthy life. Not necessarily money, but whatever a man has of encouragement and sympathy and understanding.

JOHN D. ROCKEFELLER, JR.

•

In 1902, Theodore Roosevelt went on a hunting trip in Mississippi. Nearing the end of the hunt, the president was faced with the prospect of going home empty handed. In an effort to ease the president's disappointment and boost his ego, well-meaning guides captured a large female bear and suggested he shoot it.

In an act of mercy and compassion, Roosevelt refused. He would rather go home without a trophy than take the bear's life.

The humane gesture captured the imagination of cartoonist Clifford Berryman, who published a cartoon titled "Drawing the Line in Mississippi" on November 16, 1902. It displayed the president preserving the life of a bear cub. The widely reprinted cartoon inspired two candy store owners in New York to sew a stuffed bear and call it "Teddy's Bear." The lovable, huggable stuffed toy known as the teddy bear became a national craze.

Roosevelt never lived to see the full impact of his small act of mercy. A hundred years later, teddy bears are the most popular of all plush toys and are estimated to be half of the United States' multibillion dollar plush toy industry. Their warm, cute faces are still used to bring comfort and encouragement during our nation's most challenging moments, including the events of September 11.

No Matter the Cost

Hope is the companion of power and mother of success;
for whoso hopes strongly has within him the gift of miracles.
SAMUEL SMILES

•

DeWitt Wallace, a pastor's son from St. Paul, Minnesota, developed a unique idea for a magazine. It would contain 31 condensed articles of interest and value (one for every day of the month) from leading magazines. Instead of advertising, the publication would rely on circulation for support.

He submitted the magazine proposal to major publishers around the nation and even to some lesser ones. In the end, all rejected the idea. Even the famed publisher William Randolph Hearst turned down the idea, with a note that explained that the magazine could only hope for a circulation of 300,000—a size too small to concern his company.

As the rejection notices piled up, Wallace grew more and more discouraged and even sank into depression. But one voice, his new wife, Lila, believed the idea was "gorgeous." She supported the couple and the fledging magazine on her income for more than two years. When Wallace wanted to quit, Lila persisted. She faithfully stood by his side, and her support as a loving wife helped launch one of the most successful publications of all time: *Reader's Digest.*

If you love someone, you will be loyal to him no matter what the cost. You will always believe
in him, always expect the best of him, and always stand your ground in defending him.
THE BOOK OF FIRST CORINTHIANS

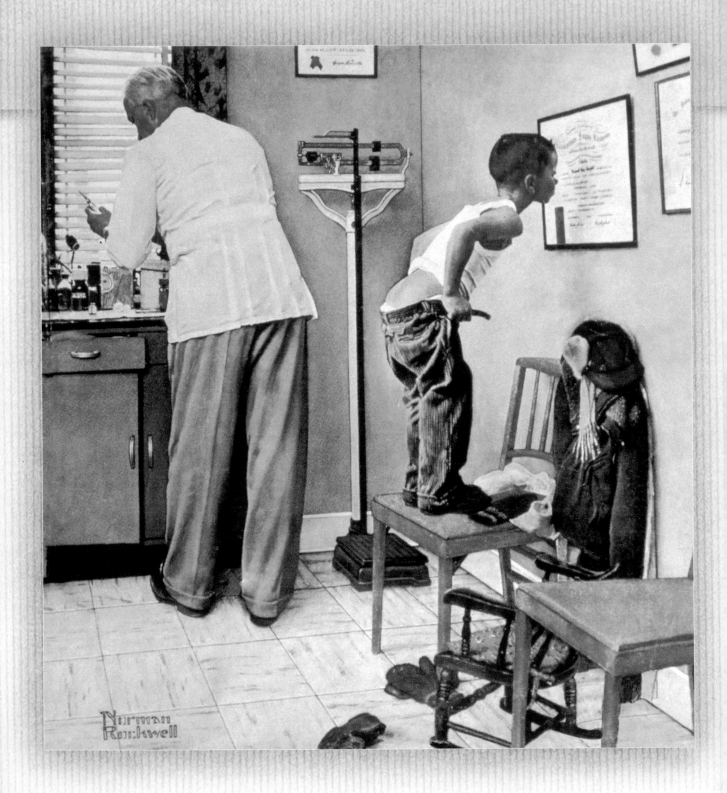

All the Difference

God has given us two hands—one to receive with and the other to give with.
BILLY GRAHAM

•

The man faced the prospect of open heart surgery with an uncomfortable blend of concern and fear. The day before the scheduled operation, a nurse walked into the man's hospital room and grabbed his hand. She asked him to do something a little odd: Take her hand and hold it. The man agreed to the strange but pleasant request, noting the size of her palm and fingers.

Then she explained.

During the surgery, the man's heart would be disconnected from his body, and machines would keep him alive. Following the operation, he could expect to wake up in a specially designed recovery room, but for up to six hours, the man would be completely immobile. Though unable to communicate or move, he would be consciously aware of everything going on around him. During those hours, the nurse promised, she would be sitting beside him, holding his hand exactly as she was now. The nurse solemnly promised to remain with him until he recovered.

The operation went well, and when the man awoke, he could feel the nurse's hand. She held it for hours. Reflecting on the experience, the man says this one act of comfort—holding his hand—made all the difference.

For God has said, "I will never, never fail you nor forsake you."
THE BOOK OF HEBREWS

One Simple Question

If it's nothing more than a smile—give that away and keep on giving it.
BETH BROWN

•

With a tall but unassuming frame, jolly belly, and whips of graying hair, Dr. Fred Horton looks more like Santa Claus than a typical college professor. But don't let the nonpretentious, gregarious Episcopalian priest fool you. As former head of the Religion Department at Wake Forest University, Dr. Horton is an accomplished and well-respected John Thomas Albritton Professor of the Bible.

There are two things I remember from the fateful moment I met Dr. Horton: First, despite all the chaos of electronic equipment, books, and ungraded papers, I did not doubt for one millisecond Dr. Horton could locate anything in that office at a moment's notice. Second, I remember him asking the most common question and really meaning it: "How are you doing?"

I tried to squeeze by with a quick knee-jerk response of "fine" and move on to other topics, but he insisted I have a seat (after clearing off the chair) and offer some detailed response. I sat for a few moments, gushing in less than eloquent terms the excitement and fear of being a college freshman. We talked for some time, and he ended the exchange, "Come back anytime...even just to talk."

I accepted the invitation.

In fact, I returned so many times, I eventually became a religion major. Dr. Horton became both a mentor and friend. I learned volumes from this man, but the greatest lesson I learned was the importance of loving others, most of which can be summed up in one question, "How are you doing?"

Norman Rockwell

Just As I Am

Let your lives overflow with joy and thanksgiving for all he has done.
THE BOOK OF COLOSSIANS

•

Sometimes golden nuggets of wisdom land in our palms at the oddest times. I was sitting at my father's sixtieth birthday party reminiscing with old friends when the conversation slowly drifted toward religious matters. A married man shared with me how he had felt led to begin each morning with a simple prayer, "Thank You, God, for my wife." After praying this for several months, he felt led to expand the prayer to "Thank You, God, for my wife, just as she is."

He commented on how the small addition "just as she is" made such a difference in his heart. The conversation drifted to other issues, but after the party ended the little prayer swirled in my mind. I began to offer similar prayers to God. "Thank You, God, for my life, just as it is." "Thank You, God, for my family, just as they are." "Thank You, God, for my job, just as it is." As I tagged on a four-word admonition of gratitude to my prayers, my demeanor began to change.

Since that fateful day, I've found myself more grateful for the little things and more accepting of other people and life's circumstances. Even when the nights are long and the days are tough, I am thankful to God and somehow that little acknowledgment—a simple act of faith—makes everything better.

One Man's Problem

I have held many things in my hands, and have lost them all;
but whatever I have placed in God's hands, that I still possess.
MARTIN LUTHER

•

Frustration led Sean Milliken to look for an alternative. As a development executive at the Boys and Girls Club of Metro Atlanta, he was tired of having to say "no" to many well-meaning donors who wanted to give nonfinancial gifts that don't meet the mission of the nonprofit organization.

He decided to do something about the quagmire and developed the nonprofit organization MissionFish (www.missionfish.com) in Arlington, Virginia. The online auction allows anyone to donate items—of any size and value—and the cash from the sale will go to the nonprofit of the donor's choice. The website helps turn donated goods into a revenue stream. Items for sale include antiques, sports memorabilia, artwork, and vacation packages.

With more than 300 nonprofits joining the MissionFish community, the site has raised funds for a long list of organizations including the Alzheimer's Association, the American Cancer Society, Boys and Girls Clubs, Farm Aid, and St. Jude Children's Research Hospital. Because of one man's innovative search for a solution, hundreds of thousands of dollars have been raised for charity organizations.

One Mother's Prayer

The earnest prayer of a righteous man has great power and wonderful results.
THE BOOK OF JAMES

•

When the Valdés family fled Cuba in 1966, ten-year-old Jorge arrived in Miami to a host of financial and emotional challenges. It didn't take the child long to learn the power of money, and he quickly turned his back on the basic values and faith of his family. Before he fully understood what he had become involved in, Jorge Valdés was part of a cocaine empire known as the Medellin Drug Cartel, eventually becoming the key leader in the United States. Though he never killed anyone directly, he was indirectly responsible for the death and destruction of countless lives through the drugs he sold.

During this time his mother never quit praying for him. Eventually, Valdés met Jesus Christ. The former cartel member used his time in prison to earn a bachelor's degree. He also earned a master's degree from Wheaton College and eventually earned a Ph.D. in New Testament Studies. He is founder of Coming Clean Ministries, which is committed to helping young people who are on destructive paths redirect their lives and become contributing members of society. Because of one mother's refusal to give up on her son, Jorge Valdés is a powerful reminder that no one is beyond redemption.

For nothing is impossible with God.
THE BOOK OF LUKE

45

Norman Rockwell

The Little Things

If you have only one smile in you, give it to the people you love. Don't be surly at home, then go out in the street and start grinning "Good morning" at total strangers.

MAYA ANGELOU

•

Bible teacher Joyce Meyer tells a poignant story of service in her book *Help Me, I'm Married!* She says that some days God tells her to serve her husband, Dave, and in her heart, she really doesn't want to.

Waking up one morning, she went downstairs to brew a pot of coffee. All she wanted to do was quietly return to her room and spend time with God praying, but she felt an unmistakable nudge of the Holy Spirit encouraging her to make a fruit salad for her husband.

She knew how her husband loved to eat fruit salad for breakfast. It was a simple request, but she didn't want to do it.

Joyce resisted the quiet nudge, responding, "I don't want to—I want to go pray." At that moment, she felt the Lord respond, "Joyce, serving Dave is serving Me."

So, she made the fruit salad and was reminded that the little things we do don't just bless others, they also bless God.

Dear friends, let us practice loving each other, for love comes from God and those who are loving and kind show that they are the children of God, and that they are getting to know him better.

THE BOOK OF FIRST JOHN

Notes

"A Boy and His Bike," quote by Lance Armstrong is taken from *It's Not About the Bike* by Lance Armstrong (New York, NY: Berkley Books, 2001), p. 19. Used by permission of the publisher.

"Just Say Hello" is adapted from *Sam Walton: Made in America* by Sam Walton (New York, NY: Doubleday, 1992), p. 15.

"Saint Jean" is adapted from "Comfort Foods" by Frank Rubino, *Hope Magazine* (September/October 2002), p. 7. Used by permission of the author. For more information, please visit www.Hopemag.com.

"An Unexpected Question" is adapted from "Frank Peretti" by Margaret Feinberg, *New Man Magazine* (March/April 2001), pp. 27–28. Used by permission of the publisher.

"The Dictionary Project" is adapted from interviews with Mary French.

"The Real Winner" is adapted from a 2002 commencement address given by Fred Rogers at Catham College.

"Share the Light" is adapted from *A Passion for God* by Greg Laurie (Eugene, OR: Harvest House Publishers, 1998). Used by permission of the publisher.

"Simple Acts" is adapted from *Ten Mistakes Parents Make with Teenagers* by Jay Kesler (Brentwood, TN: Wolgemuth & Hyatt Publishers, Inc., 1988), pp. 29–30. Used by permission of the author.

"Love Your Enemies" is adapted from "Steve Saint: In My Father's Footsteps" by Margaret Feinberg, *New Man Magazine* (September/October 2001), pp. 41–43. Used by permission of the publisher.

"No Matter the Cost" is adapted from *Words to Die For* by Lawrence Kimbrough (Nashville: Broadman & Holman, 2002), pp. 15–20. Used by permission of the publisher.

"All the Difference" is adapted from *Healing for Damaged Emotions* by David Seamands (Colorado Springs, CO: Cook Communications, © 2002, 1981 by David A. Seamands). Adapted with permission from Cook Communications Ministries. May not be further reproduced. All rights reserved.

"One Man's Problem" is adapted from interviews with Sean Milliken.

"The Little Things" is adapted from *Help Me, I'm Married!* by Joyce Meyer (Tulsa, OK: Warner Books, 2000), pp. 87–89.

Outsourcing Library Operations
in Academic Libraries

Outsourcing Library Operations
in Academic Libraries
An Overview of Issues and Outcomes

Claire-Lise Bénaud
Head, Catalog Department
University of New Mexico General Library
Albuquerque, New Mexico

Sever Bordeianu
Head, Serials Cataloging Section
University of New Mexico General Library
Albuquerque, New Mexico

With a Foreword by Katina Strauch

1998
LIBRARIES UNLIMITED, INC.
Englewood, Colorado

In Memory of Our Friend and Colleague
MaryBeth Johnson

LIBRARIES UNLIMITED, INC.
P.O. Box 6633
Englewood, CO 80155-6633
1-800-237-6124
www.lu.com

Production Editor: Kay Mariea
Copy Editor: Diane Hess
Proofreader: Sebastian C. Hayman
Indexer: Nancy Fulton
Design and Layout: Pamela J. Getchell

Library of Congress Cataloging-in-Publication Data

Bénaud, Claire-Lise.
    Outsourcing library operations in academic libraries : an overview
of issues and outcomes / Claire-Lise Bénaud, Sever Bordeianu with a
foreword by Katina Strauch.
    xix, 215 p. 19x26 cm.
    Includes bibliographical references (p. 175) and index.
    ISBN 1-56308-509-7
    1. Academic libraries--Administration--Contracting out--United
States.   I. Bordeianu, Sever.   II. Title.
Z675.U5B37   1998
025.1'977--dc21   98-17118
                                                         CIP

Contents

7—Cataloging (*continued*)

8—Retrospective Conversion 119

Foreword

Librarians have their own perceptions about outsourcing: "the bane of our existence," "a practice that leads to the perception that professional librarians' output and skills are not important or are easily replaced," and "the market has invaded the library, and competitive forces, not librarians, are shaping the library." As 1998 began, the first issue of *American Libraries* asked pointedly "Is Outsourcing the Solution or Is It Fiscal Wizardry?" The caption on the magazine's cover calls it "Outsourcery." A sense of fear and threat pervades these definitions of outsourcing. But, as authors Claire-Lise Bénaud and Sever Bordeianu point out, "outsourcing is a complex relationship between a library and a vendor and is constructed to satisfy a set of unique circumstances" that simple definitions cannot convey (chapter 1).

Whether we agree on these definitions or not, the practice of outsourcing has come to libraries with a vengeance. What is outsourcing? Is it an approval plan? Is it paying a vendor to catalog all materials received in a library? Is it engaging in retrospective conversion activities? Can it be applied to reference? Or preservation activities? In this book Claire-Lise Bénaud and Sever Bordeianu, practicing librarians with a stake in outsourcing decisions, do an excellent job of answering these and other questions.

Outsourcing Library Operations in Academic Libraries: An Overview of Issues and Outcomes takes a thorough and perceptive look at all the processes surrounding outsourcing in academic libraries. Pointing to many of the lessons of industry, chapter 1 outlines the fact that libraries, faced with the harsh realities of the marketplace and declining budgets, must consider outsourcing. Chapter 2, "Outsourcing and Academic Libraries," points out historical underpinnings of the outsourcing debate as well as the threat underlying the debate concerning the future of technical services. Moving beyond the debate to the actual planning, implementation, and management of outsourcing is the subject of the third chapter, "The Three Phases of Outsourcing." Perhaps one of the most compelling chapters in this book is chapter 4, "Outsourcing Survey Results," in which the authors compile extensive data from a survey sent to 109 Association of Research Libraries (ARL) member libraries as well as 110 medium-sized academic libraries. Chapters 5 through 11 address various aspects of outsourcing in academic libraries, including collection development, acquisitions, and serials management (chapters

5 and 6); cataloging, attendant functions of retrospective conversion, and authority control (chapters 7, 8, and 9); preservation (Chapter 10); and public services and systems (chapter 11).

In the concluding chapter 12, Bénaud and Bordeianu reflect on the importance of outsourcing for academic libraries. Is it a fad, or is it a trend that will continue? In their concluding remarks, Bénaud and Bordeianu give us food for thought. "Librarians have to learn how to integrate these alternatives in such a way that they will be beneficial, not detrimental, to the profession."

As we enter the millennium and technological capabilities and interconnectivity improve, outsourcing takes on new dimensions offering further challenges. This book demystifies some of the controversy regarding outsourcing. Not only do Bénaud and Bordeianu offer solutions for current problems, but they hint at how to meet future concerns. *Outsourcing Library Operations in Academic Libraries: An Overview of Issues and Outcomes* is a must-read monograph for all academic libraries which are considering (and even participating) in outsourcing.

Katina Strauch
Charleston, SC

Preface

The impetus for this book was provided by a visit from our AMIGOS representative, who was at the University of New Mexico on a training assignment in the fall of 1995. AMIGOS workshops are often held at our library, since Albuquerque is centrally located in the region. What was atypical about this particular visit was the trainer's request to meet informally with the associate dean, who in our library oversees technical operations, and with members of the cataloging department. The two authors—one the head of the Catalog Department and the other the head of the Serials Cataloging Section—attended the meeting. The one-hour meeting involved a presentation about OCLC's new cataloging program, PromptCat, and a discussion about OCLC's new Internet connections.

After the visit, it became obvious that the associate dean was interested in our pursuing implementation of PromptCat, and we began investigating its use in our library. Suddenly, we were faced with a situation we had thought would affect only others: the possible need to outsource some of our own operations. We embarked on a fact-finding mission, both theoretical and practical, and had lengthy conversations with our colleagues in the Acquisitions and Systems Departments and with representatives of OCLC, AMIGOS, and our materials vendor, Yankee Book Peddler (YBP). We also contacted several libraries that were already using PromptCat and read every article available on the subject, which at the time was a fairly small number. Since our local online system could not automatically accept OCLC PromptCat records because of incompatibility problems with acquisitions records, we could not implement PromptCat. However, our research on PromptCat made us aware of the larger context in which this particular operation was taking place, namely outsourcing.

Outsourcing was gaining prominence in the literature, and we found that the profession was abuzz with discussions about its pros and cons. Predictions of doom and the end of libraries, librarianship, and librarians alternated with glowing reports that presented outsourcing as a money-saving alternative that would allow libraries to flourish despite the severe budget reductions that everybody was experiencing. The idea was intriguing and timely. We wanted to find out what outsourcing was all about and how it would affect libraries in general, not just in specific areas such as technical services.

Therefore, we began to research every area in which outsourcing is performed in academic libraries and to investigate the pervasiveness of outsourcing in each key area of librarianship. We wanted to go beyond the rhetoric, the paranoia, and the circumstantial to find out how this new phenomenon was truly affecting libraries. We decided from the beginning that this would not be a how-to book but rather a book to address all major issues and provide a snapshot of the state of outsourcing in academic libraries today.

As we started our research, we noticed a flurry of activities about outsourcing. Numerous conferences, workshops, and discussions were taking place, but most were restricted to the direct experiences and perceptions of the protagonists and did not address the issue in a more global, detached manner. Available books and articles dealt with specific instances of outsourcing technical services. Most writers also cautioned that they were not prescribing outsourcing for others but instead relating an experience that worked for them. It was clear from the start that we would not be able to attend all the conferences devoted to outsourcing. Monetary and time constraints prevented it. We had to resort to more traditional research methods, such as a thorough investigation of the literature and the time-honored survey. The results have been rewarding. The good response rate to our survey, the feedback from colleagues, and the continued presence of the topic in the literature confirmed that we had picked an important subject.

Introduction

Outsourcing has risen to the top of libraries' agendas in the 1990s. Outsourcing is a phenomenon that is sweeping industry and affecting all sectors of the economy: private, public, and academic. Is outsourcing part of the reengineered and reinvented world that is being talked about so much? Is it part of the wider movement toward shaping a more productive and less wasteful world? Is it a rush to lean management or just a reaction to the ever-increasing complexity and competitiveness of business processes?

Academic libraries are not immune to this trend. Outsourcing has recently become a divisive and controversial issue in the library community and has generated many articles and discussions. It has become such a prevalent topic that entire library conferences are devoted to it.[1] Two responses are guaranteed when the topic comes up: Librarians always have an opinion about it, and everybody has an outsourcing story to tell. What effects does outsourcing have on academic libraries and how is it transforming librarianship? In an attempt to answer these questions in an unpartisan fashion, we will discuss some of the trends that have influenced how librarians have worked over the past 20 years. This is not a how-to manual. Interested readers can consult some of the recently published books that report case studies from the field.[2] The intention here is to explore the many facets of outsourcing and highlight and evaluate the impact that recent developments have had on the nature and quality of service in academic libraries.

Some librarians contend that whereas the term *outsourcing* is new, the practice has been around for many years.[3] In the early days, however, outsourcing was limited to narrow and well-contained areas of librarianship; today it has expanded to more complex and wider-ranging operations, and more responsibilities are being passed on to the vendor. Outsourcing has evolved from contracting out limited functions to the outright replacement of entire functional areas in the library.

Principal among those early outsourced operations were peripheral ones such as library security, photocopy services, courier services, and janitorial services. Many academic libraries have also outsourced some of the more central library functions such as preservation, collection development, and retrospective conversion, gaining much confidence and experience in the process. The latest trend is to outsource technical services with cataloging at the forefront.

In this book we describe the economic circumstances that gave rise to a new wave of outsourcing in academic libraries and present a detailed analysis of library functions that can be outsourced. The first chapter presents an overview of outsourcing and describes the main issues associated with this practice. Chapter 2 addresses the issue of outsourcing as it relates to academic libraries. The trend toward outsourcing in academia has been less prevalent than in industry, but libraries have witnessed outsourcing on a larger scale than other academic departments. Chapter 3 covers the phases of the outsourcing process, namely planning, implementing, and managing. The survey findings presented in chapter 4 provide a snapshot of outsourcing in academic libraries today. Chapters 5 through 11 deal with specific areas that are being outsourced by libraries. Chapter 5 addresses collection development; chapter 6 covers acquisitions; chapter 7 deals with cataloging; chapters 8 and 9 focus on retrospective conversion and authority control, respectively; in chapter 10 we look at preservation; and chapter 11 covers public services, document delivery, and systems. In the final chapter we reflect on the outsourcing trend as it applies to libraries. The appendix contains the survey questions and libraries' responses. The book is designed to give librarians a broad understanding of outsourcing issues.

NOTES

1. Two of these conferences are "Outsourcing: By You, for You, or in Spite of You?" Conference of Southern California Online Users Group, City of Industry, CA, May 3, 1996; "In or Out—In-House Innovation and Outsourcing: Technical Services Alternatives for the 90's," ALA Annual Conference, ALCTS Preconference, New York, July 5, 1996.

2. Arnold Hirshon and Barbara A. Winters, *Outsourcing Technical Services: A How-to-Do-It Manual for Librarians* (New York: Neal-Schuman, 1996); Karen A. Wilson and Marylou Colver, eds., *Outsourcing Library Technical Services Operations: Practices in Public, Academic, and Special Libraries* (Chicago: American Library Association, 1997).

3. Sandra Herzinger, in *Creative Outsourcing: Assessment and Evaluation* (Chicago: American Library Association, ALA-644, 1996). 2 audiocassettes.

List of Acronyms

ALCTS	Association of Library Collections and Technical Services
ARL	Association of Research Libraries
BCR	Bibliographic Center for Research
BIBCO	Bibliographic Record Cooperative Program
CIP	Cataloging-in-Publication
CLS	Chicago Library System
CONSER	Cooperative Online Serials Program
DEZ	diethyl zinc
EDI	electronic data interchange
EDX	electronic data exchange
EKI	Electronic Keyboarding Incorporated
FTP	file transfer protocol
HTML	HyperText Markup Language
ILL	interlibrary loan
IP	information processing
LACAP	Latin American Cooperative Acquisition Plan
LBI	Library Binding Institute
LC	Library of Congress
LCSH	Library of Congress subject heading
NACO	Name Authority Cooperative Program
NUC	National Union Catalog
OCLC	Ohio College Library Center
OCR	optical character recognition
OLUC	OCLC's Online Union Catalog
OMS	Office of Management Studies
PCC	Program for Cooperative Cataloging
RFP	request for proposal
RLG	Research Library Group
SACO	Subject Authority Cooperative Program
SALALM	Seminar on the Acquisition of Latin American Library Materials
TQM	total quality management
VABS	value-added banks
VANS	value-added networks
YBP	Yankee Book Peddlar

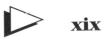

1  *Outsourcing: An Overview*

There seems to be general agreement in both the library and the business literature that outsourcing is here to stay.[1] A survey of academic libraries that we conducted for this book reveals that outsourcing is common. Similarly, a recent business survey indicates that 40 percent of the Fortune 500 companies have outsourced some department or service.[2] It was estimated that in 1996 U.S. companies would spend $100 billion on outsourcing, and as a result, cut their costs by 10–15 percent.[3] The question then becomes not whether to outsource but what to outsource. Naturally, the answer to this seemingly simple question is quite complex, and the right answer depends on a variety of factors. Outsourcing is a complex relationship between a library and a vendor and is constructed to satisfy a set of unique circumstances. No two academic libraries are alike, and outsourcing reflects this diversity. However, all libraries have to ask themselves the same questions before embarking on an outsourcing project. By having a good understanding of the basic issues, an organization increases the chances that its outsourcing operation will be successful.

WHAT IS OUTSOURCING?

Definitions of outsourcing reflect two decades of evolution—some might call it a revolution—of the outsourcing trend.[4] In the 1970s, outsourcing simply involved a supplier managing and operating a function formerly carried out in-house. During the 1980s outsourcing evolved toward closer collaboration between two companies; in the 1990s the trend is toward fuller partnerships. A similar trend is apparent in the world of academic libraries.

Definitions of Outsourcing

Outsourcing is defined as "the transfer of an internal service function to an outside vendor."[5] In its most basic form, outsourcing "is a fancy term for having someone else do your work."[6] Typically, outsourcing is performed off-site, but there are instances when it occurs on-site. Like the rest of U.S. industry, libraries first used the term *contracting out* or *subcontracting* to denote buying a product or a service from an outside supplier rather than providing it in-house. The terms are often used interchangeably. *Outsourcing* has become the preferred term in the United States; Great Britain retains *contracting out*, abbreviated as CO in its library literature.

Even though the 1993 unabridged edition of the *Random House Dictionary* describes outsourcing as "the buying of parts of a product to be assembled elsewhere, as in purchasing cheap foreign parts rather than manufacturing them at home," the business world has redefined outsourcing as a new way of doing business. The concept of outsourcing has gone beyond mere contracting out. It has become an intricate part of the reengineering revolution. Whereas traditional outsourcing merely moves the operation from the client to the outsource supplier, transformational outsourcing provides the flexibility to accommodate business change and new and evolving technologies. Unlike traditional outsourcing, transformational outsourcing allows organizations to focus on their core competencies, and provides the tools to reengineer business processes and transform people, operations, and even technology itself.[7]

A more recent interpretation is proposed in the following definition: "Outsourcing really means finding *new suppliers* and *new ways* to secure the delivery of raw materials, goods, components and services. [It means that you] use the knowledge, experience and creativity of new suppliers which you did not use previously."[8] Others claim that "outsourcing is a mechanism for acquiring new dialogue, ideas, creativity and potentiality. The supplier may have more freedom to get things done, to do them better and cheaper, and to give more customer satisfaction."[9]

Definition of the Outsource Supplier

Outsourcing is the use of an outside agency to manage a function formerly carried out inside a company; the outsourcer is the outside agency that provides the outsourced service. Some go so far as to say that the outsourcer acts as an extension of the company's business but is responsible for its own management.[10]

Definitions of Related Terms

Other terms describing subtle differences in the practice have entered the lingo. *Multisourcing* occurs when a company combines multiple deals with vendors. A company can buy different kinds of products from the same vendor. For example, a library often buys approval books and cataloging records from the same vendor. Termination of either contract does not necessarily affect the other. The term *selective outsourcing* is used when companies outsource only specific applications. This is the model most prevalent in academic libraries and is used extensively for projects such as retrospective conversion or authority control projects. In contrast, *full* or *total outsourcing* implies closing down a department and transferring the function in its totality to an outside vendor.[11] *Temporary outsourcing* describes arrangements that have a much shorter time frame than traditional outsourcing arrangements (e.g., 12 to 24 months).[12] For example, a library may need to spend a fixed amount of money within a specific time frame. A limited approval plan can be worked out with a book vendor. When companies find themselves in a situation where rapid changes are taking place, they cannot afford to lock themselves into a long-term, inflexible arrangement with an outsourcer. *Cosourcing*, another variation of outsourcing, enables companies to maintain flexibility in the marketplace. A cosourcing agreement sets out the parameters in such a way that changes are incorporated into a contract, and it allows for the renegotiation of the contract with suppliers.[13]

Insourcing refers to bringing back in-house an application that has been outsourced. This usually occurs when technology is getting cheaper and it is more advantageous to run an operation internally. For example, many library online systems no longer run on mainframe computers and have moved from university computing centers into the library.

KEY CONCEPTS IN OUTSOURCING

The 1990s are the decade of corporate reengineering, downsizing, and rightsizing. Organizations are examining the tasks they perform vis-à-vis their core activities and are asking themselves whether the tasks really need to be done in-house, whether they can be outsourced to another company that specializes in such activities, or whether they can be eliminated altogether.

Outsourcing As a Reengineering Tool

Reengineering, which applies equally to large corporations and to one-person services, begins with "an analysis of yourself, your strategy, your staff, the other people you work with, the technology you use, and the procedures or processes you employ to do the job."[14] Michael Hammer, the foremost authority on the subject, defines reengineering as "the fundamental rethinking and radical redesign of business processes to bring about dramatic improvements in performance."[15] It is a key principle for evaluating an organization's primary activities, and then looking at how those primary activities could function better regardless of the methods or procedures already in place. The focus is on improving total performance, not on task efficiency. The driving force behind reengineering is making the organization more competitive and more profitable. The result is a more efficient and streamlined operation with improved customer service and cost reductions. Noncommercial entities, such as libraries, that opt to reengineer face some special challenges. These include identifying the mission and customers, finding ways to measure performance, and "coping with resisters."[16]

Reengineering does not invariably result in outsourcing. Instead, it gives companies the opportunity to consider outsourcing as one of the tools they can use to achieve change. Outsourcing is not a goal per se. It is merely a result of reengineering. Organizations that are prepared to think about how best to produce, market, and distribute a product or service will be forced to ask themselves whether they truly need to own all the processes within their companies and, conversely, whether inefficiencies can be discovered and corrected by in-house staff.

Why Outsource?

Outsourcing takes place in organizations across the spectrum—the manufacturing sector, the service sector, the not-for-profit sector, and the government sector. It began in manufacturing. A company bought certain parts from a subcontractor who, due to specialization and economies of scale, could produce those parts for a lower cost than the original company. The globalization of the world economy is putting increased pressure on companies to become more competitive—to look at the bottom line, to trim costs, and to be more efficient—and forcing more companies to look at alternative ways of doing business.

From the private sector, the concept moved to the public sector with governments outsourcing and privatizing operations. Today, outsourcing is equally common in the public sector; public agencies contract with a variety of organizations to supply services that they cannot or do not want to provide in-house. Most commonly an agency contracts out with a private firm, but it may also outsource to nonprofit or cooperative organizations. Outsourcing is being driven by internal and external forces. Internally, management seeks better ways of doing business. Externally, providers of outsourcing services offer to take on more and more of their customers' workloads. Outsourcing grows out of three spheres: economic, political, and ideological.

Economic Gains

The goals of outsourcing are to reduce costs, increase the level and quality of customer service, and achieve a better price and performance objective for the functions outsourced.[17] One of the main purposes of outsourcing is also to have the supplier assume certain types of investments and risks. Spreading the risks over two companies is seen as a benefit. New technologies are also part of the motivation to outsource, as many functions can be performed remotely, eliminating the need for in-house personnel.

Cost Savings

As companies become increasingly concerned about mounting labor costs, outsourcing becomes more attractive.[18] Companies outsource primarily to reduce staff and save on overhead or short-term costs, including those related to space, recruiting, training and evaluating, and management.

Competitive Edge

Although a basic motivation is to cut costs, some claim that almost all outsourcing deals are subject to failure if the organization is concerned solely with cost savings. In the view of these observers, the outsourcer's function is not only to save money for the organization but also to help the organization become more competitive.[19]

Access to Experts

Lack of in-house expertise is invariably cited as a reason for outsourcing. Employers look at outside labor resources because they do not have the people with the necessary skills in-house. Businesses outsource to get expertise. External suppliers' innovations and specialized capabilities may be prohibitively expensive or even impossible to duplicate internally.[20]

Flexibility

The need for increased flexibility to respond to changes in market conditions is another factor that leads to outsourcing. In rapidly changing markets and technological environments, outsourcing creates better responsiveness to customer needs and decreases risks.[21] In an outsourcing arrangement, there is a constant trade-off between flexibility and control.

Political Motives

Outsourcing should be seen not only in an economic light but as a political tool. Outsourcing to small contractors reduces the ability of unions to hold up production. The outside supplier can be seen as an attractive alternative to permanent and pensionable staff.[22] Outsourcing can also be used as a way to deal with difficult personnel problems and to wipe out fractures and fissures that may exist in an organization. [23]

Ideological Motives

Motives can also be ideological, especially in public agencies. Some believe that the private sector is inherently more efficient and can provide many services more economically than the public sector.[24] They contend that highly formalized organizations often "stifle, stultify and strangle good new ideas, and even necessary positive work, if for no other reason than the existence of the job description." They argue that outsourcing allows the organization to flourish.[25]

What to Outsource

As a rule, companies outsource nonessential activities and keep in-house essential functions, referred to as core competencies in the business literature.

Core Competencies

In any organization, whether private, public, for-profit, or nonprofit, certain activities give it its character. These activities, called core competencies, are essential to the identity of the organization and if taken away would eliminate the need for the company to be in business. Core competencies, also labeled as "key," "critical," or "fundamental," are not easy to define. Managers need to select and develop the core competencies "that will provide the firm's uniqueness, competitive edge, and basis of value for the future."[26] According to business writers, executives need to look beyond the company's product to the intellectual skills or management systems that actually create a maintainable competitive edge. Competencies "tend to be sets of skills that cut across traditional functions" rather than ownership of assets.[27]

Organizations cannot function only by performing core competencies. A host of peripheral operations, which provide the infrastructure, are also needed. Thus a car manufacturer, a software company, and a library all need personnel departments, janitorial services, and security services; these enable them to function properly but do not define their business. It is often these peripheral operations, perceived to be commonplace and not unique to their own organizations, that companies outsource. Outsourcing peripheral operations allows the company to give more attention to its core competencies. Tom Peters is supposed to have summed it up by saying, "You should do what you do best and outsource the rest."[28]

Although most companies do not outsource their core competencies, some outsource even these. For example, the Ford Motor Company no longer wants to build engines and has contracted out this function to Japan's Mazda. One would think that building engines is a core function for an automobile manufacturer.[29]

The example of a book publisher illustrates these concepts.[30] A book publisher may outsource all routine editing, design and artwork, printing, packaging, and delivery. But the publisher is not likely to outsource core competencies such as the original scrutiny and editing of manuscripts, the management of authors, and strategic market assessment. In this scenario, outside experts are allowed to suggest marketable products and design and develop the product, which more outsiders can produce and package. The huge burden of manufacturing and printing is also outsourced, leaving the publisher the time and energy to concentrate on the core competencies of dealing with authors and markets.

Determining core competencies is not a neutral decision. It has far-reaching consequences for the labor force. Nike, the largest supplier of athletic shoes in the world, outsources 100 percent of its shoe production and manufactures only key technical components of its Nike Air system.[31] It is a prime example of a company that defines its core competencies narrowly and outsources all other functions to "part-time or temporary workers with low wages and few benefits."[32]

Make It or Buy It

First, a company needs to make a clear distinction about which operations can be outsourced and which have to be performed in-house. Second, the company has to be able to control the quality of the goods and services that are contracted out. Ideally, this can be accomplished through a good contract and detailed benchmarking. Outsourcing has become mainstream enough in industry that a lot of expertise exists in these areas. Once a company has determined its core competencies, it then needs to evaluate its noncore activities and decide which to continue in-house and which to buy from an outside supplier. The "make it or buy it" question asked by manufacturing industries and the "do it ourselves or buy it" question asked by the service industries are central to the outsourcing decision. Others note that the issue is less whether to make or buy a product than "how to structure internal versus external sourcing on an optimal basis."[33]

THE MECHANICS OF OUTSOURCING

In order to be successful, the outsourcing project needs high status, a project leader, and top management support. There are three distinct phases to the outsourcing process: planning, implementation, and management. The planning stage, by far the most complex, consists of cost studies, proposal development, choice of a vendor, and contract negotiations. Evidence shows that this endeavor is extraordinarily time-consuming and that companies need to invest considerable staff time and expertise to achieve success. Careful consideration should be given to selecting an outsourcing vendor with expertise and financial stability. The vendor's objectives should be compatible with the company's overall objectives. The company chosen should have not only excellent technical capabilities but also a philosophy that fits with the client's goals.

The contract is of paramount importance in an outsourcing agreement. It is the most powerful tool available for both the company and the outsource vendor, ensuring that both companies operate within the agreed parameters. The contract needs to be flexible enough to accommodate the changing business climate and evolving technical environments. The company needs to incorporate flexibility into the outsourcing contract so as to avoid being locked into a service it may no longer need and to accommodate a changing business and technological environment.

Implementation consists of developing procedures and workflow and training the employees of both companies. Management involves overseeing the process and includes quality control and compliance with the contract. A problem to be avoided is micromanagement, which can be counterproductive and waste valuable resources.

ADVANTAGES AND DISADVANTAGES

When a company outsources, its interests and those of its employees frequently do not coincide. What is an advantage to the company may well be detrimental to the workers. In fact, the pros and cons are usually drawn along administrative lines with administrators as proponents and employees as detractors. A recent example of this division is the autoworkers' strike against General Motors in November 1996. The strike's primary aim was to prevent GM's future outsourcing ventures.

The Company Point of View

Pros and cons are dependent on companies' unique characteristics. What may be an advantage for one company may turn out not to work for another. Before they outsource, managers must be fully aware of the strategic implications of such a decision and fully explore the risks and side effects.

Whereas outsourcing is a trend in industry, it is not an epidemic. Some writers are suggesting alternatives to outsourcing, and some organizations that have tried outsourcing are pulling functions back in-house.[34]

The Pros

Companies embark on outsourcing ventures because of the benefits they perceive. The fact that outsourcing is so commonplace indicates that in many cases, the advantages outweigh the disadvantages. The benefits, such as economic gains and increased competitiveness, tend to operate at the macrolevel; the drawbacks occur at the detailed operational level.

The Cons

Loss of Control

Loss of control over products and services is a top concern for companies. A company is ultimately responsible for the product it delivers to its customers. Should quality suffer because of substandard components supplied by an outsourcer, the company is responsible for the costs associated with the defects. When difficulties occur, the company has no means to correct the problem promptly. In this scenario, some believe that outsourcing tends to favor vendors over users. A good contract is the only tool that gives the company leverage over its outsourcing partners.

Loss of Expertise

A common apprehension regarding outsourcing is that once an operation is contracted out, expertise leaves the company. Loss of expertise diminishes the company's chances of bringing the operation back in-house at a future time. This, in the view of many, makes the company vulnerable and dependent on outsiders. For example, when U.S. companies outsourced the manufacture of what seemed to be minor components, such as semiconductor chips and bicycle frames, they later found out that their suppliers were unable or unwilling to supply them as required. By then, they had lost the skills they needed to reenter manufacturing.[35] A certain level of internal expertise is needed to manage the outsourcing arrangement and to negotiate present and future contracts. Likewise, innovations and unexpected insights or solutions resulting from interactions among in-house employees in different functional areas can be lost. Outsourcing makes such cross-functional serendipity less likely.[36]

Risks

Outsourcing implies having to establish an ongoing, long-term relationship with a vendor; significant complexities and business risks are associated with this relationship. The impediments to withdrawing from this decision once it has been made and implemented are high. For example, in the information-technology field, administrators are able to plan for only three years or less, but the average length of a contract is nine years.[37] Potential traps also include arbitrary price increases by the vendor against which the company has no protection.

Insourcing

An organization entering into an outsourcing contract must be prepared to take the outsourced function back in-house if the need arises. However, reversing an outsourcing decision and bringing the function back in-house after it has been relinquished can be a demanding and expensive task.

Lack of Accountability

In extreme cases, outsourcing can lead to a complete neglect of quality control. The ValuJet disaster of 1996 brought to light a host of problems that can build up when outsourcing goes unchecked. In the case of the infamous airline, all primary functions, including hiring and training of personnel and the all-important task of maintaining aircrafts, were outsourced. The company had actually been referred to as a "virtual airline." After the crash of one of its airplanes in summer 1996, it was difficult to pinpoint where the mistakes had occurred and who was responsible. What was clear was that not all outsourcers adhered to the high standards necessary to maintain safe flight operations. This example illustrates the most negative elements of outsourcing.[38]

The Employee Point of View

Downsizing

To fully comprehend outsourcing, consider it in the light of another management decision: downsizing or rightsizing. Rightsizing, a euphemism for downsizing, means finding the right size or the right number of people for an organization. Even though outsourcing is not strictly a function of corporate downsizing, companies frequently lay off personnel when outsourcing major parts of their activities, or they may postpone new hires. One rarely finds reports of companies increasing their workforce as part of a rightsizing effort.

Three categories of professionals are "likely to suffer the most" in cases of outsourcing: 1) professionals who put little emphasis on keeping up their skills and who are then unable to learn something new quickly; 2) ultraspecialists, that is, professionals who do not broaden their knowledge base and have difficulty adapting to a new facet of their profession; 3) and people who are not attentive to the corporate environment and are oblivious to business-cycle changes and focus solely on their day-to-day job. Employees can guard against being laid off by taking courses, attending industry conferences, and routinely reading professional magazines to polish their skills.[39]

There are two philosophies regarding personnel decisions. Some argue that when outsourcing an operation, a company should try to retain its best employees; others claim that the best way "to deal with redundant staff" is to declare to an entire group that its job is gone and then allow employees to bid for existing jobs within the organization.[40]

Internal Communications

Press coverage of the issue reveals that many organizations manage outsourcing or downsizing badly and that staff issues are not handled properly. Hammer asserts that when a company turns a new process design into a reality, change affects people directly, and when "change bites people, they bite back."[41] Outsourcing creates massive morale problems among employees. Once a company begins to outsource, most employees feel threatened even if their own jobs are not targeted.[42] No matter how small the percentage of people affected, all of the staff will be worried about change. It takes open and frank communication between the administration and the employees to deal with this uncertainty.

OUTSOURCING: A NATIONAL DEBATE

Corporate Responsibility

Outsourcing inevitably brings up the issue of corporate responsibility—or the lack thereof. Corporations that try to get rid of long-serving and higher-paid staff, thus robbing the employees of their due, are labeled irresponsible. This view is also widespread in librarianship. Michael Gorman sees the terms *modernizing, restructuring, downsizing, reengineering, rightsizing,* and *outsourcing* as code words for the administration's refusal to see personnel as a long-term asset.[43] Even though most agree that it is not the role of an organization to provide employment and wealth for its larger community, it seems that any organization has an obligation to reward its employees so they can contribute positively to the community. Decent salaries, benefits, and a stable employment situation certainly are critical to a solid citizen base. Ultimately, these are ethical issues. At what point does the bottom line take precedence over providing a healthy and supportive environment for employees so that they can be prosperous and responsible members of the community?

Costs and Wages

There are strong opinions for and against outsourcing, and it is unclear how it will affect society in the long run. Some challenge the outsourcing trend altogether and maintain that long-term outsourcing contracts might be a corporate time bomb for manufacturers.[44] They maintain that outsourcing contracts provide front-end incentives and near-term savings but that the long-term costs can be extremely high. They profess that the benefits promised by many outsourcing companies are based on historical—usually inflated—projections of in-house operating costs.

Although lower wages are not always the prime motive for outsourcing, they are often the result.[45] The shift of jobs from a company to an outsourcer often depresses wage levels for that sector. For example, as part of a cost-cutting effort, American Airlines outsourced its ticket agents. The agents in Oakland, California, are newly hired employees of Johnson Controls, Inc., making $7 to $9 an hour, whereas American Airlines paid its veteran agents $19 plus benefits.[46] We may admire innovation and the drive of businesses to conquer new markets, but outsourcing "sharpens the division into insiders and outsiders and reinforces the long-trend toward the polarization of American earnings."[47]

Outsourcing changes the way employees relate to their work. Job security is a constant preoccupation. The 1950s phenomenon of people working in one corporation, moving up, and getting a pension is quickly vanishing in the 1990s.[48] Long-term allegiance to an employer is becoming obsolete. The result is a shift in loyalty from a corporation to a profession, as employees hone their skills to be more marketable.[49]

Global Outsourcing

It is not far fetched to imagine that some libraries could outsource some of their functions overseas. Unlike manufactured goods, information can be transported quickly and cheaply. Constant improvements in computers and communications, particularly modems, are "subjecting millions of white-collar Americans to the same global pressures that their blue-collar counterparts have long faced."[50] The trend toward global outsourcing can be traced primarily to two factors: cost-reduction pressure and advances in telecommunication technology. Corporations are paying educated foreigners to do the same chores as Americans for a fraction of the cost.[51] Daniel Minoli reports that wages of data entry clerks in the Philippines can be as low as one-tenth those in the United States; those in India, one-sixth; and those in Singapore, one-half.[52] Thus tasks that involve information can be relocated to another country. Such countries offer low wages, an educated and talented English-speaking workforce, and a modern telecommunication infrastructure. It is not implausible to envision Filipinos, for example, performing cataloging for a university library and transmitting records electronically to any library's online catalog.

CONCLUSION

Whereas outsourcing helps companies cut costs in the short term, the broader economic implications are less clear cut. Some note that income is merely transferred from employees to shareholders. Operating costs go down, and profits go up, thus driving the company's stock up. This is indeed good for stockholders but leaves the American worker in the cold. Economists see this trend as detrimental to the economy.[53] At the other end of the spectrum, there are those who maintain that the employment of outsiders and the new dialogue that can ensue give rise to creativity and spontaneity. They contend that "the maintenance of the status quo within large organizations will eventually breed lethargy and boredom, a corporate mediocrity and finally the demise of the enterprise."[54]

Outsourcing is growing and service providers are expanding their range of offerings. Because this growth involves more concentration on core competencies by the principals who are passing work to outside providers, this trend may also reflect the fact that industry is coming to terms with a more demanding environment and a need to maximize resources and reduce waste. Whether outsourcing is part of a larger movement, there is no doubt that the world of lean resources is dictating lean management.

It would be foolish to suggest that all the assumptions about outsourcing from the private sector relate to academic libraries. There are vast differences between outsourcing capital-intensive operations, such as information technology, and staff-intensive operations, such as cataloging.[55] However, libraries can benefit from many of the lessons learned by industry. Academic libraries, struggling with the harsh realities of the marketplace and declining budgets, cannot ignore this all-pervasive phenomenon. How libraries fit into this paradigm will be addressed in the following chapters.

NOTES

1. Rusty Weston, "It's Hard to Buck Outsourcing Tide," *PC Week* (July 15, 1996): 105.

2. Hal Lancaster, "Saving Your Career When Your Position Has Been Outsourced," *Wall Street Journal*, sec. B1, December 12, 1995, eastern edition.

3.   "The Outing of Outsourcing (Corporate America's Enthusiasm for Subcontracting Has Made This One of the More Enduring Management Fads of the 1990s)," *Economist* 337 (November 25, 1995): 57.

4.   Michael Hammer, *The Reengineering Revolution* (New York: HarperBusiness, 1995).

5.   Jennifer L. Wagner, "Issues in Outsourcing," in *Emerging Information Technologies for Competitive Advantage and Economic Development*, ed. Mehdi Khosrowpour (Harrisburg, PA: Idea Group, 1992), 214.

6.   Robert R. Falconi, "Don't Bother Me with Work; I'm Contemplating the Universe," *Financial Executive* 11 (September/October 1995): 13.

7.   John R. Oltman, "Preface," in Daniel Minoli, *Analyzing Outsourcing* (New York: McGraw-Hill, 1995), x.

8.   Brian Rothery and Ian Robertson, *The Truth About Outsourcing* (Hampshire, England: Gower, 1995), 4.

9.   Ibid., 32.

10.   Ibid., 4.

11.   Clare B. Dunkle, "Outsourcing the Catalog Department: A Meditation Inspired by the Business and Library Literature," *Journal of Academic Librarianship* 22, no. 1 (January 1996): 33.

12.   Daniel Minoli, *Analyzing Outsourcing* (New York: McGraw-Hill, 1995), 18.

13.   Rothery and Robertson, *The Truth About Outsourcing*, 9.

14.   Ibid., 11.

15.   Hammer, *Reengineering Revolution*, 3.

16.   Ibid., 288–89.

17.   Minoli, *Analyzing Outsourcing*, 166.

18.   Tom Durbin, "Juggling Too Much While Walking the Tightrope? Outsourcing Can Keep Busy Executives from Falling into the Pit," *Colorado Business* 22 (March 1995): 25.

19.   Dennis Livingston, "Outsourcing: Look Beyond the Price Tag," *Datamation* 38, no. 23 (November 15, 1992): 93.

20.   James Brian Quinn and Frederick G. Hilmer, "Strategic Outsourcing," *McKinsey Quarterly* 1 (1995): 49.

21.   Ibid.

22.   Rothery and Robertson, *The Truth About Outsourcing*, 30–32.

23.   Minoli, *Analyzing Outsourcing*, 19.

24.   Murray S. Martin, "Outsourcing," *Bottom Line* 8, no. 3 (1995): 28.

25.   Rothery and Robertson, *The Truth About Outsourcing*, 26.

26.   Quinn and Hilmer, "Strategic Outsourcing," 50.

27.   Ibid., 52.

28. Rothery and Robertson, *The Truth About Outsourcing*, 63.

29. P. Morley, "The Advantages to Outsourcing," *Networking Management Europe* (January/February 1993): 24.

30. Rothery and Robertson, *The Truth About Outsourcing*, 61.

31. Quinn and Hilmer, "Strategic Outsourcing," 49.

32. Bennett Harrison, "The Dark Side of Flexible Production," *Technology Review* 97, no. 4 (May/June 1994): 41.

33. Quinn and Hilmer, "Strategic Outsourcing," 63.

34. Minoli, *Analyzing Outsourcing*, 5.

35. Quinn and Hilmer, "Strategic Outsourcing," 65.

36. Ibid., 66.

37. George Harrar, "Outsource Tales," *Forbes* 151 (June 7, 1993, suppl. ASAP): 38.

38. Seven J. Hedges and Peter Cary, "The ValuJet Crash in the Everglades Raises New Questions About the FAA's Oversight of Start-up Airlines," *U.S. News & World Report* 120, no. 21 (May 27, 1996): 36.

39. Minoli, *Analyzing Outsourcing*, 254.

40. Ibid., 255.

41. Hammer, *Reengineering Revolution*, 23.

42. Barbara A. Winters, "Guidelines for Successful Outsourcing," paper presented at "Outsourcing: By You, for You, or in Spite of You?" Conference of Southern California Online Users Group, City of Industry, CA, May 3, 1996.

43. Michael Gorman, "The Corruption of Cataloging: Outsourcing Erodes the 'Bedrock' of Library Service," *Library Journal* 120 (September 15, 1995): 32.

44. "CIOs Are Uncomfortable Making Out-sourcing Predictions," *Quality Progress* 25, no. 9 (September 1992): 18.

45. Aaron Bernstein, "Outsourced—and Out of Luck," *Business Week* 3433 (July 17, 1995): 61.

46. Ibid., 60.

47. Bennett Harrison, "The Dark Side of Flexible Production," 42.

48. Kirk Johnson, "Workplace Evolution Alters Office Relationships," *New York Times*, October 5, 1994, B1(L).

49. Durbin, "Walking the Tightrope?" 25.

50. Keith Bradsher, "Skilled Workers Watch Their Job Migrate Overseas," *New York Times*, August 28, 1995.

51. Ibid.

52. Minoli, *Analyzing Outsourcing*, 243.

53.   Harrison, "The Dark Side of Flexible Production," 45.

54.   Rothery and Robertson, *The Truth About Outsourcing*, 29–30.

55.   Arnold Hirshon and Barbara A. Winters, *Outsourcing Technical Services: A How-to-Do-It Manual for Librarians* (New York: Neal-Schuman, 1996), 155.

2 Outsourcing and Academic Libraries

Outsourcing is more prevalent in libraries than in other academic departments on campuses. An exhaustive search of the ERIC database shows that outsourcing in academia is confined primarily to ancillary functions such as parking, food services, the bookstore, facilities, housing, and safety.[1] Libraries find themselves in sharp contrast to this overall situation. Outsourcing in libraries has an interesting history and has existed in some form or another for more than one hundred years. For decades, libraries have relied on commercial vendors to perform some of their functions. Until recently, these outsourcing ventures were small in scope and fairly well contained and affected distinct operations. Moreover, it was the smaller libraries with limited resources that bought these services, primarily because of a lack of in-house expertise and resources. The relationship between libraries and vendors was limited to buying a service or a product. Libraries did not form true partnerships with vendors, the underlying basis of outsourcing today.[2]

Historically, outsourcing has been used to supplement library operations; today it is replacing entire library departments. Full or total outsourcing has begun to displace the selective outsourcing that libraries have traditionally practiced.[3] As libraries reexamine their mission, library administrators need to face the challenge of maintaining a high level of services in the face of declining budgets and staffs. When libraries reengineer their operations, outsourcing receives considerable attention. Outsourcing, driven by budget cuts, is seen as one way to maintain essential services.[4] The library literature, paralleling the business literature, stresses that a library should not embark on an outsourcing venture without extensive prior examination. Making the right decision about whether and what functions to outsource requires a careful analysis of the library's operations. One knowledgeable source cautions: "The rush to outsourcing . . . is a classic case of finding the answer before asking the question."[5]

A recent survey we conducted shows that the practice of outsourcing in academic libraries is commonplace and on the rise. Eager proponents see it as a panacea to all libraries' problems and argue that maintaining efficient service no matter what process is chosen, be it outsourcing or restructuring, is what truly matters. Ardent opponents argue that outsourcing "strikes to the very heart of our identity as librarians"[6] and may ultimately result in the demise of librarianship. The vast majority of librarians do not perceive outsourcing as good or bad in itself. They recognize it for what it is, namely, one tool in an arsenal to improve productivity and cut costs. The pioneers, such as Wright State University in the area of cataloging and the Hawaii State Library in technical services, that took the risk to outsource in the first place and then to participate in the national polemic need to be commended. They opened themselves to questions and criticism and allowed for a healthy discussion. Outsourcing will undoubtedly continue to be controversial within librarianship, but "the profession is richer for the debate."[7]

BRIEF HISTORY OF OUTSOURCING

More than 100 years ago, academic libraries began buying "indexing of magazine articles from the H. W. Wilson Company and book cataloging information, in card form, from the Library of Congress."[8] Although outsourcing in academic libraries has existed on a moderate scale for years, its popularity as an alternative to direct in-house services grew rapidly in the 1960s and again in the 1990s. An interesting progression of outsourcing operations has been noted in the literature with an increase occurring in the relatively prosperous decades of the 1950s and 1960s and a virtual disappearance of the topic from the library literature until the celebrated Wright State University case of 1993, when Wright State's complete closing of its cataloging department brought the topic back to the forefront.

For many years, academic libraries outsourced noncore services. The outsourcing of peripheral areas such as security, maintenance of the library building, and courier services has been much accepted. With some exceptions, other operations such as binding and photocopy services have been outsourced by most academic libraries. In the 1960s with the development of approval plans, part of collection development and acquisitions was outsourced. Collection development could not hire bibliographers fast enough to cope with large budgets and turned toward the private sector for help. In the 1970s and 1980s, some cataloging functions began to be outsourced. Libraries contracted with vendors for the provision of retrospective conversion records, microform set records, federal documents records, and authority records. In the acquisitions area, libraries began to rely on vendors for preorder searching, verification, and claiming functions. Today, budget cuts coupled with new communication standards, library automation, and new partnerships among vendors and libraries are leading to greater opportunities for outsourcing cataloging, collection development, and acquisitions. Outsourcing of what some would consider core library services such as original cataloging, interlibrary loan, book selection, and even reference services is being deliberated.

OUTSOURCING TODAY

Since the mid-1970s libraries have faced continuous budget crises; the cost of materials and services has gone up faster than budget increases. Libraries have tried varied methods of dealing with these crises; for the most part the solutions were short-term and addressed the specific problems at hand. By the 1990s the crisis situation had matured into a hard reality that could no longer be dealt with by short-term solutions. Today, library administrators are faced with a dilemma: how to continue fulfilling the library's mission and provide quality services under the stress of ever decreasing resources, or, to put it differently, how to maintain the integrity of the institution in the face of these adversities. Library administrators have come to realize that the environment in which libraries operate and provide services has changed. At the same time, library vendors and service providers have begun to offer a variety of services designed to alleviate some of the burdens experienced by libraries. Library budget-cutting strategies have generally concentrated on one of three areas: cutting the acquisitions budget for books and serials, implementing hiring freezes, and, more recently, outsourcing internal library operations.

Outsourcing in Academic Libraries

Taking cues from their colleagues in industry and government, academic administrators both in and outside of libraries see outsourcing as an increasingly attractive alternative in the face of shrinking budgets and increased workloads. Moreover, vendors are gearing to provide more services that libraries can purchase off the shelf rather than produce in-house. Some of these products result from increased technological capabilities; others are brought out as vendors compete with each other to capture a larger portion of the existing market by offering innovative services purported to save libraries time and money. The library profession has recognized that "outsourcing has become a standard business practice."[9] At the 1994 ALA Midwinter Conference, one of the Association of Library Collections and Technical Services (ALCTS) discussion groups concluded that "shrinking library budgets and advances in technological capabilities make this topic [outsourcing] one of continuing importance."[10]

Despite a common general mission statement of libraries regarding service to a primary clientele, library operations and routines can be quite varied. Some argue that the mission of the library is the direct provision of library services to the patron and that behind-the-scenes areas such as acquisitions, cataloging, systems, and document delivery should be questioned. Should these backroom operations be outsourced? As a result, library positions that are invisible to the patron are at risk.

The latest wave of outsourcing is taking place in technical services departments, and the future of technical services is now debated across the country.[11] For example, Florida Gulf Coast University, the state university system's tenth campus, opened in summer 1997 with most of its collection development and cataloging completely outsourced to Academic Book Center and OCLC.[12] Outsourcing of its library's technical services occurred in the larger context of a new way to conduct business. (Florida Gulf Coast University also made the news when it decided to offer most of its faculty multiyear contracts rather than tenure.) Clearly, technical services functions lend themselves more easily to outsourcing. Many technical services functions are repetitive in nature, can be performed off-site, and can benefit from the reduction in per-unit costs resulting from a high-volume operation. An outsource vendor can perform the operation once and then sell the product to many libraries. Thus ideally a book can be cataloged only once, and the cataloging record sold to hundreds of libraries at a fraction of what it would cost various libraries to catalog that same book in-house.

Despite librarians' justified contention that libraries are underfunded, most libraries still enjoy considerable budgets, which they use to acquire materials, services, and other products. Most of these products are purchased from outside vendors; it is the exception rather than the rule that a library creates and packages the information it provides to the public. Even though libraries are nonprofit organizations, they are closely connected with the profit sector. Therefore, it is not surprising that some of the solutions that purport to ease libraries' budget problems come from the commercial sector.

Libraries usually shop around for the best value; they may at times offer suggestions for improved products or services but seldom originate any such services themselves. Some successful projects have begun in libraries but, once they began growing, became separate operations. NOTIS, which was begun as an automation project at Northwestern University and is now owned by a private information conglomerate, is a case in point. As a rule, vendors can develop new and better tools that are beyond the capacity of even the largest academic libraries.[13] Table-of-contents services were developed by vendors. Libraries do not have the scanning capabilities to add such data to the cataloging record on a large scale.

There is good reason why few of these projects start in libraries. As nonprofit service organizations, libraries do not have the resources or the expertise to develop products and sell them to other libraries. They also do not have marketing departments or the infrastructure to support a new product in the marketplace. When a library develops a new and innovative service, such as the University of Michigan's MITS (which provides document delivery to commercial customers worldwide on demand, for a fee), other libraries can follow suit, but they generally do not subcontract with other libraries for the service except on a limited basis.

The commercial sector has a vested interest in supporting libraries, since many of the services constitute a new source of revenue for them. Such new sources of revenue are an important consideration for vendors because the budget difficulties experienced by libraries have reduced their income from traditional sources such as journal subscriptions and book acquisitions.[14] This does not mean that all outsourcing is being offered by vendors that have lost revenue from traditional library business. It does show that in the marketplace, libraries and their suppliers are dependent on each other. Ultimately, robust libraries are crucial to the well-being of library suppliers and vendors.

Outsourcing in Special Libraries

Outsourcing has been far-reaching in special libraries. In the corporate library world, private library consulting companies have begun to take over the internal libraries serving some of the nation's largest companies. For example, General Electric outsourced its library services to Teltech.[15] Teltech also offers outsourcing options such as facilities management, research services, and document delivery. Some worry that this phenomenon will prove to be the end of corporate libraries and may even do away with all types of libraries.

Outsourcing in Public Libraries

Public libraries have also outsourced their operations to a greater degree than their academic counterparts. However, Bart Kane, Hawaii State librarian, still made the news when he announced that the Hawaii State Library would outsource most of its technical services functions. The Hawaii State Public Library system's organization chart was flattened through reengineering. It focused intently on core competencies and services, outsourcing or abolishing noncore functions, and on customer needs and satisfaction.[16] First a reengineering project was initiated in February 1995. This process included mapping the current process, identifying the steps that added value for the customer, eliminating the steps that did not add value, and identifying and challenging the basic assumptions that underlay the current design. July 1995 brought devastating news to the library—a proposed budget cut of nearly 35 percent and the possibility of laying off 18 percent of the library staff. As a result of the reengineering process, the library decided that its core competencies consisted solely of customer-service functions. The reengineering of the library was driven from a customer-first perspective, one of the key elements of reengineering.[17] The library decided to outsource automation to Ameritech and Dynix, library collections—including acquisitions, selection, and cataloging—to Baker & Taylor, and serials to Information Access Corporation. The saga of the Hawaii State Library is not over. In response to strong negative reactions from librarians and the library profession, the state terminated the Baker & Taylor contract in July 1997. In November 1997 Baker & Taylor sued the State of Hawaii, the Hawaii State Library System, and its director, Bart Kane, to defend its performance in court. By Spring 1998, the Hawaii Board of Education decided to terminate Bart Kane's contract.

Outsourcing in Federal Libraries

Contrary to the current trend in academic libraries, the federal government has moved away from outsourcing entire federal libraries as heavily as it did in the past.[18] In the mid-1980s, the federal government's long-term strategy was to shift public functions to private enterprise.[19] This movement toward privatization included federal libraries, which were defined as a commercial activity in Circular A-76 issued by the U.S. Office of Management and Budget. As a result, a number of federal libraries were contracted out to the private sector. Many librarians questioned the appropriateness of considering federal libraries as commercial activities[20] and strongly opposed this practice, arguing that libraries could not be considered products that could be purchased off the shelf.[21] This movement eventually fizzled out because privatization costs became higher than anticipated.

It is clear that no single solution will fit every library. Different libraries may choose different outsourcing strategies to suit their specific situation. Vendor services reflect this diversity as they try to satisfy individual libraries' needs.

WHAT ARE THE LIBRARY'S CORE SERVICES?

What constitutes a library's core services is at the heart of the outsourcing debate. Most experts believe that organizations should not outsource core competencies. Consequently, libraries should invest "their own energies into doing as well as possible that which they are in business to do, and to purchase high-quality replacements for other services."[22] Therefore, the first step is to identify a library's core services. The main activities performed in libraries are building collections, organizing them, and making them accessible to the public. These functions have traditionally been organized along the lines of technical services and public services. To what extent any of the technical and public services functions qualify as core services depends on the degree to which a library would cease to be a library if the particular function was outsourced.

Outsourcing Core Competencies:
A Contradiction in Terms?

Neither the library nor the business literature provides a foolproof method for identifying core competencies. There is little theory or consistency about what "core" really is.[23] A thorough analysis of library functions might reveal that some operations commonly considered core services are not. Librarians have differing perceptions of where core services end and peripheral services begin. For example, cataloging and selection, once taken for granted as core services, are now being outsourced by some libraries. The debate occurs on two levels: Are these services outsourced because they are no longer considered core, or are libraries outsourcing core competencies? Ultimately, the debate is resolved not in the realm of semantics but in the practical realm of day-to-day work. Pragmatically, if a function can be outsourced but the library can still provide the same level and quality of service, it is irrelevant whether that function is categorized as core or peripheral to librarianship. The implications then shift from who performs the function and where, to how the library can maintain control over the quality of the outsourced function. The nature of libraries is such that outsourcing core functions within the library can cause difficulties stemming from the interdependence of all parts of the library. Indeed, fragmenting the library into units for contracting out is a complex task.

Technical Services

Clearly, selective outsourcing has occurred more extensively in technical services than in public services. Yet these services have traditionally been considered essential. As libraries move to full outsourcing of technical services departments, is the premise still valid? Are technical services still a core competency in libraries? Would a library lose any of its characteristics if the buying, preservation, processing, and cataloging of its materials were outsourced? Would it lose these characteristics if it retained control over decision making on what to buy and over the quality of the material's cataloging and preservation? Each library needs to determine to what extent distinct areas of technical services can be purchased from outside rather than provided in-house.

Arnold Hirshon points out that if a library can measure "the type and quality of the work performed . . . then [the] service is likely to be non-core." He adds that the final output generated by technical services operations "may be a core service but that the operations themselves are not" and concludes that most of the work done in technical services falls in this area.[24] Clare Dunkle argues that this argument is flawed and should be a supporting point rather than a central one. She adds that, indeed, a number of businesses can measure the type and quality of their core services and questions the validity of whether the output of a noncore operation may be a core service.[25]

Public Services

On the other hand, most agree that the public service functions tend to be more closely related to the identity of the library. Outsourcing reference, for instance, would entail transferring the responsibility of providing the library's primary function to another entity. This entity would then in essence become the library. Circulation and interlibrary loan would likewise be difficult to outsource because they depend directly on the collection of the particular library.[26] If these departments were moved out of the library, they would be physically separated from the primary materials with which they perform their work.

WHY DO LIBRARIES OUTSOURCE?

Ideally, libraries should reexamine their operations periodically to determine if certain assumptions still hold or if new, more efficient technologies are available. Periodic reassessment of the library's operations, whether with an eye to eventual outsourcing or not, provides a comprehensive view of library operations. This process uncovers activities that get too high a priority, often at the expense of more significant activities that are slighted. A full-scale reexamination is more easily described than done. Reengineering results in drastic changes and should not be confused with "the usual adjusting, tinkering, and fine tuning" that libraries do on a regular basis.[27] Such radical changes generate strong internal resistance in libraries because they challenge powerful vested interests.

Outsourcing is not the only option available to achieve these goals, as inefficiencies could be corrected by in-house staff and resources. The insights gained from such evaluations make it possible to improve library services and products without outsourcing. Through internal changes, many libraries have been able to achieve cost savings comparable to those provided by vendors and to increase productivity significantly.

As noted throughout this text, the overall goals of an outsourcing arrangement are to reduce costs and maintain or increase the quality of library services. On one hand, library users want greater access and more books and serials. On the other, libraries need to learn to operate with leaner budgets. In order to achieve this, libraries need to examine the costs associated with every library operation rather than focus solely on the cost of isolated tasks, as has been the case lately in discussions about cataloging.

Outsourcing is not a one-size-fits-all process. A library contemplating outsourcing must understand the implications of such a move as it pertains to its own situation. Management must determine whether the purported advantages apply to the library's unique environment. Management must then consider the balance and determine whether, in the specific situation, the advantages outweigh the disadvantages. For example, the outsourcing of cataloging affects a library using several approval plans more severely then it does a library using just one approval plan. Outsourcing binding has different consequences for a library with an extensive rare-book collection than for one collecting mainstream materials.

What Questions Should We Ask?

Outsourcing requires lots of groundwork. Wide-ranging considerations in the technical, political, and legal domains need to be taken into account. Before jumping on the bandwagon, a library considering outsourcing should ask these fundamental questions: How would it affect the integrity of the data? What are the cost advantages and disadvantages? What is the reputation and the reliability of the contractor? How would outsourcing this function affect corporate memory?[28]

Measuring the success of outsourcing presents special complications. Libraries often have difficulty in specifying output. Few academic services lend themselves to easy specification because of the importance of quality in determining users' satisfaction. Whereas output associated with most commercial services is relatively easy to quantify and satisfaction can be measured through the marketplace, areas such as finding the right books for one's research present significant problems of measurement.

Other concerns should also be weighed whenever embarking on an outsourcing venture. Can the library maintain control over the operation? Can the library retain key skills to manage outsourcing and to restart the function in-house if needed? Does the library have a contingency plan if the vendor does not deliver a satisfactory product or goes bankrupt? Can it change vendors if it needs to? There are no yes or no answers to any of these questions. The final decision depends on how much risk the library is willing to take.

Advantages and Disadvantages

Because libraries outsource for different reasons, generalizations are hard to make. What one library may regard as an advantage may be seen as a disadvantage by another. It is clear, though, that there are disadvantages to outsourcing. In particular, strategic problems associated with loss of control and other risks should not be overlooked.

The literature tends to present one point of view, for or against. The opinions of administrators appear to dominate; the voices of employees who are in the direct line of fire are seldom heard. Usually, the stories of those individuals directly affected by outsourcing are reported on listservs. Many of the benefits and drawbacks summarized here were compiled by Karen Wilson and presented at the 1996 ALA preconference on outsourcing technical services.[29] This list is not unique. Many articles on outsourcing present similar compilations.

Advantages

Cost Savings

Cost-cutting is the primary motive for outsourcing. Contracting out forces libraries to evaluate services in terms of their costs. In order to compare in-house versus outsourcing costs, libraries need to assess the true costs of an operation by including such intangibles as employee benefits. Outsourcing reduces overhead costs—meetings, committees, sick or vacation time.[30] Equipment and supply needs will be reduced. Benefits from cost savings occur when the library is able to retain the funds in the library budget. These funds can then be reinvested in other library areas such as the materials budget or automation.[31] Libraries need to understand how vendors can provide an identical service for less money. Economies of scale are the typical rationale. Also, vendors may pay their staff less and give them fewer or no benefits, or quality may be reduced. Cost reductions outside the context of qualitative evaluations are meaningless, as libraries can spend less money for an inferior product.[32]

Buying Expertise

Outsourcing allows a library to acquire expertise that is not available in-house, thus saving the library considerable resources and at the same time providing a necessary product or service. This has been true in libraries both for peripheral functions and for specialized core functions. For example, a majority of libraries are buying preservation expertise from commercial vendors.

Productivity

The culture of the library omits productivity as a central goal.[33] In contrast, outsourcing typically increases productivity and often results in reduced turnaround time. Vendors are more production oriented than libraries, as evidenced in their job ads. For example, a recent vendor job ad for a cataloger stressed the need for a "production-oriented" individual.[34] In contrast, productivity is seldom mentioned in library ads. Unless the library can hire an army of selectors and catalogers, more books can be ordered and cataloged through vendors. In some instances, productivity is increased dramatically, as in the case of consolidating book orders with one jobber or receiving shelf-ready materials. In other cases, productivity increases are more modest, as in retrospective conversion when in-house staff often have to fix numerous post-conversion snags.

Control over the Library Budget

Parent institutions such as universities often question the ratio between personnel and materials expenditures in libraries and pressure libraries to lower their staffing level, which in turn would lower the university's total expenditures on salaries and fringe benefits. Thus academic libraries aim to reduce their payroll in order to increase other lines in the budget. Outsourcing fits well into this scheme, since the outsourcing budget is not in the personnel category.

Concentration on Core Services

Outsourcing allows libraries to commit more resources to core services and eliminate time and effort spent on marginal areas. It enables the library to meet critical institutional goals. Outsourcing redirects staff to other areas within the library, making it possible for new services to be implemented. Often, technical services staff are reassigned to public services. Outsourcing allows administrators to carry out such personnel transfers while technical services activities continue to be performed. Some do not perceive such staff transfers as being advantageous to the library. They note that for years the focus of technical services has been effectiveness and cost reductions. They feel that the pattern of shifting staff from technical services to other library areas does not encourage the areas receiving staff to question their approaches to the same degree as was done in technical services.[35]

Control over Vendors

Through the contract, a library may have more control over a vendor and its performance than over its own employees. Libraries can ensure the consistent delivery of a quality product. If the quality is not satisfactory, libraries can always cancel the contract. However, this extreme measure is disruptive and requires that the library find another supplier for the same service.

Staff Reduction

Libraries spend a great deal of time and effort in hiring, training, and evaluating staff. Going to a vendor decreases the need to hire and train new staff. A smaller number of staff members means that supervisors spend less time on day-to-day supervision and evaluation.

Problem Employees

Libraries spend an extraordinary amount of time dealing with incompetent employees, and firing unsatisfactory employees is a laborious process. By outsourcing, the library passes on these problems to the vendor. Vendors are better equipped to deal with issues "of employee resistance and lack of productivity" because in the private sector, employees' job security is linked to adaptability and productivity.[36] In contrast, libraries rarely fire employees and prefer to transfer them within the library or the university.

New Culture

Outsourcing requires considerable cooperation among many areas of the library, promoting teamwork. It allows for greater communication between departments and across the library.[37] Outsourcing may break organizational bottlenecks and may eliminate barriers between library departments.

Value-Added Services

The outsource vendor can provide services not offered by the library. For example, an outsource cataloging vendor can provide table-of-contents services not typically provided by in-house library staff.

Disadvantages

Loss of Control

Loss of control over the outsourced operations is the most critical problem faced by the library, as staff have to relinquish some control to vendors. Loss of control can take many forms, and its implications differ according to the type of operation that is being outsourced. For example, in collection development a library loses to varying degrees the control of what books are added to the collection. In the case of the Hawaii State Public Library System, Baker & Taylor added 470 duplicates and other inappropriate titles.[38] In the area of cataloging, loss of control occurs when the option of rush cataloging disappears if processing is performed off premises. Libraries have no control over the amount of time commercial binders keep materials out of the building and therefore out of the reach of patrons. Another aspect of losing control exists in the library's relationship to a vendor. A library may be locked into a long-term contract for a service or product it no longer needs. The library thus becomes less flexible and may be unable to respond to new demands or adopt new trends effectively. Getting out of the contract creates innumerable problems for the library, the least of which is an interruption of service.

Loss of Intellectual Capital

Outsourcing may deplete the intellectual capital of the library. Over time, the library will lose expertise because the skills to perform a particular task are no longer needed. The library may not be able to bring back this know-how in case it is again needed in-house. This decline in the library's overall intellectual repertoire is troublesome. Some library leaders recommend against outsourcing professional and intellectual activities and suggest outsourcing routine activities instead.[39]

Loss of Institutional Memory

Contract workers lack institutional memory. Many current policies are based on practices peculiar to the institution. They were developed to best serve that particular library's clientele. A lack of institutional memory leads to chaotic, contradictory, and inconsistent practices. For example, many libraries experienced difficulty when outsourcing retrospective conversion projects because vendors could not comprehend the idiosyncrasies of catalog cards. Furthermore, when the historical perspective is gone, the ability to be involved in "future procedures and policies for the tasks being outsourced" is lost.[40]

Staff Morale

Outsourcing affects staff morale on many levels. First, the change inevitably associated with outsourcing produces high levels of stress. Second, many employees whose jobs have been outsourced will be transferred, against their will, from one department to another, typically from technical to public services. Although a transfer is preferable to being laid off, the possibility of losing one's position reduces employee self-worth and creates insecurity. Once a function has been outsourced, other staff members may see all library administration decisions in the context of outsourcing. A climate of pervasive fear and suspicion may linger in the library. The distrust of management may be so strong that some even caution that if managers come seeking information, they may have already made the decision to outsource.[41] The administration has to take this morale problem seriously and use every means at its disposal, including the provision of counseling for staff, in order to rebuild trust and create a positive work environment.

Although libraries' outsourcing ventures to date have not resulted in significant layoffs, the possibility is very real. Despite the low number of layoffs, it is understandable that employees will feel that their job security is threatened by outsourcing. It is logical to anticipate that if outsourcing spreads in the library world, layoffs will eventually occur. This is a major cause of stress among employees.

Traditionally, libraries and their employees have felt a mutual loyalty.[42] A primary consequence of outsourcing, discussed extensively in the literature, is loss of staff loyalty. A climate of anger and mistrust toward the library administration occurs. When a library outsources a function that has been performed in-house for many years, it creates a new environment that engenders an us-versus-them attitude. Staff, feeling betrayed, get the impression that what they did for years was inconsequential. Regaining staff loyalty is a long and arduous process. The library must be ready to deal with such issues by the same methods of open communication and support that are used to deal with low staff morale.

OUTSOURCING AND LIBRARY JOBS

Outsourcing is changing the world of library employment itself, for library professionals working both for libraries and for the outsource vendor. Once the decision has been made to outsource an operation, the professionals displaced by this action need to figure out what their new role is in the organization, if indeed they still have a role. Those left in charge need to focus on the continuation of quality service. It is seldom the case that the professionals directly involved in the performance of specific tasks propose the outsourcing of those tasks. Typically, outsourcing is a management decision. Outsourcing presents library managers with sensitive human relations challenges because it can affect many employees and sometimes an entire department. Too often, employees at the lower level believe that if they can convince the administration that their operation is important, or core, the function will be kept in-house. Ultimately, the success or failure of outsourcing does not depend on them but on those who take on the new responsibility.

Whose Jobs Are Eliminated?

Outsourcing and downsizing are intimately connected. The jobs that have been eliminated as a result of outsourcing will not be replaced. Paraprofessional positions are most often eliminated as a result of outsourcing. Unlike in the private sector, the library literature reveals that in almost all cases, libraries do not lay off employees when outsourcing. In June 1997, we conducted a survey to determine the effects of outsourcing on staffing. The survey was posted electronically to three library listservs, AUTOCAT, LIBADMIN, and LIBPER. Of the 42 respondents, only one said that an employee was laid off. Of 26 libraries that answered a question on hiring patterns, 15 libraries indicated that hiring slowed down, while 11 indicated it did not. Seventeen libraries reported that they transferred staff to other departments, and nine reported they did not. This survey indicates that libraries transfer some staff out of the area being outsourced, and they fill vacancies at a slower rate.

When Central Michigan University, for example, outsourced its cataloging operations, all library staff members were retained by the university.[43] Transfer to another position within the library or the university is the chosen option even though the overall goal of library management is to decrease the payroll. Attrition is the preferred method used to decrease payroll. Some library staff also decide to leave their position, feeling their job got swept from under their feet.

In considering transfers or layoffs, the administration must comply with "federal and state laws governing changes in the workplace."[44] Even private academic libraries must follow an array of rules and regulations. For this reason, it is imperative that the library work with its human resources department and the university's human resources department to make sure that employees' rights are respected. In some cases, labor laws prevent the library from transferring employees to other departments and compel it to rehire its own employees.

A Personal Perspective

The employee whose job has been outsourced is rarely heard. Nonetheless, outsourcing touches individuals profoundly. A library employee whose job was outsourced told her story on a listserv. After 24 years of employment, "she felt a bond to the university as a whole and to the library in particular." She knew that some positions would be eliminated but did not know her job was one of them. After finding out that most of the department would be eliminated, she felt "alienated from the university" and that all those years of honing her craft and following every cataloging rule had been a waste of her time. She said that for the next three months, "low morale, tension, and fear were palpable" and that classified staff wondered who would be next. She took another position in the acquisitions department at a lower classification and later regained her previous classification. Even though the university was generous in offering career counseling and free psychological counseling, she concluded that the element of surprise was the staff's worst enemy.[45]

The Administrator's Perspective

Most articles focus on the big picture and how outsourcing affects the totality of library operations. Bart Kane, Hawaii State librarian, presents the point of view of the administrator and cites four key lessons he learned while outsourcing most of the technical services operations of the Hawaii State Library:

1. Success requires long-term commitment on the part of the library administration, measured by the "willingness to pay for results in dollars, lost productivity over an initial period, the investment of time . . . and the personal pain that will be involved in making change happen."[46]

2. The goals must be superior performance, defined as excellence in service, and a work environment that supports people in doing their best. Reengineering should not be done solely for the purpose of cost-cutting or downsizing. Cost-cutting most often leads to a reduction in quality and organizational viability.

3. Success requires sacrifices on the part of the library administration. Administrators must be willing to exert leadership while making unpopular decisions and must let go of excessive control.

4. The library administration must make a compelling case for change and reinforce the message repeatedly in a variety of media. Library administrators should be scrupulous in ensuring that all organizational actions and communications are in alignment with the principles and purposes of change. They should believe that "educated, experienced, motivated adults who are in your work force are capable of full authority and responsibility."[47]

THE OUTSOURCING DEBATE IN THE LIBRARY COMMUNITY

The outsourcing controversy expresses itself in various ways. Both negative and positive perceptions are reflected in the library literature.

Library World Versus Business World

Commercial goals and academic interests are often at odds.[48] Librarians and academics are frequently suspicious of the business world and wary of importing its models of operation. There are often legitimate reasons for this suspicion. Double-digit inflation of journal prices over the past decade is an example that comes to mind. Librarians, rightly, feel that journal publishers unreasonably inflate prices. Libraries are also wary of fads. The management literature periodically embraces grand ideas that supposedly will save American industry. Some of these ideas, such as total quality management (TQM), are adopted wholesale by industry only to be discarded a few years later. Libraries sometimes jump on the bandwagon, often belatedly, only to find out that these miracle solutions do not work. It is understandable, then, that some librarians are skeptical of jargon-laden solutions that promise to alleviate most of libraries' problems.

In the commercial world, where making money is the raison d'être of the organization, outsourcing is just another way to increase profits. Clearly, outsource suppliers are in business to make a profit. On the contrary, libraries are not in the business of making money; they "are in the business of losing money."[49] As a result, libraries have a difficult time putting a price tag on services, making it hard to evaluate outsourcing realistically. Another major obstacle that librarians encounter relative to outsourcing is psychological. Too often they consider it wrong to spend money on a service if a vendor can make a profit from it.[50]

Proponents of outsourcing often perceive the private sector to be inherently more efficient than the public sector. In the current economic climate, public-sector organizations are regarded as inefficient bureaucracies that "need to be shaken up, if not eliminated altogether."[51] The solution to this problem is to outsource or privatize such inefficacious establishments. In contrast, opponents argue that "indirect" delivery reduces accountability, democratic control, and quality of service.[52] Even though some note that there is no evidence that employees in the private sector work harder than their counterparts in the public sector, they point to the rigidity of public institutions, which are burdened by "excessive legislative oversight [and] rampant proceduralism," as the reason the public sector is less efficient.[53] Outsourcing is a way of bypassing some of these burdens.

The dichotomy between the library and business cultures manifests itself in their approach to the bottom line: Libraries are in for the long term—building collections for future generations—whereas vendors need to become profitable quickly in order to stay in business.[54] For example, the long-term value of collections or cataloging records is critical to libraries and should not be sacrificed in the name of efficiency; for vendors, efficiency takes precedence over long-term considerations.

One may ask if academic libraries should run like businesses. Jane Miller argues that librarians worried about being outsourced should become educated on how to run information centers in a businesslike way. She adds that librarians "have to look at the bottom line, so they can get the best bang for their buck."[55]

The bottom line in business is cost; libraries emphasize quality. As librarians have had to cancel journals and trim their book budgets, they have had to grapple with cutting quality. The private sector is more concerned with doing well (making a profit) than with doing good (advancing the general welfare),[56] and outsourcing is seen as another attempt to decrease the quality of library services. The library assumes that vendors should be able to provide a high-quality product and cut costs. Dunkle notes that, unfortunately, unless the library states up front that high quality is a measurable part of the outsourcing arrangement, vendors will not provide it.[57] Vendors, in order to have competitive prices, will deliver only what libraries ask for.

Librarians Versus Management

Coalitions for and against outsourcing are, to a large extent, drawn along administrative lines. Proponents include library and university administrators. Opponents of contracting out are less homogenous in outlook and belief. Foremost among them have been the librarians whose jobs are in jeopardy. These two sides have waged an active battle of words in an attempt to influence decision makers. One has portrayed contracting out as a cure for the ailments of the academic library; the other has suggested that this particular approach is unsuitable and will prove detrimental to the long-term health of the institutions involved. One of the main challenges for administrators is to balance their desire for radical change with the staff's desire for certainty.[58] This conflict is inherent in the process and can seldom be resolved to the satisfaction of all.

Outsourcing Versus Cooperation

There is a long tradition of cooperation among academic libraries. Libraries have been genuinely successful in building cooperative networks ranging from cataloging to interlibrary loan to collection development. They have learned to collaborate to stretch their resources to offer better service at a lower price.[59] Such agreements do not have a price tag and cannot be duplicated by outsource vendors. Libraries' cooperative ventures have created products that vendors are now using to their advantage. The controversy in cataloging, for example, stems from the fact that librarians themselves built huge databases cooperatively (OCLC being an excellent model of cooperation) and that commercial vendors, including the bibliographic utilities themselves, are reselling the work created by librarians to other libraries, making a profit on the way.

Outsourcing: A Tool for Addressing Personnel Problems

Some claim that outsourcing is, foremost, a way to get rid of library staff rather than a way to cut costs per se. They assert that the library administration uses economic arguments to promote outsourcing when personnel issues are the crux of the matter. Some argue that most, if not all, of these outsourcing arrangements were born in an environment of poor internal relations and high political tension. For example, it was established that Wright State had been facing personnel problems.[60] Therefore, it has been said that Wright State cannot be considered representative of less politicized environments. Ann C. Davidson points out that in some cases outsourcing of in-house services may be a sign of a company in trouble. She asserts that outsourcing should not be considered when the real solution is the removal of the employee.[61]

Outsourcing As a Catalyst for Change

Advocates of outsourcing claim that all libraries should evaluate the feasibility of outsourcing. These proponents take the position that much can be gained simply from the evaluation process even if the ultimate decision is not to outsource. The process may serve as a catalyst for performance assessments and quality improvements. Karen Wilson emphasizes that undertaking this reassessment with outsourcing in mind allows the library to gain a fresh perspective or implement a new approach to a traditional process. Deliberations about outsourcing stimulate creative thinking and develop strategic alliances between library and vendors, force library-wide discussions, and standardize approaches.[62] If nothing else, library management can become more knowledgeable and aware of the organization's posture, and individual library departments can become more sensitive to financial issues.[63]

Inconclusive Evidence

The literature on outsourcing, from both library science and business, delivers a mixed message. There is a wealth of information about selective outsourcing—approval plans, specialized cataloging projects—but the literature on total outsourcing is sparse. The library literature mirrors the business literature: There are those who are total believers in the virtues of outsourcing, and others are utter skeptics. Analyzing the respective claims of the protagonists is not easy. Only a handful of contracts—especially in the case of cataloging—have been operating for any length of time, and the information gathered from these is as yet inconclusive.

Both sides have supported their claims by documenting the experiences of libraries that have shifted some of their operations from in-house to outsourcing, but the data employed in these exercises are uniformly partisan and highly suspect. Evidence often focuses on short-term phenomena such as the level of cost savings or the inevitable hiccoughs that characterize the transition from in-house to outsourcing. Many of the facts used by both sides are exaggerated and present more a political than a fiscal argument. Librarians have made false accusations about contractors' performances, and their opponents have been shown to overstate the level of savings achieved by outsourcing. Some maintain that the case for outsourcing is unproven and that it is harmful to force areas of a library to undertake a costly and disruptive process that might not yield any benefits in the end.

CONCLUSION

Just because an activity "can be outsourced does not mean that it should be outsourced."[64] The library may not want to give up control of some of its functions, the function may be performed economically in-house, or vendors could charge more for providing an identical service. Most librarians predict that full outsourcing will not be the major outcome of budget cuts and that although it is a very valuable tool, it is one of several available to large academic libraries.[65] Many anticipate that cooperation with the private sector will continue to include outsourcing and that libraries will keep vendors under pressure to provide the best services for the best price.[66]

Many academic librarians see outsourcing as a threat to the library profession. Librarians may need to adopt the same job-survival strategies as their counterparts in the private sector, where job skills are tied to a profession rather than an organization. They need to start thinking, "I own my own skills" and go where the jobs are. Outsourcing creates a loyalty to a profession, not a company.[67]

Full outsourcing challenges the centrality of technical services itself. In this debate, there is wide disagreement about the future of technical services. Michael Gorman writes that the future of technical services has been debated for nearly a century and that librarians should "succumb neither to despair or euphoria."[68] He asserts that there is still a future for technical services staff to provide order to an increasingly disorganized world of information.

NOTES

1. Kenneth L. Ender and Kathleen A. Mooney, "From Outsourcing to Alliances: Strategies for Sharing Leadership and Exploiting Resources at Metropolitan Universities," *Metropolitan Universities: An International Forum* 5, no. 3 (winter 1994).

2. Vendor Panel, "In or Out—In-House Innovation and Outsourcing: Technical Services Alternatives for the 90's," ALA Annual Conference, ALCTS Preconference, New York, July 5, 1996.

3. Clare B. Dunkle, "Outsourcing the Catalog Department: A Meditation Inspired by the Business and Library Literature," *Journal of Academic Librarianship* 22, no. 1 (January 1996): 33.

4.   William Miller, "Outsourcing: Academic Libraries Pioneer Contracting Out Services," *Library Issues* 16, no. 2 (November 1995): [1].

5.   Murray S. Martin, "Outsourcing," *Bottom Line* 8, no. 3 (1995): 30.

6.   Ellen Duranceau, "Vendors and Librarians Speak on Outsourcing, Cataloging, and Acquisitions," *Serials Review* 20, no. 3 (1994): 69.

7.   Miller, "Outsourcing," [3].

8.   Ibid., [1].

9.   Arnold Hirshon, Barbara A. Winters, and Karen Wilhoit, "A Response to 'Outsourcing Cataloging: The Wright State Experience'," *ALCTS Newsletter* 6 (1995): 27.

10.   Nancy J. Gibbs, "ALCTS/Role of the Professional in Academic Research Technical Services Department's Discussion Group," *Library Acquisitions* 18, no. 3 (1994): 322.

11.   I offer two conferences as examples: "Revisioning Technical Services: Building on the Tradition of Excellence," workshop sponsored by Dougherty and Associates, Ann Arbor, MI, October 13 15, 1996; "The Information Wave. Sink, Swim, or Surf," conference sponsored by Potomac Technical Processing Librarians, Bethesda, MD, October 25, 1996.

12.   "OCLC, Academic Book Center, SOLINET to Provide Automated Collection and Technical Services to New Florida University," *OCLC Newsletter* no. 225 (January/February 1997): 10.

13.   Martin, "Outsourcing," 29.

14.   Joyce L. Ogburn, "An Introduction to Outsourcing," *Library Acquisitions* 18, no. 4 (1994): 364.

15.   Barbara Quint, "Teltech: Tool or Rival?" *Searcher* (February 1996): 3–7. Reprint.

16.   Bart Kane, *Service First* (Honolulu: Hawaii State Public Library System, April 1996), 6.

17.   Michael Hammer, *The Reengineering Revolution* (New York: HarperBusiness, 1995), 7.

18.   Ogburn, "An Introduction to Outsourcing," 364.

19.   Marc A. Levin, "Government for Sale: The Privatization of Federal Information Services," *Special Libraries* 79 (summer 1988): 207.

20.   Anne A. Heanue, "Fed Librarians Meet As More Libraries Face Contracting," *American Libraries* 17 (December 1986): 822.

21.   "Berger Testifies Against Contracting-Out," *Wilson Library Bulletin* 60 (January 1986): 11.

22.   Arnold Hirshon, "The Lobster Quadrille: The Future of Technical Services in a Re-engineering World," in *The Future Is Now: The Changing Face of Technical Services: Proceedings of the OCLC Symposium, ALA Midwinter Conference, February 4, 1994* (Dublin, OH: OCLC, 1994), 16.

23.   James Brian Quinn and Frederick G. Hilmer, "Strategic Outsourcing," *McKinsey Quarterly* 1 (1995): 51.

24.   Hirshon, "The Lobster Quadrille," 16.

25.   Dunkle, "Outsourcing the Catalog Department," 39.

26.   Sheila S. Intner, "Outsourcing—What Does It Mean for Technical Services?" *Technicalities* 14, no. 3 (March 1994): 4.

27.   Brian Alley, "Reengineering, Outsourcing, Downsizing, and Perfect Timing," *Technicalities* 13 (November 1993): 8.

28.   Barbara Quint, "Professional Associations React to the Challenge: Interviews with SLA's David Bender and AIIP's Jane Miller," *Searcher* (May 1996): 15. Reprint.

29.   Karen A. Wilson, "Evaluating Outsourcing Services," paper presented at "In or Out—In-House Innovation and Outsourcing: Technical Services Alternatives for the 90's," ALA Annual Conference, ALCTS Preconference, New York, July 5, 1996.

30.   Hirshon, "The Lobster Quadrille," 17.

31.   Ibid.

32.   Herbert S. White, "What Price Salami? The Federal Process of Contracting Out Libraries," *Library Journal* 113 (January 1988): 59.

33.   Barry Fast, "Outsourcing and PromptCat," *Against the Grain* 7 (April 1995): 50.

34.   Library Technician 3, Job announcement, WLN, Lacey, WA. Listserv LIBJOBS @INFOSERV.NLC-BNC.CA. Thurs., 28 Nov 1996 13:21:00.

35.   Dilys E. Morris, "Technical Services Costs and Resource Allocation," paper presented at "In or Out—In-House Innovation and Outsourcing: Technical Services Alternatives for the 90's," ALA Annual Conference, ALCTS Preconference, New York, July 5, 1996.

36.   Jack G. Montgomery, "Outsourced Acquisitions? Let's Meet the Challenge," *Against the Grain* 7, no. 2 (April 1995): 66.

37.   Wilson, ALCTS Preconference, July 5, 1996.

38.   "Honolulu Is Talking," *Newsweek* (October 28, 1996): 8.

39.   White, "What Price Salami?" 58.

40.   Rick J. Block, "Cataloging Outsourcing: Issues and Options," *Serials Review* 20, no. 3 (1994): 74.

41.   Quint, "Professional Associations," 17.

42.   Pam Bigus, "Outsourcing—One Paraprofessional's Experience," Listserv ASSOC-L. Fri., March 1996.

43.   "Central Michigan University Libraries Use TECHPRO," *OCLC Newsletter* (July/August 1995): 30.

44.   Arnold Hirshon and Barbara A. Winters, *Outsourcing Technical Services: A How-to-Do-It Manual for Librarians* (New York: Neal-Schuman, 1996), 148.

45.   Bigus, "One Paraprofessional's Experience."

46.   Kane, *Service First*, 6.

47.   Ibid., 7.

48.   Warren J. Haas, "America's Libraries, Distinguished Past, Difficult Future: A Supplement to ARL #172, January 1994," *ARL: A Bimonthly Newsletter of Research Library Issues and Actions* 172 (January 1994): 2.

49.   Daniel CannCasciato, "Tepid Water for Everyone? The Future OLUC, Catalogers, and Outsourcing," *OCLC Systems & Services* 10 (spring 1994): 7.

50.   Randall Marcinko, "Keynote Address," presented at "Outsourcing: By You, for You, or in Spite of You?" Conference of Southern California Online Users Group, City of Industry, CA, May 3, 1996.

51.   Martin, "Outsourcing," 28.

52.   Kate Ascher, *The Politics of Privatization: Contracting Out Public Services* (New York: St. Martin's Press, 1987), 11.

53.   Levin, "Government for Sale," 209.

54.   Dunkle, "Outsourcing the Catalog Department," 38.

55.   Quint, "Professional Associations," 19.

56.   Levin, "Government for Sale," 213.

57.   Dunkle, "Outsourcing the Catalog Department," 37.

58.   Hirshon, "The Lobster Quadrille," 15.

59.   Martin, "Outsourcing," 30.

60.   Dunkle, "Outsourcing the Catalog Department," 35.

61.   Ann C. Davidson, " 'Obedience to the Unenforceable': The Ethics of Outsourcing," *Searcher* (April 1996): 12. Reprint.

62.   Wilson, ALCTS Preconference, July 5, 1996.

63.   Daniel Minoli, *Analyzing Outsourcing* (New York: McGraw-Hill, 1995), 143–44.

64.   Miller, "Outsourcing," [4].

65.   Colleen F. Hyslop, "PromptCat Prototype: Accelerating Progress in Technical Services," in *The Future Is Now: The Changing Face of Technical Services: Proceedings of the OCLC Symposium, ALA Midwinter Conference, February 4, 1994* (Dublin, OH: OCLC, 1994), 38.

66.   Martin, "Outsourcing," 30.

67.   Tom Durbin, "Juggling Too Much While Walking the Tightrope? Outsourcing Can Keep Busy Executives from Falling into the Pit," *Colorado Business* 22 (March 1995): 25.

68.   Michael Gorman, "Innocent Pleasures," in *The Future Is Now: The Changing Face of Technical Services: Proceedings of the OCLC Symposium, ALA Midwinter Conference, February 4, 1994* (Dublin, OH: OCLC, 1994), 42.

3

The Three Phases of Outsourcing

For outsourcing to be successful, one has to recognize that quality service depends on a highly professional staff within both the library and the vendor organizations. Before a library embarks on the outsourcing project, numerous issues need to be addressed by management. It needs to know how staff resources are used, evaluate in-house processes and costs, identify potential benefits and risks, establish objectives, and make a recommendation to outsource. Outsourcing causes major disruptions to the library and to staff. Getting people "to let go of their old ways and embrace new ones" is tough.[1] Resistance to change cannot be underestimated, and advocates of change may eventually give in. This prospect of disruption, coupled with fears about losing control of essential functions, is a key concern.

Measuring success is another obstacle encountered by libraries. Libraries do not function as businesses in the sense that they do not have customers with well-defined information needs and performance measures expressible in financial terms. Furthermore, libraries have goals and values that often override financial concerns. If the success of outsourcing is ultimately based on customer satisfaction and cost savings, it is quite difficult for libraries to measure success in concrete terms.

There are three clear phases to outsourcing: planning, implementing, and managing.[2] Libraries need to devote a lot of time and energy during each phase of the process.

PLANNING

Outsourcing is a project of paramount importance that will have wide-ranging implications throughout the library. Consequently, a structure must be put in place, plans must be made, and a detailed methodology must be employed. Planning requires by far the largest expenditure of time and effort.

Role of Library Management

Outsourcing decisions are made by the library management. For management, this is a more difficult matter than adopting a new local system or implementing new policies. Management should strive to obtain a commitment from key people in the library for the outsourcing project, a decision that is usually fraught with threatening implications. This is indeed hard, since it will undoubtedly be a divisive issue among the library staff. Once the decision has been made to outsource, management should clearly support the decision, and this message must be communicated to the library staff and periodically reinforced.

The administrator responsible for the decision will either manage or pick the best person available to oversee all phases and aspects of the project. For outsourcing to be a valid option, management must identify the actual costs both of providing the service in-house and of buying it from an outsource vendor. This requires a substantial learning process.[3] Management needs to know "what it costs to order and process a monograph, a serial, an audiotape, etc."[4] This is fundamental if the primary motivation is to reduce operational costs. The management may also want to provide a better service at the same price rather than just achieve a lower-cost service. In either case, cost studies are paramount. Evaluating the library's existing processes and costs is a complex undertaking that involves many, and perhaps all, functional areas within the organization. To accomplish the analysis, management must be prepared to support the individuals performing the evaluation as they develop performance and cost-study models and attempt to quantify productivity.

The organization can benefit from the evaluation in several respects. The area under scrutiny may become better equipped to work in a more cost-conscious manner, and library management may develop a better understanding of the library function's actual, rather than perceived, value. There also will be greater insight into the role the function plays within the organization and how it can better support the other areas within the library.

Higher Initial Costs

Libraries need to realize that there are high initial costs associated with entering an outsourcing agreement. Planning for outsourcing is a staff-intensive operation and takes away resources from the library. Planning for outsourcing is time-consuming, and involves in-depth examinations and lengthy discussions with potential vendors.

Understanding Existing Processes

In order to be successful, existing processes need to be analyzed. Many librarians excel at understanding workflows and writing meticulous procedures. As a group, they may not be willing or able to change or simplify processes because so many constituencies may be affected. In considering outsourcing, librarians are called upon to see the big picture.

Workflow, workload, and employee productivity all affect cost. Convoluted workflows hamper efficiency and increase cost with little tangible benefits. Workload is another matter to be taken into consideration when determining costs. Often librarians' workload encompasses more responsibilities than just the activity being outsourced. Productivity varies among employees. Every library department has star employees and some that are less stellar.[5] Employee effectiveness will indeed affect cost, especially in smaller departments.

The person chosen to conduct the analysis should understand how tasks fit together to form a process and how process designs and organizational designs fit together to form the library. This person should have a "congenial inability to accept things as they are" and have the patience to "listen to the needs, fears, and concerns" of everyone who will be affected.[6]

Measuring Costs

Costs are often more difficult to evaluate than processes and require long and tedious studies to assess the soundness of the outsourcing decision and the reasonableness of the charges proposed by the vendor. The library's organization structure, different levels of staff performing identical tasks, and the spread of PCs and networks throughout the organization can make cost analysis virtually impossible. Other considerations such as local online catalogs and salary structures make it difficult to establish meaningful costs. This is especially true in libraries where technical services and public services functions are decentralized and run across departments. Nonetheless, some areas, chiefly technical services functions, are more feasible to cost out than others. For areas such as reference and service, it is particularly difficult to devise output measures.

Cost analysis has its critics. Some argue that we are in danger of knowing the cost of everything and the value of nothing. Others contend that achieving a high degree of precision and completeness and spending an inordinate amount of time doing so, is wasteful.[7] In their opinion, cost benefits can only be estimated.

Many libraries have little idea of what it costs them to design, run, and manage a specific area. It is easier to identify the costs of dealing with external suppliers than to identify internal costs.[8] Let's take the example of cataloging: Workflow, telecommunication costs, interactions with other library departments—specifically acquisitions, systems, and collection development—all affect cost. Cost studies in cataloging "from the point of view of personnel time and overhead, are rare."[9] Moreover, catalogers in most academic libraries do not merely catalog. Their responsibilities are often multifaceted. Most have additional duties within the library and university such as committee work, hours on the reference desk, or selection duties. They contribute to their profession through local, state, or national organizations, and many have research and publication requirements. A method for quantifying the value librarians add to an institution needs to be developed. There are no hard data on added value to the library, and information is anecdotal at best. Even though putting a price tag on a service is complex, libraries across the country have attempted to do just that.

There are basically two ways to evaluate costs in an academic library: total output measures and microanalysis or time-task analysis. At the 1996 outsourcing conference sponsored by ALCTS, Barbara Winters of Wright State University and Dilys Morris of Iowa State University reported on the cost of technical services at their institutions.[10] Each used one of the methods and described its benefits and applications.

Broad Cost Studies

Winters used broad, general figures to determine in-house cataloging costs.[11] Broad cost studies, although not as time-consuming as specific cost studies, require a sizable amount of work because libraries need to calculate direct costs and indirect costs. According to Winters, Wright State University was not in a position to do a time-task analysis. Instead it used total output measures to assess the cataloging cost of a Wright State University title. The total output figure represents the catalog department's total expenditures, both direct and indirect costs.

In their book, Arnold Hirshon and Barbara Winters present a detailed spreadsheet model designed to calculate broad output measures. It includes the following direct-cost categories: Personnel, equipment and related expenses, transaction charges, and other operating expenses. It also includes indirect cost categories, such as space, telephone, and custodial services.[12] The total figure for indirect costs is divided by the number of transactions, and that figure is added to the total direct costs to arrive at the total output. Wright State figured out that it would save approximately $10 per title if they outsourced its cataloging.[13] Any library can customize their spreadsheet to reflect its own situation.

Time-Task Cost Studies

Other libraries prefer the microanalysis method, establishing benchmarks and analyzing how much time it takes to perform each specific task. This technique requires libraries to cost out individual activities and compare local costs to those of the vendor. Library staff need to keep a diary over a period of time and painstakingly document the amount of time spent on each activity. Many technical services departments, especially cataloging and acquisitions, routinely have tried this method. Cataloging departments attempt to determine how long it takes a cataloger to catalog a certain type of title depending on the kind of copy available and the need to reclassify, to make corrections, and so on; acquisitions departments attempt to determine how long it takes acquisitions staff to order a book depending on the availability of the book and the type of order—firm order, approval plan, or blanket order plan. Another approach is to estimate the percentage of staff time spent on tasks and then evaluate these activities in terms of cost. The next step is typically for a technical services department to compare itself to a similar department, if possible, one at a similar institution. Technical services staff who have participated in such comparative studies know that the variables from one institution to the next are endless.

Dilys Morris of the Iowa State University Library reported on a time and cost study that has been in place at her institution for nearly a decade. She noted that it is not difficult to do a time and cost analysis but that it "does require perseverance and time."[14] She presented concrete data on how automation has affected technical services, specifically cataloging and acquisitions, and reported that technical services made significant cuts in total staff costs and increased services and productivity. Libraries can time activities and factor in other staff costs such as training, policies and procedures development, and problem solving. At her institution, all time for all staff is sampled and analyzed on an ongoing basis to gather data for short- and long-term planning and for future decisions. She reported the considerable costs of activities such as administration, meetings, professional service and scholarship, and other overhead costs. In addition to salary costs, librarians must take into account other costs such as equipment, supplies, the number of supervisory staff, and use of space to see whether savings can be achieved in these areas.

An accurate method for sampling or estimating staff time is important for a valid analysis. For the year 1994–1995, Morris reported the data for her institution's cataloging and acquisitions departments.[15] Percentages for time and cost varied, reflecting the different salary structures found in the library and whether librarians, library staff, or students were involved in a specific type of activity. In order of importance she reported that in technical services, professional involvement, such as research, committee work, and administration, was the most expensive category, representing 28 percent of the total cost and 21 percent of time spent, since librarians with the highest salaries are actively involved in such work. Acquisitions was in second position with 22 percent of costs and 24.5 percent of time spent. Cataloging was in third position, representing 16 percent of costs and 15 percent of time. Leave was the fourth most expensive category: Annual leave, sick leave, and holidays represented 15 percent of costs and 14 percent of time. Conversion represented 10 percent of costs and 12 percent of time. Catalog maintenance represented 5 percent of costs and 7 percent of time. Cataloging operations are today the most likely area to be outsourced because of their perceived high cost. The data collected at Iowa State University do not reflect this cost relationship.

Morris also commented that outside of technical services, selection at her institution was undoubtedly the most costly category in her library. Her study clearly shows that cost studies are essential to make an informed decision.

A Comparison of Methodologies

Time-task analyses and total output studies are strikingly different. In the former, the entire staff of a department is involved in recording data; in the latter, only administrators perform the study. Time-task studies have to be repeated periodically in order to get usable data, whereas broad output figures need to be generated only once.

Hirshon and Winters point out that total output measures are more accurate than time-task analysis because they better reflect total activity over a longer period of time. Time-task analysis has several disadvantages. Employees tend to be more productive when observed, and the "whole is greater than the sum of its parts," which implies that observing individual activities does not necessarily generate a complete picture.[16] Time-task studies would be more meaningful if more libraries would replicate them.[17] Unfortunately, when they do, they use different definitions and methods, thus making comparisons weak. The inordinate amount of time devoted to time-task studies may also discourage libraries from conducting this kind of analysis. For these reasons, broad output studies are both more practical and more useful.

Overhead Costs

Regardless of the method favored by individual libraries to assess costs, overhead costs must be factored in. Overhead costs are those not directly related to producing a product or providing a service. These costs exist in all parts of the library, technical services and public services, and constitute a significant part of total costs. Sick leave, vacations, and holidays have to be taken into account. Research and publications, university work, committee work, and meeting attendance are also a major component of librarians' duties in academic libraries. Other technical costs need to be factored in, such as automation and bibliographic utility charges. Different types of library employees have different overhead costs. Librarians with professional activities have higher overhead costs, since they spend time in activities that do not produce a service or a product.

Academic libraries have little control over overhead costs, since librarians are expected to contribute to professional service and are required to publish, especially when they have faculty status. A vendor clearly has lower costs in that area. In order for a library to compete with outsourcing services, these overhead costs must be driven down.[18] In addition, most of the overhead costs should influence decisions about what work is assigned to which level of staff and should clarify the contributions expected of staff. There is another type of overhead cost that is even more difficult to measure; that is, space needs, electricity needs, and supplies as they relate to the level of staffing. These factors do not appear on the library budget and are seldom factored into cost studies.

Measuring Quality

Libraries also encounter difficulties when they attempt to specify with output measures the quality aspects of a service. Outsourcing creates the expectation of improved or sustained levels of quality. Even though librarians may have a knack for intuiting quality, in an outsourcing context it is imperative to be able to define it in measurable terms. Joyce L. Ogburn remarks that "librarians probably do not have a clear idea of how to measure quality."[19]

Further complicating matters, the final product is often not evaluated by the department involved in creating that product. Thus problems in acquisitions are most often detected by selectors or patrons, and problems in cataloging are often discovered by reference librarians or patrons. Therefore, even if a department has strict quality-control measures in place, it needs to rely heavily on input from outside departments. This situation creates a double jeopardy, since it is a politically sensitive matter for one department to critique or evaluate another department, and the feedback may get lost somewhere along the way. Nevertheless, each department has to take responsibility in creating a high-quality product or service that can withstand the scrutiny of peers and the public.

Too often librarians assume that the vendor will provide a quality product. The vendor, however, will not do so unless quality is specified in the contract.[20] In order to specify quality in the contract, the following areas need to be defined: completeness, consistency, accuracy, and adherence to standards. Furthermore, an acceptable error rate and the manner in which quality control will take place have to be spelled out.[21] Since the definition of quality depends entirely on what product or service is being measured, it has to be stated for each specific instance. In all cases, acceptable levels as well as steps to be taken to redress a slippage in quality need to be specified.

Informing the Staff

The success of outsourcing is more likely to be hindered by human problems than by technological problems.[22] As the library literature reveals, outsourcing is sometimes viewed less than favorably by librarians. The staff need to be informed that outsourcing is being considered or has been selected; if the staff find out through the rumor mill, the department could become paralyzed by worries about job change or loss. In-house staff currently providing the service may view outsourcing as threatening or as a reflection on their performance. Some staff may believe that the announcement that their operation will be outsourced is only a tactic aimed at improving their performance. Some individuals will not agree with the process, the analysis, or the conclusions, especially if their job security is at stake. Some individuals may go out of their way to make the analysis even more difficult to complete. The staff may find it difficult to acknowledge that change should occur or to accept that change is going to happen. In some libraries where outsourcing is a reality, many fear the possibility that other operations will be outsourced.

When staff recognize that outsourcing will indeed take place, numerous concerns surface. Employees are "thrown into a period of uncertainty and feel that they lack control over their future."[23] Even though jobs are fairly secure in most libraries, career progression is uncertain, and often transfer to another area of the library or the university is a strong possibility. During the entire process, communication must be continuous. There is no such thing as overcommunication,[24] and communication should not cease when implementation begins.

The Request for Proposal Process

When a service is performed in-house (i.e., firm ordering or cataloging), a department typically has a well-established rapport with other departments, a rapport that is taken for granted. Outsourcing will change this. Library employees will have to adjust to dealing with a colleague one day and a vendor who has commercial motives the next. Some areas of the library, such as collection development or preservation, are used to dealing with vendors; other areas, such as cataloging, are new at it.

Once the library administration has decided that outsourcing is the best solution to optimize a library function, management needs to decide on administrative and technical specifications. The most widely used method is a request for proposal (RFP) specifying the library's needs and the vendor's responsibilities. The RFP "is a statement of mandatory and desirable conditions that a vendor (also known as a 'bidder' or 'proposer') must meet to fulfill the requirements of an intended contract."[25] Both mandatory and desirable conditions must be specified because no vendor can fulfill 100 percent of the library's expectations.

The RFP process is crucial to the success of outsourcing. Academic libraries are very experienced in this area and have been writing RFPs for many years. RFPs have been used by libraries to purchase automation systems, bindery contracts, approval plans, and a whole array of other products or services from vendors.

The RFP is complex and provides a structured approach to the planning process. It forces the library to carefully analyze and break down the operation to be outsourced into distinct components and by doing so, it presents to the prospective vendors a complete picture of the library's expectations. This detailed picture allows vendors to assess realistically their ability to provide the service. The RFP also presents a blueprint for future benchmarks that the library can use to measure vendor performance.

The literature on RFPs is quite extensive, and it is relatively simple for most librarians to educate themselves about the process. There are two distinct areas that the RFP has to cover. The first, called boilerplate, "gives institutional requirements for the contract" and includes specifications about the description of the institution, the service to be provided, the duration of the contract, pricing of the service, and instructions and deadlines for the bidder.[26] For an institution, the boilerplate section will be used for all RFPs regardless of what service or product is being bid for. The second area consists of functional specifications that are unique to the activities being outsourced. For example, for an approval plan, the RFP can include type of publisher, reader level, and languages in which materials can be provided; for cataloging, the RFP can include type of cataloging copy, level of editing, provision of item records, authority control, and physical processing.

Selecting a Vendor

Choosing the right vendor is critical. The vendor needs to understand and support the library's goals, and this requires a good cultural fit. When the library finds a compatible partner, the relationship can flourish over many years. However, certain pragmatic criteria need to be considered for the business relationship to be successful.

Vendor reputation and financial stability are the primary considerations to look at when choosing an outsourcing provider. Confidence that the vendor can meet the service levels and evidence that it has done so for other libraries need to be established as part of the vendor selection process. Vendor commitment can be checked from references provided by current customers.

Libraries should ask themselves the following questions: What is the vendor's attitude? What is the vendor's quality of written communication? Does its brochure have badly thought-out claims or overstatements? Is the vendor interested in responding to your needs or trying to sell you something else? A library should check on the supplier's electronic network and decide if the supplier and the library will need to share the same network. Libraries also need to understand how the vendor will make money. Where can it achieve efficiencies the library cannot? Where will it realize savings? What steps in the process will it cut out? Are there any points on which it is inflexible? One worry is that the vendor will make it difficult to change to another vendor and that the library will be coerced into continuing with a vendor whose services or products are unsatisfactory.

A cultural fit between the library and the vendor is fundamental. It is difficult to form a workable library-vendor partnership without trust. Does the proposed partner feel right? Do the library staff and the vendor's staff work well together? Do they speak the same language? Libraries and vendors often have to go back to the table either to cover an unexpected situation or to clarify language that may be subject to different interpretations. A positive disposition based on mutual trust is key to making this aspect of the relationship work in a professional manner.[27] In order to determine how the vendor's culture and work style fit with that of the library, vendors can be invited to give presentations during the RFP process. The library thus has the opportunity to interview different vendors, and compare them, and then choose the most compatible one.

Negotiating the Contract

The contract is the main tool for enforcing vendor performance. The RFP specifications need to be contained in the contract. One way to achieve this is to incorporate the entire RFP, including vendors' responses and related correspondence, in the contract. In the case where the parent institution requires a separate document, the library needs to incorporate all the RFP specifications into the contract. Libraries have some expertise with contracts, but vendors live and breathe them. Academic libraries, however, have at their disposal the legal counsel of the parent institution. Because contract negotiations can be intimidating, the library has to be careful to avoid signing an unsatisfactory contract. There is no such thing as a standard contract, and libraries can negotiate every single point. Libraries should be careful to negotiate reasonable requirements. Otherwise the vendor has the option to develop expensive new services or refuse to do business with the library.

The contract consists of the following categories: definitions, which ensure that vendor and library have a common understanding of key terms; institutional responsibilities, which outline the library's obligations to the vendor; vendor's responsibilities, summarizing the services the vendor will provide; the duration of the contract; and a non-compliance clause, which specifies when the contract can be dissolved.[28] Outsourcing contracts in the information-technology sector have an average length of nine years.[29] In contrast, library contracts are in force for three to four years,[30] placing libraries in a better situation to react to changes. Evidently, a longer contract benefits the vendor, and a shorter contract is advantageous to the library.

Libraries should consider several factors before entering into an agreement with a vendor. The contract has to be flexible; both sides should be allowed to initiate changes. The library should also try to anticipate situations that might require renegotiating the contract. There may be a reduction in requirements as a result of a drastically reduced materials budget, a new computer system, or a library reorganization. Alternatively, an increased volume of business may lead to an increased service need.

Renegotiating or terminating a contract after signing is not simple. Even a meticulously negotiated contract could become a burden in the years to come. One needs to consider the importance of defining situations that justify termination or renegotiation, such as a failure to comply with stated services, a takeover of another company, or vendor bankruptcy. An outsourcing arrangement needs to be viewed not just as a service contract but as a strategic alliance involving a long-term partnership between the organization and the outsourcing vendor.[31]

IMPLEMENTATION

After the basic issues concerning planning, proposal development, and contract signing have been worked out, the implementation phase begins. The real work starts at this point.[32] Implementation consists of activating the actual functions that are outsourced, such as data transmission and processing by the vendor. The implementation stage is the most difficult and disruptive stage of the agreement, as both library and vendor need to design and introduce new workflows. The vendor's involvement in implementing the process is crucial. First, the vendor needs to understand completely the library's needs. The vendor then trains the library staff in the new procedures in order to integrate the outsourced service into the library's workflow. Library employees need to learn how to access the vendor's system and to use it fully. Again, each operation has its peculiar needs, and vendor involvement differs accordingly. For example, if a library outsources some of its acquisitions functions, library staff need to become familiar with the new vendor's online system. If a library outsources cataloging, less training by the vendor may be required, and the changes are instituted in the library. During the implementation phase, staff will need to modify initial policies and procedures to achieve the maximum benefits of outsourcing. When a library changes vendors for an outsource operation, the new vendor typically assists the library in the transition process. This help is crucial in achieving a smooth transition of services and guarantees a minimal disruption of operations.

In the early stages, the library needs to check and test its assumptions at regular intervals. Many libraries want the option of conducting a pilot project or want to start the outsourcing on a small scale. However, this is not always possible. Unexpected problems will arise and will require fine-tuning by both the library and the vendor. The library's workflow may need to be adjusted again in order for the outsourcing process to be efficient.

MANAGING

The library needs to retain experienced technical and managerial staff to oversee the outsourced operation. Questions that come into play at this stage include the following: What internal expertise is needed to ensure that expected levels of service and performance are met? How is the library going to exercise control over the outsourced function? For example, in collection development, an experienced bibliographer needs to manage the project to make sure that the books sent to the library match the profile and to identify gaps.

At the beginning of the contract, the library needs to review every piece of work that is completed. For example, the manager of outsourced cataloging needs to check that the bibliographic records match the books, that all required fields are included in the MARC record, that the editing of required fields is correct, and that errors are noted.

After a few months, the process should run smoothly enough to require only random checking. Micromanagement of the outsourcer is a common problem that negates the benefits of outsourcing. Instead, the vendor needs to meet the agreed-upon levels of quality and quantity of service. Libraries should require all vendors to produce periodic performance reports comparing performance against standards established in the contract.

Just as in-house operations cannot be taken for granted and need to be looked at periodically in order to assess their usefulness, outsourced operations should also be reevaluated periodically. Yet staff cannot constantly analyze whether they or a vendor can perform a function more efficiently than someone else. In time the operation may need to be brought back in-house or outsourced differently. The library needs to focus on long-term benefits and goals and give the outsourcing process time to work, but it also has to be prepared to reverse the process at a future time if needs dictate.

CONCLUSION

It is imperative that libraries do not ignore the three formal phases described in this chapter. Shortcuts will undermine the final success of the operation. Librarians should not allow themselves to make decisions based on gut feelings at the expense of careful analysis. Although a manager may feel intuitively that he or she knows the exact cost of an in-house activity, only a detailed study can produce this information. Further analysis will yield additional necessary information, such as the impact of outsourcing on other library operations. Throughout this process, communication is of paramount importance. There are many interested parties in an outsourcing operation, such as the various departments in the library that will be affected by outsourcing, the library itself, one or more vendors, and the bibliographic utilities. The communication lines among all these parties have to be open to achieve the best results.

Planning takes the longest. The manager has to be aware of two pitfalls associated with planning: First, no matter how well designed a plan is, it will contain some fallacies that will have to be corrected by trial and error;[33] second, the entire process has to be implemented within a finite, usually short, period of time. Michael Hammer states that the organization "must do an amazing amount of work in a very short period of time."[34] If the process drags on, its chances of success diminish because administrators and other employees lose interest and become skeptical. The vendors may also lose interest and not take the library's intentions seriously. Hirshon and Winters affirm that complete outsourcing is not for the faint of heart. Indeed, the decision may be one of the most controversial ever made by a library's administration. However, with proper planning and careful monitoring, outsourcing can also be extremely beneficial to the library.

NOTES

1. Michael Hammer, *The Reengineering Revolution* (New York: HarperBusiness, 1995), 117.

2. Daniel Minoli, *Analyzing Outsourcing* (New York: McGraw-Hill, 1995), 16.

3. Clare B. Dunkle, "Outsourcing the Catalog Department: A Meditation Inspired by the Business and Library Literature," *Journal of Academic Librarianship* 22, no. 1 (January 1996): 38.

4. Jack G. Montgomery, "Outsourced Acquisitions? Let's Meet the Challenge," *Against the Grain* 7, no. 2 (April 1995): 66.

5. Dilys E. Morris, "Technical Services Costs and Resource Allocations," paper presented at "In or Out—In-House Innovation and Outsourcing: Technical Services Alternatives for the 90's," ALA Annual Conference, ALCTS Preconference, New York, July 5, 1996.

6. Hammer, *Reengineering Revolution*, 58–59.

7. Ibid., 31.

8. James Brian Quinn and Frederick G. Hilmer, "Strategic Outsourcing," *McKinsey Quarterly* 1 (1995): 58.

9. James E. Rush, "A Case for Eliminating Cataloging in the Individual Library," in *The Future Is Now: The Changing Face of Technical Services: Proceedings of the OCLC Symposium, ALA Midwinter Conference, February 4, 1994* (Dublin, OH: OCLC, 1994), 2.

10.   Morris, "Technical Services Costs"; Barbara Winters, paper presented at "In or Out—In-House Innovation and Outsourcing: Technical Services Alternatives for the 90's." ALA Annual Conference, ALCTS Preconference, New York, July 5, 1996.

11.   Arnold Hirshon and Barbara A. Winters, *Outsourcing Technical Services: A How-to-Do-It Manual for Librarians* (New York: Neal–Schuman, 1996), 32.

12.   Ibid., 42.

13.   Winters, "In or Out."

14.   Morris, "Technical Services Costs."

15.   Ibid.

16.   Hirshon and Winters, *Outsourcing Technical Services*, 32.

17.   Dilys E. Morris, "Staff Time and Costs for Cataloging (at Iowa State University)," *Library Resources & Technical Services* 36 (January 1992): 90.

18.   Ibid.

19.   Joyce L. Ogburn, "An Introduction to Outsourcing," *Library Acquisitions* 18, no. 4 (1994): 365.

20.   Dunkle, "Outsourcing the Catalog Department," 38.

21.   Ogburn, "Introduction to Outsourcing," 365.

22.   Minoli, *Analyzing Outsourcing*, 251.

23.   Ibid., 252.

24.   Hammer, *Reengineering Revolution*, 47.

25.   Hirshon and Winters, *Outsourcing Technical Services*, 50.

26.   Ibid., 59–60.

27.   Minoli, *Analyzing Outsourcing*, 176.

28.   Hirshon and Winters, *Outsourcing Technical Services*, 139.

29.   George Harrar, "Outsource Tales," *Forbes* 151 (June 7, 1993, suppl. ASAP): 38.

30.   Hirshon and Winters, *Outsourcing Technical Services*, 139.

31.   Minoli, *Analyzing Outsourcing*, 176.

32.   Dunkle, "Outsourcing the Catalog Department," 38.

33.   Hammer, *Reengineering Revolution*, 26.

34.   Ibid., 28.

4   *Outsourcing Survey Results*

    In fall 1996, the authors sent out a survey to all 109 academic members of the Association of Research Libraries (ARL) libraries and to 110 medium-sized academic libraries with holdings between 300,000 and 900,000 volumes (the majority having about 500,000 volumes). The sample of non-ARL libraries was chosen to supplement data collected from ARL libraries, the largest academic libraries, in order to provide a more balanced picture of outsourcing across the spectrum. The non-ARL sample includes private and state universities and colleges. Libraries from every state in the United States were surveyed; the more populous states such as California and New York had more entries. One hundred thirty-nine (63%) of the libraries responded. The survey, addressed to the chief administrator for each library, covered every aspect of library operations that has the potential to be outsourced: collection development, acquisitions, preservation, reference, interlibrary loan, document delivery, systems, cataloging, authority control, and retrospective conversion. Each question also provided the opportunity for librarians to indicate future plans and to comment. The importance of outsourcing with library administrators was underscored by the timely responses to the questionnaire. A copy of the survey is included in the appendix.

    The comments provided by the respondents made it clear that checking a particular category did not mean that the library outsourced that particular area completely. Oftentimes there was a balance between in-house and outsourced operations, such as approval plans or blanket orders supplementing individual ordering, or preservation being performed both in-house and through a vendor. Library practices run the gamut from no outsourcing at all to full outsourcing of some areas. The vast majority of libraries engaged in outsourcing; eight libraries, two ARL and six non-ARL, reported no outsourcing at all. There seems to be no correlation in outsourcing activities among different areas of the library. For example, one library may totally outsource cataloging and not outsource preservation at all.

Respondents also showed differences in their understanding of what outsourcing means. One library indicated that it does not outsource even though it uses approval plans, another indicated that it has been using approval plans for more than 10 years and contended that it no longer considered this outsourcing, and two libraries noted that they contracted with individuals rather than a commercial vendor to perform original cataloging and retrospective conversion in-house and considered this outsourcing because they did not use their regular staff. Another marked that it does not outsource preservation, since all these functions have always been done by vendors and as such do not meet the technical definition of outsourcing. One respondent questioned why the survey did not contain a question regarding the use of OCLC for cataloging, since in the respondent's opinion this too is outsourcing. This variation in interpretations shows that outsourcing can be an ambiguous concept.

COLLECTION DEVELOPMENT

Respondents were asked to check if they outsourced the following collection development areas: approval plans, blanket orders, bookstore, and "other."

Overall Findings

Ninety-seven (70%) of the libraries reported that they outsource collection development; 41 (29%) of the respondents reported that they do not. Of the libraries that outsource collection development, 96 (69%) use approval plans, 45 (32%) use blanket orders, and 4 (3%) have arrangements with bookstores. Five libraries (4%) marked the category "other." In this category, libraries listed purchase plans, depository arrangements with agents in foreign countries, arrangements with vendors for special collections and archival materials, and (one instance) renting best-sellers and popular reading materials.

Comparison of ARL and Non–ARL Libraries

ARL libraries outsource in larger numbers than non-ARL libraries. Fifty-nine (86%) of the responding ARL libraries outsource some aspect of collection development; only 38 (54%) of the non-ARL libraries do. This is reflected in the difference between the prevalence of approval plans and blanket orders in ARL versus non-ARL libraries: 58 (84%) of ARL libraries use approval plans, and only 38 (54%) of the non-ARL libraries do; 36 (52%) of ARL but only 9 (13%) non-ARL libraries use blanket orders. Moreover, only 10 (14%) ARL libraries indicated that they do not outsource collection development at all; the number for non-ARL libraries is 31 (44%). Few respondents indicated that they plan to change their practices in the future, indicating a stable situation in this area.

ACQUISITIONS

Respondents were asked to check if they outsourced the following acquisitions functions: preorder searching, serials check-in, subscription agents, claiming, and "other."

Overall Findings

In addition to the fact that a large number of libraries indicated the use of approval and blanket order plans through vendors, 82 (59%) respondents indicated that they outsource some acquisitions functions. Eighty libraries (58%) use subscription agents; 9 (6%) outsource claiming. Even though the interface between library and vendor computer systems is improving, only one library outsources preorder searching and another used a vendor for serials check-in but brought the operation back in-house. Fifty-seven (41%) of the libraries indicated that they do not outsource acquisitions. Respondents' answers indicate that the majority of outsourcing in acquisitions consists of using vendors and subscription agents. One comment supports the findings from the literature that auditing requirements and the necessity of maintaining control of purchase orders in-house is preventing libraries from outsourcing acquisitions functions on a larger scale. One respondent noted that outsourcing cataloging through PromptCat in effect eliminates the need for acquisitions departments to search OCLC and to download records. The great majority of respondents indicated that they have no plans for changing acquisitions routines.

Comparison of ARL and Non-ARL Libraries

The bulk of outsourcing of acquisitions functions revolves around the use of book and serials vendors; the percentage of ARL libraries that do so is higher than for non-ARL libraries—64% versus 51%, respectively. Little outsourcing is taking place in other categories related to acquisitions, such as preorder searching, serials check-in, and claiming, and there is no difference in the practices of ARL and non-ARL libraries in this respect.

PRESERVATION

Respondents were asked to check if they outsourced the following preservation functions: binding, mending, microfilming, photocopying, digital scanning, conservation, and "other."

Overall Findings

The vast majority of libraries, 110 (79%) outsource some preservation functions. Binding is by far the most prevalent (106 libraries, or 76%), followed by preservation microfilming (52 libraries, or 37%), conservation (24 libraries, or 17%), preservation photocopying (21 libraries, or 15%), and mending (6 libraries, or 4%). Preservation is one area in which several respondents indicated that the same functions are performed both by vendors and in-house. For example, one respondent commented that his library is considering outsourcing conservation of selected atlases and digital scanning of selected cartographic materials. Another library indicated that only color microfilming is outsourced, and other preservation microfilming is performed in-house. Several libraries indicated that they outsource only preservation that is under grant programs. One library indicated that it outsources not only preservation microfilming but also target preparation for preservation filming, prospective cataloging, and record completion. Only 8 libraries (6%) overall indicated that they are investigating additional outsourcing options for preservation; 25 libraries (18%) indicated no plans for future outsourcing. Those libraries that specified that they are investigating future outsourcing possibilities mentioned primarily microfilming and scanning options.

Comparison of ARL and Non-ARL Libraries

In the area of preservation, even though ARL libraries outsource more than non-ARL libraries, the difference is not dramatic. Fifty-seven (83%) ARL libraries outsource some preservation function compared to 53 (76%) non-ARL libraries. Both groups outsource bindery extensively—56 (81%) ARL libraries and 50 (71%) non-ARL libraries. The differences are more pronounced in the areas of microfilming (33, or 48%, of ARL versus 19, or 27%, of non-ARL libraries), preservation photocopying (16, or 23%, of ARL versus 5, or 7%, of non-ARL libraries), and conservation (17, or 25%, of ARL versus 7, or 10%, of non-ARL libraries). Only ARL libraries outsource digital scanning. There was no indication from the non-ARL libraries whether scanning occurs at all.

REFERENCE

Respondents were asked to check if they outsourced the following reference functions: reference assistance, library instruction, online searching, weekend or evening desk hours, and "other." Not surprisingly, the academic libraries surveyed do not outsource reference functions. No library indicated that it outsources reference, library instruction, and weekend or evening desk hours. One library indicated that it outsources online searching, and another plans to outsource reference functions for its distance education sites. No instance of outsourcing reference at a main campus was mentioned. Two libraries engage in reverse outsourcing of reference. The libraries actually provide reference services for a publisher and a small private university that do not have libraries. There is no variation in the practices of ARL and non-ARL libraries. Both groups of libraries indicated that they do not plan to outsource in this area. The survey findings fully support the reports from the literature, which show that there is little outsourcing activity taking place in public services.

INTERLIBRARY LOAN

The vast majority of libraries, 132 (95%), do not outsource interlibrary loan. Of the four libraries that reported outsourcing in this area, two are ARL and two are non-ARL. Activities consist of obtaining documents from commercial document-delivery centers for patrons. Although the survey did not mention unmediated document request and delivery, two libraries mentioned this activity as an example of outsourcing. Of the two, one uses a commercial vendor, the other a cooperative arrangement with other libraries through a consortial online catalog. It is probable that many libraries engage in this type of practice but do not consider it outsourcing. Only six libraries reported that they are investigating options for outsourcing their ILL functions.

DOCUMENT DELIVERY

Probably the most surprising part of the survey was the overwhelmingly consistent response from the majority of libraries that they do not outsource document delivery. One hundred twenty-nine libraries (93%) reported that they do not outsource document delivery. Eight libraries indicated plans to outsource this area in the future. The question on the survey specifically asked respondents not to refer to the use of unmediated searching of services such as CARL/Uncover or FirstSearch as outsourced document delivery. These services do not involve the library's contracting out with an outside contractor for the specific purpose of locating and making available documents. Rather, the library facilitates patron access to the databases. Depending on the arrangement, either the library pays for an unlimited supply of documents to patrons or patrons pay for the articles themselves. Cooperative agreements among libraries that allow each other's patrons to borrow from their collections either in print or electronically was also mentioned as an example of outsourcing by some.

These findings were surprising because of the striking contrast with reports from the literature indicating that a large number of libraries use document-delivery vendors. However, comments made on the individual survey responses are much more in sync with the literature and show that the line between document delivery and interlibrary loan is blurry. Oftentimes, an activity that is considered interlibrary loan by one library is reported as document delivery by another.

SYSTEMS

Respondents were asked to check if they outsourced any of their systems functions to campus computing centers, consortia, vendor automation centers, and "other."

Overall Findings

Slightly more than half the respondents, 71 (51%), outsource some of their systems functions. The greatest number, 56 (40%), depend on the campus computing center for automation support. Another 20 libraries (14%) belong to consortia that manage the online catalog. In some cases a library may belong to a consortium as well as have its computing center manage the system. Seven libraries (5%) reported that they completely outsource their system functions to an outside automation vendor.

Comparison of ARL and Non-ARL Libraries

Slightly more non-ARL libraries (37, or 53%) outsource system functions than ARL libraries (34, or 49%). Whereas both groups report working with the campus computing center, 31 (45%) ARL libraries and 25 non-ARL (36%), the situation is different in regard to consortial agreements. Only 5 (7%) ARL libraries outsource some system functions to their consortium but 15 (21%) non-ARL libraries do so. Another difference is that only ARL libraries (6, or 9%) indicated plans to outsource in this area if they do not currently or to increase their activity in this area.

Types of activities reported as outsourced or under investigation are some of the network support tasks, library systems software development, network drops and cabling, preinstallation of software and hardware components, the operation of mainframe and servers, and CD-ROM LAN installation and support.

CATALOGING

Respondents were asked to answer questions regarding the outsourcing of cataloging in three areas: vendors used, types of records acquired, and value-added services acquired.

Overall Findings

Outsourcing in cataloging is a dynamic area and generated the most comments. Whereas outsourcing in some of the other heavily outsourced areas such as preservation and collection development has reached a steady level, cataloging is experiencing vigorous developments in a variety of areas ranging from pure cataloging to value-added services and the physical processing of books. Eighty-eight (63%) respondents indicated that they engage in some form of cataloging outsourcing, and 50 (36%) indicated that they do not. Sixty-one (44%) libraries use Marcive, 35 (25%) use TECHPRO, 11 (8%) use PromptCat, 2 (1%) use Diogenes, and 29 (21%) use other cataloging vendors. Regarding the types of records acquired, the highest number of libraries (63, or 45%) buy bibliographic records for U.S. federal documents, 19 (14%) buy records for unique collections; 16 (12%) buy records for unique languages such as CJK, Judaic languages, and Arabic; another 16 (11%) acquire Library of Congress 050 bibliographic records; and 21 libraries (15%) report that they buy other types of records.

The survey revealed that libraries purchase a remarkable variety of records for a remarkable variety of materials. Libraries reported buying records for all monographs received through approval plans, all monographic cataloging, original cataloging only, member input records only, English-language materials only, foreign-language materials only, original cataloging of Latin American collection materials only, scores, sound recordings, special collections materials only, children's literature only, generic backlog material, HTML (HyperText Markup Language) processing of texts, item records, upgrading of CIP records, and videos. The scope of outsourcing is also extreme. One library reported that it outsources all its cataloging, consisting of 45,000 records a year; another library indicated outsourcing no more than 35 records a month.

Thirty-eight (27%) libraries purchase value-added services; 48 (35%) reported that they do not. Twenty-three (17%) buy labels, 17 (12%) buy table of contents, and 21 (15%) buy security taping. Nine libraries (6%) report buying additional value-added services and acquire shelf-ready materials consisting of bibliographic records, labeling, pockets, date-due slips, property stamping, security taping, and barcoding.

Outsourcing cataloging seems to be more haphazard than outsourcing collection development or preservation, as libraries experiment with and sometimes drop their arrangements with vendors. For example, one library reported using TECHPRO for one year during the absence of the CJK cataloger.

A few libraries commented on the successes and failures of their outsourcing endeavors. One reported that outsourcing was not successful; others reported that it works well. Two libraries considered outsourcing but encountered strong opposition from librarians, who mobilized the faculty. As a result, plans for outsourcing were dropped.

The number of libraries that have plans for outsourcing cataloging in the future is virtually the same as the number of libraries that do not have such plans. Thirty-nine libraries (28%) indicated plans to outsource some aspect of cataloging; 41 libraries (29%) indicated that they do not. Future plans include table-of-contents enhancement, approval plan books through PromptCat, security taping, cataloging of technical reports, buying cataloging records for large microfilm sets, and multimedia cataloging.

Even in this area, the interpretation of what constitutes outsourcing is quite broad. At least two libraries mentioned cooperative cataloging agreements with other libraries as outsourcing. Some libraries reported that they acquire value-added products such as tables of contents through a consortium and are unclear if this activity is considered outsourcing.

Comparison of ARL and Non-ARL Libraries

ARL libraries are outsourcing cataloging more than non–ARL libraries. Forty-nine ARL libraries (71%) outsource some cataloging; 39 non-ARL libraries (56%) outsource some cataloging. This difference carries over in the individual categories that the two sets of libraries outsource: 35 ARL libraries (51%) outsource U.S. federal documents records versus 28 (40%) of the non-ARL libraries; 12 ARL libraries (17%) outsource cataloging of unique languages versus 4 (6%) non-ARL; 16 (23%) ARL libraries outsource the cataloging of unique collections versus 3 (4%) non-ARL libraries. However, the difference between ARL and non-ARL libraries is not as pronounced in the area of value-added services. Twenty-one ARL libraries (30%) buy value-added services versus 17 (24%) non-ARL libraries. More ARL libraries plan to outsource cataloging in the future than non-ARL libraries. Twenty-three ARL libraries (33%) indicate such plans compared to sixteen non-ARL (23%). Moreover, the number of non-ARL libraries, 28 (40%), that indicate that they do not plan to outsource cataloging is higher than that for the ARL libraries, 13 (19%).

The data indicate that libraries with larger collections outsource more than libraries with smaller ones. A survey of academic libraries conducted in January 1997 by Katherine A. Libby and Dana M. Caudle confirms that there is a correlation between the size of the collection and the decision to outsource: the larger the collection, the more likely the library is to outsource cataloging.[1]

AUTHORITY CONTROL

Seventy-six (55%) of the libraries that responded to the survey indicated that they outsource or have outsourced authority control functions. Twenty nine (21%) do not have plans to outsource in this area and 20 (14%) have plans to do so. Again, ARL libraries outsource authority control more than their non-ARL counterparts. Forty-two ARL libraries (61%) outsource in this area versus 34 non-ARL libraries (49%). Some libraries mentioned that they stopped outsourcing authority control because their retrospective conversion projects ended; others continue to outsource authority control for current cataloging. Typically, libraries contracted with a vendor for their initial load into an online catalog or when migrating from one online system to another.

RETROSPECTIVE CONVERSION

Overall Findings

Most activity in this area took place in the 1980s when libraries began implementing automated catalogs. Although the task of converting card catalogs to machine-readable form was daunting, those projects were by definition finite. Some libraries also indicated using retrospective conversion vendors to update their bibliographic records to full MARC. The majority of libraries, 83 (60%), outsource all or some of their retrospective conversion. Many of these libraries used several vendors during the span of their conversion. Fifty-seven libraries (41%) converted in-house. Not surprisingly, few libraries, 10 (7%), have plans to outsource in this area; 33 (24%) indicated that their conversion is complete. Of the libraries that indicated that they have future plans for conversion, all mentioned the use of a vendor for this activity. Several indicated that they plan to convert their government documents collection.

Comparison of ARL and Non-ARL Libraries

In the area of retrospective conversion, ARL libraries outsource considerably more than non-ARL libraries. Fifty-two ARL libraries (75%) outsourced conversion; nineteen (28%) did not. Conversely, the majority of non-ARL libraries did not outsource conversion with 38 libraries (54%) reporting that they did not use a vendor, and 31 (44%) indicating that they did.

GENERAL COMMENTS

The survey included a section asking if there were any areas in which the library outsourced that were not covered by the questionnaire. Ninety-six libraries (69%) responded that there are no additional areas in which they outsource; 30 libraries (22%) responded with additional comments. The main areas that were mentioned as outsourced clearly fell outside the scope of this book and included such ancillary activities as security, janitorial services, photocopy services, microfilm and laser printer support, collection storage and moving services, and equipment maintenance. Others mentioned areas that clearly meet the definition of outsourcing and fall within the category of library activities that could be considered core services such as shelving, loose-leaf filing, relabeling collections from OCRs (optical character recognition) to barcode, inventorying, developing staff courses, maintaining some Web consortial sites, programming to perform statistical analysis for benchmarking, dealing with management reports from book and serial vendors, and preparing library instruction for distance education.

The survey also included a section that allowed respondents to share opinions and relate their experiences about outsourcing. Several people commented that outsourcing worked for them; others expressed frustration because of the limitations of the interface between vendor and library systems. Others expressed disappointment in the results of their outsourcing ventures. One library indicated that it intends to outsource in order to save money, particularly staff monies. Not surprisingly, a few also noted staff resistance to the notion of outsourcing.

CONCLUSION

The survey sheds light on several aspects of outsourcing that are not apparent when reading the library literature. Several libraries indicated that they would like to outsource more but do not have the budget to support this activity. The discrepancy between the amount of outsourcing taking place in ARL versus non-ARL libraries, with the assumption that ARL library budgets are stronger, also supports this supposition. Yet it counters the arguments used in the literature for outsourcing, namely that it saves money. One library actually suspended its approval plan due to lack of funds, another indicated that it plans to implement an approval plan when funds become available, and another library specifically noted that serial check-in and claiming is cheaper in-house. A telling comment from Western Washington University—"the answers to this survey, a year from now, may be very different"—summarizes the fluid status of outsourcing today.

The survey does show that there is a lot of outsourcing activity in technical services, specifically in cataloging, and virtually no outsourcing going on in public services. Nearly all the libraries indicated that they do not outsource reference; over 60 percent indicated that they outsource some aspect of cataloging. The survey also shows that there is a greater variety of outsourcing options in the area of cataloging than in any other area surveyed. Libraries surveyed outsource the cataloging of government documents more than any other type of record. A sizable number of libraries use OCLC's TECHPRO service. The survey also confirms that some aspects of collection development and preservation are outsourced by the majority of academic libraries. In all areas in which outsourcing occurs, libraries use several vendors, contributing to the complexity of the process.

The survey does not reflect a trend toward an all-out outsourcing of technical services, as might be indicated by the current controversy surrounding outsourcing in the Hawaii Public Library system. Rather, it indicates that libraries are taking a cautious, albeit serious, approach toward outsourcing.

NOTES

1. Katherine A. Libby and Dana M. Caudle, "A Survey on the Outsourcing of Cataloging in Academic Libraries," *College & Research Libraries* 58, no. 6 (November 1997): 556.

5

Collection Development

Although collection development and management are as much core library competencies as reference and cataloging,[1] outsourcing in this area has been going on for several decades, during which time it has matured and been refined. In fact, the history of collection development shows that this area was one of the earliest to be outsourced by libraries in the form of approval plans.

Outsourcing in collection development consists of approval plans, blanket orders, standing orders, gathering plans, and all-the-books plans.[2] Some of these terms have gone out of style, and there has always been some ambiguity as to the difference between them.[3] In this chapter we use the term *approval plan* to refer to all of these plans. Ultimately, terminology is less important than the concept itself, which simply means an agreement between a library and a materials vendor—book vendor in the early days—by which the vendor automatically sends the library newly published books based on agreed criteria, called a profile. There are variations among plans in terms of coverage and added services, as will be discussed in this chapter.

HISTORICAL BACKGROUND

Traditionally, libraries had relied on full-time bibliographers for identifying the titles to be added to the library's collection. This was a labor-intensive and time-consuming process. In the early days of academic libraries, bibliographers were faculty members with an interest in books.[4] In fact, the position of librarian was generally relegated to a scholar.[5] Gradually, faculty began withdrawing from selection functions because of increasingly rigorous tenure requirements,[6] and selection was transferred to librarians with subject expertise.[7] The subject bibliographers, in many cases scholars themselves, kept close contact with the faculty. But the transition of responsibilities for building collections from faculty to librarians meant a transfer of control. Librarians became responsible for the contents of the library's collection and took control of the acquisitions budget.

Paradoxically, it was the relatively prosperous period following World War II that forced libraries to give up at least part of the responsibility for building collections. Because of a great need to expand educational facilities for returning military personnel, the government provided generous funds for universities and libraries. Often though, the funds were earmarked for material purchases with no equivalent increase for hiring personnel.[8] Libraries found themselves in a quandary. The material budgets were strong, but there was a short supply of librarians.[9] Bibliographers found themselves in the awkward position of having too much money and not enough time to spend it. Methods had to be devised for the quick and efficient spending of the increased acquisitions budgets.

In the 1940s, the Library of Congress (LC) had used approval plans, then called blanket order plans, to acquire materials from foreign countries.[10] The library bought, through a vendor, a copy of every book published in a particular country. It was the vendor's responsibility to identify the books and send them to the library. Vendors did not provide the option of returns. Unwanted books were discarded rather than returned for a refund.[11] Although not all books were added to the collection, the relatively cheap cost of books at the time made it acceptable to write off the cost for discarded books. Other examples of early blanket order plans are the Latin American Cooperative Acquisition Plan (LACAP), proposed at the first Seminar on the Acquisition of Latin American Library Materials (SALALM) meeting in 1956; the Greenaway plan, between the Philadelphia Free Library and several publishers; and PL-480, the public law that allowed libraries to purchase materials from foreign countries in local currencies obtained by the U.S. government from the sale of American agricultural products.[12]

Richard Abel is credited with the invention of the approval plan as we know it today.[13] He implemented the first such plan in the early 1960s, adding new services that made the idea appealing to libraries. The Richard Abel Company used LC proof slips, book reviews, the *Weekly Record*, and its contacts with publishers to get information about new books being published. In most cases the company had this information earlier than most libraries.[14] Abel had studied the needs of the college library for which he had a contract and ordered in advance books that would be needed by the library. Thus a substantial saving of time was achieved. This was the beginning of the profile. The books were sent to the library for review, and the library could choose which books to keep and which to return. There was no charge for returned books. The library received one invoice per shipment. The Abel Company offered regular status reports, centralized accounting, standing-order records, and cataloging either as Library of Congress card sets or in machine-readable form.[15] It was not until the 1990s that vendors reintroduced the practice of selling cataloging records with books to academic libraries. More than three decades later, these services sound very modern, and they show the true level of innovation that Richard Abel brought to collection development.

The Abel Company started with one customer, but librarians learned about its services through word of mouth, and the company's client base grew quickly. Soon, other book vendors started providing approval plans. The approval plan transferred a large portion of the effort for selection from the library to the book vendor. Approval plans provided a quick and efficient way for libraries to spend their acquisitions budgets while still allowing them to maintain control over the quality of the purchases. Most of the risk was borne by the vendor, since libraries had the option to return unwanted books.

The Controversy

Today, approval plans are commonplace.[16] Seventy percent of the academic libraries surveyed for this book reported that they outsource some collection development activities. Of those, the majority use approval plans. Blanket order plans, arrangements with bookstores and with agents in foreign countries, are used to a lesser extent.

At its inception, like any innovative idea, the approval plan did create some controversy and met considerable resistance. Initially, the service was met with "fierce resentment" by librarians and faculty who believed that only they were qualified to select books for libraries.[17] Other librarians accused vendors of "having a casual attitude toward the expenditure of funds," of presenting a "greedy demand for library dollars," and finally of setting up approval plans "to exploit the situation."[18] Many of these professionals saw the vendors' motivation as being anathema to what libraries stand for—service rather than profit.[19] Approval plans were also entering the market at the time when librarians were taking over selection responsibilities from faculty, and it is understandable that they would be unwilling to give up this responsibility easily.[20] Not surprisingly, many libraries did not embrace the idea from the beginning.[21] There were other arguments used against approval plans. In most cases approval plans deliver mainstream materials. Critics pointed out that if collections were built by approval plans, they would all look alike[22] and libraries would lose the enormous diversity and uniqueness they had enjoyed until then.

Some arguments were political in nature, and experience has shown that approval plans did not create uniform library collections. As respondents to a survey in the early 1970s about approval plans pointed out, libraries still maintain a portion of the budget for firm orders, and it is these orders that make their library collections unique.[23] Another reason this feared uniformity did not develop was the striking diversity of approval plans—a fact that certainly contributed to their success. In 1988, ARL reported a "remarkable diversity of practice" ranging from specialized plans for publishers, subjects, or formats to comprehensive plans.[24] The diversity of plans in terms of both coverage and size is probably one of the most important characteristics pertaining to the evolution of approval plans.

Over the years, an increasing number of vendors began providing approval plans. These plans could be tailored to the needs of large and small libraries, in contrast to the early plans, which served only large libraries.

The outsourcing decision has been—and remains—the prerogative of the library administration. Collection development is no exception. A 1977 survey found that library administrators were responsible more often than any other group for the introduction of approval plans in libraries.[25] In retrospect, this finding is enlightening. First, it underscores one of the major characteristics of the implementation of outsourcing: it is usually an administrative decision mandated from the top. Second, it shows that substantial opposition existed to the adoption of approval plans. These findings are telling, since today there is complete acceptance of this practice in the profession, and few librarians would argue against the concept.

The Literature on Approval Plans

It is interesting to look at the evolution of the approval plan as it is reflected in the library literature. Multiple articles, books, and even library conferences were devoted to the topic in the late 1960s and early 1970s. The articles discussed eloquently the pros and cons of approval plans. A group called the International Seminar on Approval and Gathering Plans in Large and Medium Size Libraries held three conferences, in 1968, 1969, and 1970, exclusively devoted to the issue. Luminaries of the day such as Daniel Gore, Peter Spyers-Duran, Roscoe Rouse, and Richard Boss discussed every possible aspect, positive and negative, of the approval plan. By the end of the third conference, Richard Chapin, in summarizing the accomplishments of the conferences, stated emphatically that approval plans were here to stay and there was no need for further conferences or discussions on the topic.[26] As if taking a cue from Chapin, the literature shows a noticeable gap in articles and books on the topic until the 1980s. The group met one more time almost a decade later.[27] The discussions did not present any radically new ideas. Instead they focused on techniques for administering and improving approval plans.[28] This focus is reflected throughout the literature from this time period and continues into the 1990s. Since the mid-1980s the literature has shown much less interest in the pros and cons of approval plans than with fine-tuning and improving existing plans. A modern manual on collection development published by ALA's ALCTS section entitled *Collection Management for the 1990s*[29] does not even contain the term *approval plan* in the index, demonstrating that approval plans are taken for granted today.

BASICS OF APPROVAL PLANS

An approval plan is an agreement between a library and a book vendor whereby the vendor provides a certain set of books regularly to the library. The books are selected with the help of a profile. The library reviews the books, returns to the vendor those that are unsuitable for its collection, and keeps those that are. The library pays only for the books that it keeps. The vendor sends the library one invoice per shipment, which facilitates the library's bookkeeping operations. This simple definition of approval plans covers the concept of the service. A closer look reveals several components that are common to all approval plans.

Publisher Lists

Approval plans differ most distinctly regarding the type of publishers they cover. Each vendor has a list of publishers from which it can supply books. Vendors specialize in a variety of publishers such as trade, academic, art, music, or juvenile. Besides by the type of publisher, vendors also specialize by geographic area or language. The list of publishers and the geographic and language specializations allow libraries to choose the vendor best equipped to provide the library with needed materials.

Profiles

Based on the vendor's area of specialization and the library's needs, the two parties create a profile that enables the vendor to identify materials appropriate for a specific library. The profile is the single most important tool in controlling the relevance of books sent on approval. Profiles, first introduced by Richard Abel, have evolved into sophisticated tools that allow modern plans to be more than 95 percent accurate. Each vendor uses customized profiles, but there are some general criteria that apply to all.

Profiles use subject parameters. Some vendors use the Library of Congress subject headings (LCSH); others have created their own subject thesauri. Some vendors also use the LC classification system. Most vendors also use nonsubject parameters such as geographic, language, or price restrictions. Thus a book from a country or in a language that the library does not collect will not be sent. Books over a certain price will also not be sent. Most approval plans provide the option of using a slip notification system to alert the library to additional books that do not match the profile but may still be of interest.

The Contract

The contract is equally important when dealing with an approval plan. Whereas the profile is a working document that influences specific decisions, the contract provides the legal framework for delineating responsibilities. The contract specifies the vendor's responsibilities and the library's expectations. It includes clauses that are enforceable by either party, such as penalties, and provides for termination of the contract if the level of service deteriorates. The contract is the most powerful tool that the library has to ensure a high-quality product. It is the only legally valid protection either party has against poor performance.

TYPES OF APPROVAL PLANS

Today's vendors can provide any newly published book from their inventory of publishers. Whereas approval plan vendors offer a variety of customized services based on libraries' needs, there are two major types of plans: comprehensive and specialized. Comprehensive plans offer a large number of books on a variety of topics from a large number of publishers. Libraries are familiar with plans run by companies such as BNA, Baker & Taylor, Yankee Book Peddler, and Academic Book Center. Smaller plans based on a specific area such as medicine, engineering, art books, or Latin American books, to name just a few, are also available. Examples of these types of plans would be Howard Karno's Mexican Art Book plan and Harrassowitz's European Music Scores plan. Although profiles allow a library to create a specialized buying plan with a comprehensive vendor, there are advantages in choosing a specialized vendor for these more distinct areas. The vendor's relationship with niche publishers is the most obvious advantage. The attention to detail provided by a smaller vendor is another.

CURRENT DEVELOPMENTS

In the 1990s, several developments have affected approval plans: direct access to vendors' databases; the provision of cataloging and physical processing of materials, or value-added services; and total outsourcing. The first two developments were initiated by the vendors and were based on already existing services. Total outsourcing was introduced in a public library system and paves the way for academic libraries with limited budgets.

Direct Access

Technological developments already point to many improvements in the efficiency of approval plans. The improvements range from computerized data exchange among publishers, vendors, and libraries to the electronic transmission of records,[30] the creation of lists for mechanical selection of mainstream materials,[31] the creation of customized files to monitor approval plan rejects,[32] and the use of expert systems to evaluate and predict approval plan performance.[33] Vendors are beginning to make their databases available to their customers. The library knows in real time what books have been sent on approval, can find out which books the vendor will send slips on, and can see the vendor's entire stock. In some cases, the library can order directly through this system. The service is in its infancy and is currently supported by the large vendors. Undoubtedly, most vendors will adopt this feature, and as that happens, more improvements and refinements will occur.

Value-Added Services

Another feature of modern approval plan vendors is value-added services. Vendors now supply cataloging records and a wide range of physical processing together with their books. Many academic libraries use this service, which is affecting approval plans and collection development practices. In effect, it eliminates the best feature of the approval plan. As libraries purchase books together with their cataloging, returning books is becoming less of an option. Also, the need for selectors to review these books is eliminated. In essence, the approval plan becomes a blanket order, in which all books sent by the vendor are kept by the library without being reviewed. In this scenario, the profile becomes even more critical, since it remains the only decision making tool.

Total Outsourcing

In the most extreme case of outsourcing to date, the Hawaii State Public Library system allocated all collection development decisions for the 49 branches to Baker & Taylor. No selection is performed by librarians; nor is there any money to buy materials for the specific needs of individual libraries within the system. Some of the drawbacks of such a drastic move soon became apparent. Librarians were losing expertise in book buying, were losing touch with their collections, and had no way to redress mistakes made by the vendor. Most perceived this loss of expertise as detrimental to the provision of quality reference service.[34] Loss of control, one of the pitfalls associated with total outsourcing, was evident. Ultimately, the outsourcing contract for collection development was terminated roughly two years after it was begun. Although this example comes from the world of public libraries, it is conceivable that in time the model may spread to academic libraries. For example, the newest campus of the University of Florida system opened its library in summer 1997 with a minimal level collection development and technical services operation.[35] Academic Book Center provided the library with an opening-day collection of approximately 35,000 shelf-ready books and will supply books on approval, standing orders, and firm orders.

ADVANTAGES AND DISADVANTAGES

Since the controversy over approval plans has virtually disappeared, it is useful to look at the advantages that libraries are reaping from using this service. It would be safe to state that one of the most important reasons for the success and wide acceptance of approval plans is that they do provide numerous benefits for libraries.

Discounts

First on the list is the economy of scale that vendors are able to provide. Vendors have large storage facilities and order large quantities of books from one publisher, which they then resell to several libraries, passing on the discount they receive from publishers. Discounts are part of the benefits of using an approval plan.[36] This fact testifies to the efficiency of vendor operations and to a competitive marketplace in which vendors aggressively compete; in the early days of approval plans, the practice of offering libraries discounts did not exist.[37] Although publishers avoid discussions on discounts, it is a fact that books ordered by a library directly from a publisher carry a higher price tag than books received on approval from a vendor.

Access

Vendors identify newly published books from a variety of sources. As a rule, they have wider access to information on what is being published than a library's collection development department. Vendors use all the standard tools for identifying materials, such as *Publishers Weekly*, national bibliographies, and publishers' announcements. Each vendor creates a special relationship with its publishers, which allows it to receive the books quickly after publication. It would be impractical for a library's acquisitions department to maintain such close contact with every publisher from which the library buys books.

Reliability

Approval plans offer a steadiness and reliability of coverage that is difficult to achieve by individual bibliographers over extended periods of time. Vacations, sabbaticals, and sick leave, which can take bibliographers out of the library for extended periods of time, can create wide variations in coverage of specific subjects.[38] The vendor has a built-in mechanism for making sure such variations do not take place. For the vendor, using the profile to identify the books and then sending them to the library is the primary function of operation. Extended staff leave is taken into account in such a way as to not disrupt this selection. A library can use its contract to ensure the steady delivery of books. Evidence from the field indicates that vendor performance in this area is satisfactory.

Reports

Current approval plans provide a variety of reports that enable selectors to monitor plans more easily and efficiently. Automation allows vendors to generate a multitude of standard and customized reports that provide the library with useful information about spending patterns, buying patterns, price increases, ratios between monographic and serials expenditures, and so on. Many of these reports present data in innovative ways, enabling libraries to better manage their resources and giving them new perspectives on solving problems.

Staff Savings

One of the casualties of this new arrangement between libraries and book vendors was the full-time bibliographer. This position has all but disappeared from American academic libraries. Without a doubt, the full-time bibliographer could develop the best possible collection for a library. This model, though, is expensive and time-consuming. In order to provide adequate collection support and expertise in a specific area of the collection, the bibliographer needs to have the proper education and training. Thus the larger the library and the more varied the research interests of its clientele, the larger the number of expert bibliographers needed. It therefore became impractical to build library staffs with competency in all subjects.[39]

Once part of their work was contracted out to a book vendor, these highly skilled experts were freed to perform other tasks considered more important in libraries than the meticulous selection and evaluation of individual book purchases. With approval plans, the bulk of ordering occurred almost automatically and certainly with only minimal involvement by the bibliographer. The model has continued to evolve to the point where most collection development and management activities today are performed on a part-time basis by librarians in addition to their other responsibilities.

Their expertise is used in a broader area of librarianship than before. Selectors use their skills to devise approval profiles that ensure the continued receipt of quality materials for their libraries. They monitor the plans; purchase books that fall outside the profile, thus supplementing the gaps in the approval plan; and at the same time provide other services to the library such as reference-desk coverage, teaching, and cataloging.

It is generally assumed that approval plans allow libraries to order and process increased amounts of material without a corresponding increase in staff. Indeed, approval plans arrived on the scene at a time when library staffs were not keeping up with the increase in the materials budgets. Approval plans were touted as providing support to libraries in times of higher budgets and inadequate staffing. But higher budgets were short-lived. Paradoxically, approval plans were also praised in times of budgetary restraints. At the third International Seminar on Approval and Gathering Plans in Large and Medium Size Libraries held in 1970, approval plans were described as tools that would help libraries in times of budgetary restraints,[40] and in the late 1980s some libraries cite financial austerity as the reason for using approval plans.[41]

Evidently, by the 1970s academic libraries were relying quite heavily on approval plans. Several studies indicate that indeed libraries save on staff time, realize processing efficiencies, allow selectors to expand their collection development activities, and broaden the collection's coverage.[42] Newer studies support the assertion that libraries realize efficiencies after the introduction of approval plans.[43] Other studies are not as conclusive,[44] but it is evident that libraries gained enough benefits from approval plans to make them justifiable and commonplace.

Even though bibliographers have mostly been replaced by part-time selectors, the fiscal realities of the 1990s have forced some libraries to take a hard look at the cost of selection. Despite approval plans, selection continues to be one the highest-cost activities in the library, as most of the work is performed by high-level, highly paid professionals.[45] There are still numerous steps involved in reviewing materials: Acquisitions staff open boxes and place the books on display shelves; selectors review the books and make decisions about additions to the collection, location, and treatment; acquisitions staff further process the books, pay invoices, return unwanted books, and send approved books to cataloging. This time-consuming and expensive process is being questioned by library administrators, which partly explains the trend toward purchasing shelf-ready books from vendors in the hope of reducing the overall cost of selection and acquisition.

Control

Usually, when an operation is outsourced, a certain amount of expertise is lost by the organization. Outsourcing has worked so well in collection development partially because the library has had to give up relatively little control or internal expertise in order to achieve an increase in productivity.

With approval plans, quality checking occurs on a continuous basis as selectors or bibliographers review each week's shipment of books. Unwanted books can be returned, and, at least theoretically, misses can be identified in the process. Perhaps it is this continued maintenance of control over the process by the library that has made outsourcing of collection development so acceptable.

Gaps in Coverage

By far the greatest fear experienced by libraries regarding approval plans is that of missing important materials.[46] There are two major causes for gaps. One is systemic: The vendor's coverage of publishers and subjects may not be broad enough to provide the necessary materials for the library. The other is functional: A vendor may not order enough copies of a particular title to supply all interested libraries. As a result, certain libraries are short-shipped. Systemic deficiencies are easier to identify and rectify because the vendor can provide lists of publishers with which it does business, and it is possible to predict gaps based on these lists. Functional deficiencies are not immediately apparent. Selectors need to be vigilant in identifying important titles not received and draw the vendor's attention to them. Libraries can monitor approval plan receipts and match them against lists of all titles that should have been received. This is one of the most important facets of selector involvement with approval plans besides creating the profile. Selector expertise is crucial at this juncture, since identifying gaps is more complicated and time-consuming than simply judging the quality of a book for its addition to the collection.

The profile and the contract come in handy at this stage. Monitoring the plan provides selectors with a good picture of the collection and allows them to respond quickly to the changes that inevitably arise. But monitoring should not be excessive. As was mentioned in the general discussion about outsourcing in chapter 1, selectors should be careful not to micromanage the plan because this would lead to wasteful and unnecessary duplication of effort. Once the plan is operating optimally, periodic checking will suffice. As with all outsourcing operations, a level of cooperation and trust has to be established in order to achieve the desired results, and it is expected that the two parties will communicate freely when problems occur.

COLLECTION DEVELOPMENT AS A MODEL FOR LIBRARIANSHIP

Outsourcing collection development could serve as a model for other outsourcing ventures in the library. Parts of an activity that once constituted a core competency have been outsourced. Libraries have become so dependent on this arrangement that it would be impossible for most of them to take the function back in-house and return to the full-time bibliographer model. Acquisitions departments would also be unable to handle the large number of orders with each individual publisher. Regardless of whether the bibliographer model is more desirable than approval plans and blanket orders, it is important to look at the lessons to be learned from the experience of outsourcing collection development: partnerships with vendors, internal control of the venture, lower costs, continuous evaluation, negligible loss of expertise, and so on. The lessons learned will apply to other areas of librarianship such as cataloging and acquisitions.

Outsourcing in collection development has opened the way to outsourcing other library functions. It has helped develop an industry that specializes in providing products and services for libraries. Many of the book vendors that started by selling books to libraries have evolved into the companies that today offer a whole array of products and services to libraries ranging from cataloging to electronic acquisitions functions and customized collection-evaluation tools.

CONCLUSION

Approval plans are an example of a mature outsourcing operation. Today they form an integral part of collection development in academic libraries. As an increasing number of functions in libraries are being outsourced, it is becoming more difficult to draw distinct lines between separate functions. Outsourcing arrangements in one area, such as cataloging or acquisitions, will change some of the parameters of another area, such as approval plans. This interaction will inevitably transform library processes over time.

In order to completely understand their roles, we need to view approval plans in the proper perspective. Approval plans are not the ultimate answer to all of collection development's needs. They are only a tool in a library's exercise of collection development functions. There is still ample room for individual book selection by expert bibliographers, be they part time or full time. Most libraries spend only a percentage of their budgets on approval plans, leaving funds aside for individual purchases.

The approval plan creates a stable base of core materials upon which the collection can be built. It frees selectors to engage in the pursuit of specialized materials that fulfill the unique needs of the library. It also frees them to perform other collection management functions such as collection evaluations, retrospective buying, and faculty liaison. As several studies have proved, approval plans enable libraries to process large amounts of materials without a corresponding increase in staffing. There are few deficiencies inherent in the concept of the approval plan; the only drawbacks arise from operational problems that can be monitored and corrected. Technological advances promise new developments that will further improve the quality and usefulness of approval plans. Outsourcing collection development in the form of approval plans provides a solid value for the library's dollar.

NOTES

1. Richard E. Chapin, "Summary Statement," in *Economics of Approval Plans*, ed. Peter Spyers-Duran and Daniel Gore (Westport, CT: Greenwood Press, 1971), 123.

2. Daniel Gore, "Understanding Approval Plans," in *Advances in Understanding Approval and Gathering Plans in Academic Libraries*, ed. Peter Spyers-Duran and Daniel Gore (Kalamazoo: Western Michigan University, 1970), 4.

3. Mary J. Bostic, "Approval Acquisitions and Vendor Relations: An Overview," in *Vendors and Library Acquisitions*, ed. William A. Katz (New York: Haworth Press, 1991), 130.

4. Dora Biblarz, "Approval Plan," *Encyclopedia of Library and Information Science* 56 (1995): 21.

5. Eugene R. Hanson and Jay E. Daily, "Catalogs and Cataloging," *Encyclopedia of Library and Information Science* 4 (1970): 243.

6. Geoffrey Caston, "Academic Tenure and Retrenchment: The U.S. Experience," *Oxford Review of Education* 8, no. 3 (1982): 299.

7. Joseph J. Branin, ed., *Collection Management for the 1990s* (Chicago: American Library Association, 1992), vi.

8. Ann L. O'Neill, "How the Richard Abel Co., Inc. Changed the Way We Work," *Library Acquisitions* 17 (1993): 44.

9. Biblarz, "Approval Plan," 24.

10. Biblarz, "Approval Plan," 25.

11. Ibid., 23.

12. Ibid.

13. O'Neill, "Richard Abel Co.," 42.

14. O'Neill, "Richard Abel Co.," 41.

15.   Biblarz, "Approval Plan," 25.

16.   Robert F. Nardini, "Approval Plans: Politics and Performance," *College & Research Libraries* 54, no. 5 (September 1993): 418.

17.   Daniel Gore, "Adopting an Approval Plan for a College Library: The Macalester College Experience," in *Economics of Approval Plans*, ed. Peter Spyers-Duran and Daniel Gore (Westport, CT: Greenwood Press, 1971), 24.

18.   Nardini, "Approval Plans," 417.

19.   Ibid.

20.   O'Neill, "Richard Abel Co.," 44.

21.   Roscoe Rouse, "Automation Stops Here: A Case for Man-Made Book Collections," in *Advances in Understanding Approval and Gathering Plans in Academic Libraries*, ed. Peter Spyers-Duran and Daniel Gore (Kalamazoo: Western Michigan University, 1970), 35.

22.   O'Neill, "Richard Abel Co.," 44.

23.   David O. Lane, "Total Effect of Approval Plans on the Nation's Academic Libraries," in *Economics of Approval Plans*, ed. Peter Spyers-Duran and Daniel Gore (Westport, CT: Greenwood Press, 1971), 44.

24.   *Approval Plans.* SPEC Flyer 141 (Washington, DC: Association of Research Libraries, Office of Management Studies, February 1988).

25.   Nardini, "Approval Plans," 419.

26.   Chapin, "Summary Statement," 124.

27.   Peter Spyers-Duran and Thomas Mann Jr., eds., *Shaping Library Collections for the 1980s* (Phoenix, AZ: Oryx Press, 1980).

28.   Jennifer Cargill, "A Report on the Fourth International Conference on Approval Plans," *Library Acquisitions* 4, no. 2 (1980): 111.

29.   Branin, *Collection Management*.

30.   Biblarz, "Approval Plan," 27.

31.   John C. Calhoun, James K. Bracken, and Kenneth L. Firestein, "Modeling an Academic Approval Program," *Library Resources & Technical Services* 34, no. 3 (July 1990): 374.

32.   John Earl Keeth, "Approval Plan Rejects—To Keep or Not to Keep—Is That the Question?" *Library Acquisitions* 16 (1992): 168.

33.   Lynne C. Branche Brown, "An Expert System for Predicting Approval Plan Receipts," *Library Acquisitions* 17, no. 2 (1993): 163.

34.   "Outsourcing in Hawaii's PLs: Lessons, Unresolved Issues," *Library Hotline* 25, no. 44 (November 4, 1996): 1–2.

35.   "OCLC, Academic Book Center, SOLINET to Provide Automated Collection and Technical Services to New Florida University," *OCLC Newsletter*, no. 225 (January/ February 1997): 10.

36. Kay Womack et al. "An Approval Plan Vendor Review: The Organization and Process," *Library Acquisitions* 12, no. 3/4 (1988): 364.

37. Peter Spyers-Duran, "Plans for Acquisitions of Current Library Materials: Approval Plans," *Encyclopedia of Library and Information Science* 22 (1977): 484.

38. Gore, "Understanding Approval Plans," 11.

39. Thomas C. Harris, "Book Purchasing or Book Selection: A Study of Values," in *Advances in Understanding Approval and Gathering Plans in Academic Libraries*, ed. Peter Spyers-Duran and Daniel Gore (Kalamazoo: Western Michigan University, 1970), 55.

40. Peter Spyers-Duran, "Preface," in *Economics of Approval Plans* (Westport, CT: Greenwood Press, 1971), vii.

41. Bostic "Approval Acquisitions," 130.

42. Peter B. Kaatrude, "Approval Plan Versus Conventional Selection: Determining the Overlap," *Collection Management* 11, no. 1/2 (1989): 149.

43. Barry Baker, in *Creative Outsourcing: Assessment and Evaluation* (Chicago: American Library Association, ALA-644, 1996). 2 audiocassettes.

44 Joseph W. Barker, "Vendor Studies Redux: Evaluating the Approval Plan Option from Within," *Library Acquisitions* 13, no. 2 (1989): 134.

45. Dilys E. Morris, "Technical Services Costs and Resource Allocation," paper presented at "In or Out—In-House Innovation and Outsourcing: Technical Services Alternatives for the 90's," ALA Annual Conference, ALCTS Preconference, New York, July 5, 1996.

46. John Walsdorf, "New Trends and Needed Improvements in Approval Services: A Dealers' Panel," in *Advances in Understanding Approval and Gathering Plans in Academic Libraries*, ed. Peter Spyers-Duran and Daniel Gore (Kalamazoo: Western Michigan University, 1970), 115.

6  *Acquisitions and Serials Management*

Whereas collection development is concerned with identifying materials needed for the collection, acquisitions is concerned with acquiring those materials. Today, a majority of academic libraries purchase materials from book jobbers and subscription agents. The survey indicates that 59 percent of respondents outsource some acquisitions functions; the larger ARL libraries outsource in higher numbers than their non-ARL counterparts. This includes approval plans, standing orders, and firm orders. No matter what the method, "the library depends upon the vendor for order fulfillment."[1] It is the exception rather than the rule for a library to routinely order materials directly from publishers. The dependence of libraries on vendors developed at a time when the publishing industry experienced an unprecedented growth and publishing output increased dramatically. Libraries found it impractical to order materials from a large number of publishers. Furthermore, publishers were not equipped to handle orders from thousands of individual libraries.

Acquisitions departments have less control over workload and workflow than other technical services departments. Their work is affected by the library budget cycle, publishing cycles, individual bibliographers or selectors, and the unpredictable receipt of gifts. Acquisitions has a pivotal role in the library as the interface between internal and external library operations. Thus any outsourcing operation in which other departments engage affects the acquisitions department and its workflow. The compatibility—or lack thereof—among the library's online system, the jobber's system, and the bibliographic utility determines whether outsourcing is a success or a failure.

Gary Shirk suggests the possibility that the entire acquisitions operation can be outsourced.[2] However, he admits that there are so many ifs to this premise that it is unrealistic to expect the wholesale closing down of acquisitions departments in libraries across the country. In fact, most of the literature suggests that acquisitions will never be fully outsourced because it controls the monetary resources of the library and therefore needs to remain in-house.

THE EVOLUTION OF ACQUISITIONS

Outsourcing of acquisitions started before automation. In the 1960s, the technology of the day—the telephone and surface mail—provided the foundation for outsourcing. These tools were used by librarians to communicate with the outside world, that is, book and serials vendors. In the 1970s toll-free telephone numbers and the first generation of vendor-developed, proprietary acquisitions systems were introduced. During that same period, some jobbers started offering libraries access to their databases. Others provided libraries with microfiche copies of their title lists. OCLC's database also grew during this period; it proved useful to acquisitions librarians for title verification and made machine-readable cataloging records widely available. During the 1980s many libraries purchased online auto-mated library systems, allowing acquisitions librarians to place orders electronically. In the 1990s online systems were further improved, and most libraries have moved to second-generation, integrated systems. Today, electronic ordering is common, and the adoption of BISAC and SISAC standards promises to increase the efficiency of communication between the library and the vendor. The acquisitions librarian has metamorphosed into a highly sophisticated professional who is equally conversant in the language of commerce and that of technology.[3]

ACQUISITIONS LIBRARIANS AND VENDORS: A SELECT RELATIONSHIP

Acquisitions librarians have typically enjoyed a close relationship with vendors. Staffing in acquisitions usually consists of one professional librarian and support staff. Unlike in other library departments such as reference, cataloging, and collection development, which usually have several professional librarians, the acquisitions librarian does not have professional peers working in the department. Moreover, the work of acquisitions requires knowledge and specialization that are fundamentally different from the skills employed by other librarians. This may explain why acquisitions librarians have historically been more isolated from their peers and therefore closer professionally to vendor representatives.[4]

The close relationship between acquisitions librarians and vendors has led to a unique phenomenon: Librarians often go to work for vendors (sometimes later returning to academia), and vendor representatives frequently join libraries. This fluid situation has created close partnerships, based in great part on cultural fit, that depict the ideal outsourcing arrangement. It is evident that this relationship has worked well for libraries and vendors alike and has enabled acquisitions librarians to make their needs and concerns known to vendors. In many cases vendors have responded quite willingly to librarians' requests. At national library meetings, vendors host parties for acquisitions librarians. Although controversial and certainly not approved by all librarians, these gatherings represent excellent venues of communication and professional networking for both librarians and vendors.[5]

The close connection between acquisitions departments and vendors and the two-way traffic of professionals between academia and the commercial world have led to many outsourcing innovations. These professionals, who best understand the intricacies of the process, have been able to expand existing services. These enhanced services often develop into the outsourcing opportunities of tomorrow.

BENEFITS OF OUTSOURCING

Initially, the use of vendors in acquisitions encountered opposition from librarians who feared higher costs and an increase in the delivery time of materials because of the use of a broker.[6] However, the practice prevailed and has been perfected over the years. Outsourcing of acquisitions is so common that many no longer question it. The use of vendors is not encumbered with the negative factors usually associated with outsourcing such as loss of control over the process and loss of in-house expertise. The library maintains full control over the ordering process. Loss of expertise is not an issue because a professional acquisitions librarian is typically retained by the library in order to manage the department and the vendor-library agreement. Acquisitions librarians are skilled at writing RFPs and negotiating contracts. Indeed, modern academic libraries would be severely impaired if they were not able to rely on vendor services.

Ordering through vendors is a showcase for outsourcing library services and accomplishes the main purposes of outsourcing: saving money and staff time, and achieving greater efficiency.[7] A vendor orders multiple copies of a book for resale to several libraries. For the publisher, this means one financial transaction for multiple sales. Selling in higher volume also enables the publisher to offer the requisite discounts usually associated with higher volume sales. The library is able to consolidate its ordering with a small number of vendors rather than having to conduct transactions with scores of publishers. The result for the library is fewer orders, fewer invoices to check and pay, fewer claims, and fewer problems to resolve. The transactions and workflow are speeded up because of this streamlining.

In order to determine the true costs of ordering, check-in, and claiming, acquisitions departments should cost out individual activities and compare local costs to those of the vendor. Libraries have been using book jobbers and subscription agents for so long that a comparison of vendor costs and in-house costs is not feasible. Despite the heavy reliance on vendors, acquisitions remains one of the costliest library activities.[8] For newer services such as claiming and check-in of serials, it is easier to do cost comparisons because they are still being done predominantly in-house. The low market penetration in academic libraries—only one library surveyed had experimented with a vendor's serial check-in—indicates that the verdict is not in. Clearly, such services save the library staff time, but it is unclear whether they actually save the library money because vendors charge a hefty fee for this value-added service.

As in any outsourcing arrangement, problems sometimes occur, most frequently in the following areas: The vendor sends inappropriate materials to the library; the vendor short-ships the library because it did not order sufficient quantities to satisfy all its customers; delivery time is unacceptably long; and vendor responsiveness to a library's concerns is not timely.

When a library faces such problems, it can use the contract to enforce an improvement in performance or terminate the outsourcing relationship. The number of vendors in the market enables libraries to switch vendors, albeit with some effort. Switching vendors is time-consuming and involves considerable and expensive planning. This is especially true today, when the vendor assumes added functions such as approval plans, cataloging, or physical processing.[9] Oftentimes, the new vendor will assist the library in the transition, which entails learning new routines and changing workflows. For this reason, despite the safety net offered by the marketplace, libraries would do well to see that their initial outsourcing agreement works satisfactorily.

VENDOR SERVICES

Monographic and serials vendors differ in the way they operate because of the nature of their materials. Book jobbers buy books from publishers and store them in warehouses. Subscription agents act as intermediaries: Libraries subscribe to a set number of journals for which they pay a lump sum to the vendor; the vendor places individual orders with publishers on behalf of the library; the publisher sends the journal issue directly to the library. In both instances, vendors assist libraries in the order process by verifying prices and availability.[10] These services, which have become an integral part of vendor offerings, also include rush ordering, check-in and claiming of serials, duplicate checking, canceling, and the generation of reports regarding the library's ordering patterns. These improvements, introduced by vendors over time, have benefited acquisitions departments that have been characterized by historically low staffing levels.

Price and Availability Checking

Passing on price and availability checking to the vendor saves library staff a great deal of time. It also eliminates the costs associated with accessing remote systems, for example, telecommunications charges. Vendors are in a better position than the library to perform price and availability checking, since often the items ordered are in their inventory, and thus searching costs are reduced. Some libraries have eliminated price and availability checking from their preorder searching routine and rely solely on vendors for its performance.[11] Vendors also have greater accessibility to publishers' databases, which enables them to check price and availability more efficiently. In the opinion of one experienced acquisitions librarian, this feature represents the greatest advantage that libraries realize from outsourcing acquisitions activities.[12]

Duplicate Checking and Cancellation

When fulfilling a firm order, jobbers can perform duplicate detection in several ways. Via dial-up or the Internet, they can check the library's online catalog to see if the book is already owned and check the library's order system to determine that the item is not already on order, and they must check their own database to see if it contains an order for that item. Jobbers also have the capability and authority to cancel orders if a duplicate is found. This situation requires a high level of cooperation and trust because jobbers have extensive access to a library's internal files.

Outsourcing in this time-intensive area is in its infancy and can be performed only for small projects. Larger projects could be processed by loading the library's holdings into the vendor's database to check for duplicates, but the limited capacity of most vendor systems prevents this kind of checking. Thus large academic libraries do not yet use this service. As system capabilities expand, vendors will be able to offer this service on a larger scale.[13]

Rush Ordering

Rush ordering allows libraries to call a vendor with an order and have it processed immediately. Given vendors' access to large inventories and their knowledge of publishers' inventories, placing a rush order with a vendor increases the chances for an order to be filled efficiently.

Vendor Reports

Vendor reports are based on data gathered from electronic transactions between the library and the vendor. The reports track expenditures by subject area or fund, track returns, and show the library's spending patterns over time. Reports let librarians look at the data in novel ways. For example, Faxon's analysis of serial prices, which tracks price increases based on academic discipline and geographic origin, has become a standard tool for libraries.[14] Vendors provide other useful information such as the time it takes to fill an order or lists of outstanding orders. These reports, useful to acquisitions and collection development librarians, provide data needed to evaluate current buying practices and to develop future strategies.

Claiming and Check-in of Serials

Libraries rely on their vendors for claiming serials. Acquisitions staff inform the vendor, who in turn contacts the appropriate publisher to send the missing issue. Similarly, vendors are able to check in serials for selected customers. This service, first offered to special libraries, is now marketed to academic libraries. In this scenario, the publisher sends journal issues to the vendor. Upon receipt, the vendor dials into the library's online system, checks in the issue, marks and security strips the issue, and then sends it to the library. Vendors provide different levels of check-in options, and the price varies accordingly. In addition to this basic level of service, vendors provide extra services such as sending copies of the same journal to several locations, providing routing slips, and indicating when the issue will reach the shelves.[15]

OUTSOURCING OTHER AREAS: IMPLICATIONS FOR ACQUISITIONS

A discussion of acquisitions functions in a general outsourcing context is important. The following section describes how specific outsourcing arrangements in collection development, cataloging, and public services affect acquisitions.

Collection Development

Collection development is associated more closely with acquisitions than any other library area. Acquisitions' goals are set by collection development policy and in some libraries the two functions are performed in the same department. There is a close working relationship between selectors and acquisitions staff, as selectors can provide useful sources, especially for areas that rely on materials from small or obscure publishers or for materials acquired from specialized vendors in foreign countries.

Outsourcing of collection development, specifically the percentage of materials acquired through firm orders versus approval plans or blanket orders, significantly affects ordering. Such plans enable acquisitions to streamline ordering, receiving, and payment functions. In the case of an approval plan, the vendor sends the materials, accompanied by a shipping list as well as an electronic list of the materials being sent. Invoices are received electronically, thus avoiding duplication of work. After the materials have been reviewed by the selectors, the rejected materials can be easily returned. The materials that have been selected are paid for and added to the collection.

This process demands that the vendor support certain technical capabilities that are compatible with the library's online system. At the initial stage of the order process, a brief record is sent electronically, by the vendor, to the library. This brief record, which must contain enough bibliographic information to identify the item accurately, is the basis of all future activities. Current systems operate with brief MARC-like records, but increasingly full MARC records are being used depending on the availability of a MARC record at the time of the order creation. To this record are added order and payment information as well as decisions such as approval or rejection by the selector.

Cataloging

An increasing number of jobbers are going beyond selling books and are offering bibliographic records, authority records, and physical processing. Acquisitions and cataloging departments are "becoming interwoven as integrated library systems have allowed acquisitions to participate in creating . . . the bibliographic record."[16] It is essential that in outsourcing cataloging functions, the needs of acquisitions be met. Outsourcing of cataloging creates a complex relationship among three entities: the book vendor, the library, and the bibliographic utility. The MARC records are obtained from a bibliographic utility or are created by the vendors. In this scenario, a vendor may send the library two bibliographic records: a brief order record at the time the book is ordered and a complete cataloging record when the book is cataloged. These records can come from the same vendor or from different vendors. Depending on the configuration of the library's online catalog, this operation can present problems for technical services because these two records may need to be merged into the online catalog.

The method of transmission—through tapes, file transfer protocol (FTP), or direct load from a bibliographic utility—to the online catalog also affects this process. Libraries need to make certain that the advantages received as a result of outsourcing cataloging do not negate most of the advantages gained from outsourcing acquisitions. Regardless of the way cataloging is outsourced, acquisitions needs an order record as soon as the book is ordered to have full control over its own processes.

TECHNOLOGY AND OUTSOURCING

Outsourcing is most efficient when both the library and the vendor use state-of-the-art technology. The capabilities of the systems have a major effect on the success or failure of electronic communication between libraries and vendors. The library's and the jobber's systems need to be compatible so that both entities support the infrastructure necessary to run them. The improved interfacing capabilities of modern library online systems, paralleled by developments of vendor systems, is increasing the low-cost data exchange between libraries and vendors.[17]

The Library's Online System

Some of the earliest automated systems introduced on the market were acquisitions systems. The power of these systems has increased dramatically over time, to the extent that now the entire acquisitions operation is fully dependent on automation. Consequently, book and serials vendors have developed sophisticated software that enables the library's system to interface with the vendor's system. This makes possible the automatic transmission of order and payment records between library and vendor. Too often, new advances in technology cannot be adopted by a library because the online system it has purchased does not support these functions.

Electronic Communication with Book Vendors

There are basically three areas in which acquisitions departments use automation to their advantage: electronic communication between the library and the vendor, electronic ordering, and electronic invoicing. Each of these three areas has been adopted by libraries to varying degrees. Technology promises to eventually combine these three functions and go beyond their individual application toward a complete form of electronic business interaction.

Much of the communication between library and vendor today takes place electronically. This includes both interactive discussion between library and vendor staff, such as the routine informal communication supported by electronic mail, and system-to-system communication such as FTP of vendor records.

Most vendors maintain extensive databases of all the titles they have available. Selectors can search these databases, identify the materials they need, and then instruct the acquisitions department to place an order. The order can be placed electronically, thus eliminating the extra step of rekeying the information. Claims for materials that have not been received can also be sent electronically. Finally, the vendor can send the invoice to the library electronically.

Currently, the only function not actively supported electronically is that of money transfer. Logistical and security problems as well as accounting practices at the parent institution have so far prevented the implementation of electronic fund transfers on a large scale.

Electronic Data Interchange (EDI)

Currently, even more powerful developments are taking place in the market. Spurred on by electronic commerce, new applications such as EDI, or electronic data interchange, promise to further improve efficiency and time savings in the acquisitions process. EDI enables a variety of routine transactions between libraries and vendors to occur automatically without human intervention.[18] EDI and its standard, X12, make possible the automatic exchange of business data between disparate local electronic systems such as those of a library and a jobber. X12 is defined as "the standard adopted by the business community . . . to be used for the electronic exchange of business transactions."[19] It can transmit invoices, purchase orders, price and sale catalogs, ship-notice manifests, and so on.[20] It is expected that EDI will eventually include all present and future acquisitions activities.[21] Even though EDI was not developed exclusively for libraries, its broad capabilities and adoption by the marketplace will affect library operations.

A fully integrated online system is required for the successful implementation of EDI.[22] Today, system limitations restrict libraries' ability to implement EDI. Unfortunately, libraries find themselves in a reactive situation. They do not design online systems; they simply buy them off the shelf. Libraries cannot develop these applications independently and therefore depend on the automation vendor to provide them. As EDI becomes more prevalent, systems vendors will provide EDI-capable systems.

Other impediments to the complete adoption of EDI by libraries are corporate culture and data security. Many higher-education institutions have rigid structures regarding payments of funds, dictated in part by the legality of accounting functions and the paper trail they require. EDI, which automates payments, runs counter to this practice. Currently, data security is also at risk, since the Internet does not provide the most secure environment for data transfer. The alternatives are secure networks that provide complete data protection such as value-added networks (VANs) and value-added banks (VABs). They are designed to address these security problems but they entail considerable costs.[23]

EDI has made limited inroads in libraries so far. This powerful technology, which is being adopted increasingly by the business community, will be adopted by libraries as well. After all, Marion Reid correctly states that acquisitions librarians are also businesspeople and must use business methodologies in their profession.[24] Again, acquisitions librarians are at the cutting edge of innovation in adopting modern business practices.

CONCLUSION

The central role played by acquisitions in the library and its close interaction with all departments in technical services means that the effect of outsourcing goes both ways: Any time a department outsources, it affects acquisitions; conversely, any outsourcing venture that acquisitions undertakes affects other departments. Because of this double impact, close communication, cooperation, and collaboration must be maintained among all the departments involved. Failure to do so leads not only to confusion but also to passing on tasks from one department to another. Increasing the workload in one department in order to decrease it in another is not the goal of outsourcing and does not produce the economies that libraries seek.

External communication between the library and a variety of vendors is equally important. The major area of interest in this context is system compatibility. In order for the library to take full advantage of all the services provided by vendors, its system needs to be able to communicate fully with each vendor's system. Book and serial vendors use proprietary systems that are quite different. The current technology enables libraries to interact successfully with several vendors and their systems.

NOTES

1. Joyce L. Ogburn, "An Introduction to Outsourcing," *Library Acquisitions* 18, no. 4 (1994): 365.

2. Gary M. Shirk, "Contract Acquisitions: Change, Technology, and the New Library/Vendor Partnership," *Library Acquisitions* 17, no. 2 (1993): 148.

3. Marion T. Reid, "Closing the Loop: How Did We Get Here and Where Are We Going?" *Library Resources & Technical Services* 39 (July 1995): 268–69.

4. Ibid., 268.

5. Richard P. Jasper, "Academic Libraries and Firm Order Vendors: What They Want of Each Other," *Acquisitions Librarian* 3, no. 5 (1991): 88.

6. Helen M. Welch, "Acquisitions," *Encyclopedia of Library and Information Science* 1 (1968): 69.

7. Ibid.

8.   Dilys E. Morris, "Technical Services Costs and Resource Allocation," paper presented at "In or Out—In-House Innovation and Outsourcing: Technical Services Alternatives for the 90's," ALA Annual Conference, ALCTS Preconference, New York, July 5, 1996.

9.   Reid, "Closing the Loop," 270.

10.   Carmel C. Bush, Margo L. Sasse, and Patricia A. Smith, "Toward a New World Order: A Survey of Outsourcing Capabilities of Vendors for Acquisitions, Cataloging and Collection Development Services," *Library Acquisitions* 18, no. 4 (1994): 398.

11.   Ibid.

12.   Frances C. Wilkinson, interviewed by authors, University of New Mexico General Library. Albuquerque, NM, May 23, 1996.

13.   Bush, Sasse, and Smith, "A Survey of Outsourcing," 400.

14.   Adrian W. Alexander, "U.S. Periodicals Price Index," *American Libraries*. Annual column in May issue.

15.   Susan Hillson, Faxon Company, telephone interview by authors, June 25, 1996.

16.   Ogburn, "Introduction to Outsourcing," 366.

17.   Bush, Sasse, and Smith, "A Survey of Outsourcing," 398.

18.   Carol Pitts Hawks, "EDI, the Audit Trail and Automated Acquisitions: Report of a Presentation," *Library Acquisitions* 18, no. 3 (1994): 351.

19.   Wilbert Harri, "Implementing Electronic Data Interchange in the Library Acquisitions Environment," *Library Acquisitions* 18, no. 1 (1994): 115.

20.   Hawks, "EDI," 352.

21.   Rosann Bazirjian, "ALCTS/Automated Acquisitions/In-Process Control Systems Discussion Group, American Library Association Conference, New Orleans, June 1993," *Technical Services Quarterly* 11, no. 4 (1994): 67.

22.   Harri, "Implementing Electronic Data Interchange," 116.

23.   David Barber, "Electronic Commerce in Library Acquisitions with a Survey of Bookseller and Subscription Agency Services," *Library Technology Reports* 31, no. 5 (September/October 1995): 506.

24.   Reid, "Closing the Loop," 270.

7   *Cataloging*

Outsourcing cataloging has become one of the most contentious library issues of the 1990s. Cataloging costs are perceived as too high, cataloging standards as too rigid, cataloging production as too slow, and cataloging service as too removed from patron needs to be relevant.[1] In this context, administrators see outsourcing as increasingly attractive, and cataloging itself is being questioned as a professional endeavor. Sixty-three percent of the respondents to the survey engage in some form of outsourcing, and an additional 28 percent indicated that they have future plans for outsourcing cataloging.

Academic libraries have long outsourced some of their cataloging operations. Until recently, these outsourcing ventures supplemented existing cataloging operations. Even though retrospective conversion projects and discrete cataloging projects were contracted out, in-house cataloging was accepted and indeed preferred as the most effective way to provide access to library collections. Whereas earlier discussions about outsourcing revolved around the accuracy of the bibliographic records, the speed of cataloging, and the careers of catalogers,[2] today's concerns center on the future of cataloging.

When Wright State University, in 1993, became the first academic institution to hand over to OCLC the entire responsibility for its cataloging—21,000 titles per year—the outsourcing debate moved to new heights. Suddenly, people started asking themselves whether outsourcing "regular" cataloging, the bread-and-butter of catalogers, had become the new world order. Florida Gulf Coast University, which opened its library in summer 1997 with minimal staff in cataloging, elevates outsourcing to a new status. It outsourced the cataloging of its opening-day collection and most future cataloging to Academic Book Center in cooperation with OCLC and SOLINET.[3] These two examples, although not reflecting the current level of outsourcing in academic libraries, show that total outsourcing can be a viable option. Accuracy of the bibliographic record, once catalogers' main concern regarding outsourcing, becomes overshadowed by a much larger concern, namely, the deprofessionalization of cataloging[4] or, worse, its disappearance.

The growth of outsourcing cataloging can be attributed to budgetary shortages and technological advances, and maybe cataloging's lack of visibility in the library. Most academic libraries will not get substantial fund increases. If new acquisitions have to be made, if the library hours have to be maintained, if reference desks have to be staffed, the funds to support these services must come from within the library's budget. Cataloging is an invisible operation to patrons and administrators, and most other library staff consider it laborious. This aspect contrasts with the glamour of reference service, online and Internet searching, and teaching; when combined with the high cost associated with processing every book and serial, it makes cataloging a quick target for budget cuts. As a result, some libraries have begun to redirect their technical services staff, primarily catalogers, to public services areas as they outsource the functions of these departments.

Technology will continue to be one of the driving forces behind outsourcing cataloging. The increased capacity of telecommunications is making outsourcing of cataloging viable. Optical-scanning technology and automated tools in the areas of electronic classification and authority processing may further reduce the amount of time it takes to catalog titles. Vendors are already taking advantage of this emerging technology. The catalog is no longer the library's central database. It is one of many finding aids available to library users; others include vendor-produced indexes and full-text databases such as CARL/Uncover, FirstSearch, and Expanded Academic Index. Newly created libraries may follow the same logic for the library catalog, that is, have it produced by a commercial vendor rather than the library.

HISTORICAL BACKGROUND

Historically, cataloging and classification have been the primary functions of the keepers of libraries. In modern times, American libraries began to emphasize public services. Early in the twentieth century, cataloging departments began to outsource some of their cataloging by subscribing to the Library of Congress card service[5] and the H. W. Wilson Company. In 1967, with the advent of OCLC, libraries began to purchase their catalog cards and, later, machine-readable records from OCLC. Soon, other bibliographic utilities such as RLIN, WLN, and UTLAS came on the scene, providing essentially the same types of services.

These two events, both early forms of outsourcing, marked important turning points in the history of cataloging. At each stage, pundits predicted the extinction of cataloging. Despite this limited outsourcing, the demand for skilled professional catalogers remained high in academic libraries, and departments maintained the expertise to perform original cataloging in-house. Cataloging remained alive and well. The emergence of total outsourcing is a third turning point in the long history of cataloging, and some are convinced that it will finally spell the death of cataloging.[6]

Catalog Card Services

Beginning in 1901, the LC catalog card service supplied cataloging copy, in the form of catalog cards, for every book cataloged by the Library of Congress. In 1938, the H. W. Wilson Company also began selling catalog cards.[7] For most libraries, these services covered all their needs, and at the time, some predicted that fewer catalogers would be needed. The remaining "super catalogers"[8] would mostly manage clerical and paraprofessional employees and activities and perform occasional "snag" cataloging. This proved to be a false assumption. First, catalogers did not readily accept cards without making changes. They routinely altered the cards, changing the edition statement, the publisher, the classification, and so on to "better" reflect the book in hand and to make it fit the local collection. Second, the Library of Congress did not assume responsibility for cataloging all the materials acquired by most libraries. In fact, by the 1990s, LC began accepting copy cataloging from other libraries because it could not keep up with its arrearages.

In the 1960s there was renewed interest in vendor-supplied cataloging as libraries began to buy cataloging cards from nonlibrary agencies operating for profit. This commercial cataloging and physical processing business was aimed primarily at school libraries, setting the precedent for other types of libraries.[9]

Bibliographic Utilities

In the late 1960s, when automation was just beginning to affect libraries, it was believed—again—that the Library of Congress would become the only significant employer of original catalogers in the United States, and many predicted that with networks and shared cataloging, fewer and fewer catalogers would be needed. Before OCLC, each library cataloged its own title of a book or modified the LC cards. Libraries had access only to cataloging records created by LC and lacked access to records created by other libraries. It was in this area that libraries spent enormous amounts of time duplicating each other's work. National cooperative products such as the National Union Catalog (NUC) were developed to alleviate this problem, but in the era of pre-automation, this was cumbersome and time-consuming. With OCLC, libraries began to contribute new titles to an ever-growing database, making them available to the rest of the library community. By the mid-1970s, cataloging online became the norm, and libraries began to create their own cards through services offered by the bibliographic utilities, mainly OCLC and RLIN. The utilities made available cataloging from a multitude of libraries. As with the LC cards, catalogers found it necessary to revise the records for local use.

When OCLC was still called the Ohio College Library Center, many were contemplating a day when cataloging departments would be dramatically reduced. Paradoxically, cataloging departments did not disappear, and knowledge of electronic tools was added to the cataloger's job description. In 1988, Roxanne Sellberg pointed out that "the central importance of the cataloger's art was reaffirmed with the development of online catalogs."[10] She noted that rather than simplifying cataloging, technological advances increased the complexity of creating, managing, and automating catalog records. Cataloging has become a more and more complex activity due to automation, standardization, and new material types (nonbooks, computer files, Internet files).

Selective Outsourcing

Besides card production, libraries selectively outsourced some of their cataloging for special formats, foreign languages, or other esoteric materials. This type of contract cataloging provided expertise that individual libraries did not have in-house. Selective outsourcing continues to be used extensively. A good example is outsourcing U.S. federal documents through a vendor such as Marcive or Brodart. Nearly half the libraries surveyed outsource their documents cataloging to a vendor. Libraries also report outsourcing the cataloging of unique collections and languages, 14 percent and 11 percent, respectively. In the 1990s, expanded outsourcing services entered the marketplace, and contract cataloging began to supply ongoing cataloging for all the library's needs. Rather than focusing on specific projects, outsourced cataloging entered the regular workflow of cataloging departments. The wholesale outsourcing of cataloging dominated discussions on cataloging listservs such as AUTOCAT.

THE CONTROVERSY

The main concerns for library administrators are cost and productivity; the main concern for catalogers remains the accuracy of the bibliographic record. There is a debate going on between these groups, and libraries need to find the balance between pragmatism and perfectionism. The debate is necessary, and it is important that both sides argue their views vigorously. Only this will result in sound decisions that will provide the maximum benefits to the library and its patrons.

Is Cataloging a Core Function?

The questions regarding outsourced cataloging are the same basic questions asked about the outsourcing of any other operation. The central question boils down to the issue of core competencies: Is cataloging mission-critical? And if so, to what degree can it be outsourced? For years, cataloging was central to the mission of the library, and many still consider that "cataloging is one of the perennial activities of librarianship."[11] The "coreness" of cataloging is now under scrutiny.

There is no credible argument that explains how a function once considered "core" ceases to be "core." Paul Strassman, referring to information technology, finds no valid reason for this change in status and contends that the move from core to noncore includes imaginative stories about "why a function once seen as a critical success factor can now be reassigned to outsiders."[12] This argument seems to describe the situation in which cataloging finds itself today. Part of the explanation lies in the fact that the paradigm has changed. Cooperative cataloging and advances in automation make it possible for large amounts of cataloging data to be shared and distributed to a virtually unlimited number of libraries. Arnold Hirshon offers another explanation and contends that although the product of cataloging is a core function, its creation is not.[13] Total outsourcing clearly means that cataloging is no longer considered a core competency and no longer represents a basic professional activity.

The Ivory Tower of Cataloging

Cataloging, with its sets of rules and hair-splitting interpretations, is often described as arcane and cryptic and catalogers as holding onto knowledge that few understand or appreciate. Clare Dunkle warns that "if cataloging staff fail to couch cataloging issues in terms that make sense to management, they may see their manager reaching for outsourcing as a way to understand what is going on."[14] Even Michael Gorman, the champion of catalogers, admits that the reputation of cataloging "as a branch of librarianship that was inferior to other branches, inefficient, wasteful, and fit only for hermits and misanthropes" is not entirely unjustified.[15]

This does not mean that the low status of cataloging is entirely due to this "wretched reputation." The failure of the library administration to understand the subtleties of cataloging causes a lack of appreciation of its contributions. Outsourcing tackles "the ivory tower of cataloging" and draws fire from "some of the more thoroughly entrenched bastions of traditional librarianship."[16] Clearly, proponents of these views consider outsourcing a cure-all, always preferable to in-house operations, and propose the wholesale closing of catalog departments in libraries. However, a mature approach to outsourcing needs to be based not on polemical arguments that portray catalogers as some kind of misfits or the process as irrelevant but instead on objective, quantifiable criteria that clearly measure both the benefits and the limitations of in-house cataloging.

The Inevitability of Outsourcing

Naturally, catalogers feel resentment regarding the outsourcing of their skills. Part of the bitterness stems from a belief that regardless of the arguments brought forth about the intrinsic value of cataloging, library administrators will decide to outsource. Many believe that administrators fail to recognize the importance of cataloging to library services and see outsourcing as a quick fix. This feeling is reflected in the name of one outsourcing conference "Outsourcing: By You, for You, or in Spite of You?" which took place in May 1996 in California.[17] One of the organizers, Barbara Quint, calls outsourcing the "O" word.

The Cookie-Cutter Approach

In-house departments can be responsive to public services special needs. Catalogers work closely with the reference staff, and many reference librarians consult with catalogers on how to find items or have them recataloged to improve accessibility.[18] At the University of New Mexico General Library, this translates into working with reference departments, special collections, collection development, and the library development officer. Catalogers at the University of New Mexico General Library routinely alter classification to help patrons browse the reference collections, improve access to New Mexicana by adding contents notes for the benefit of special-collection patrons, reclassify general collection materials so patrons can find books within the same series together, add subject headings, and add electronic bookplates to gift books when library benefactors need to be recognized.

One of the results of using an outsource vendor is that the library loses its flexibility to provide customized cataloging. This contributes to the McDonaldization of cataloging and results in decreased variety and a fairly low level of quality.[19] Vendors are less capable and often unwilling to provide customized cataloging.[20] If they do, it certainly affects the price, making it too expensive for libraries to request this type of service on a regular basis. The logistics of requesting customized treatment by the vendor are infinitely more complex than communication with in-house cataloging staff. Requests from public services would most likely have to be funneled through a technical services department to the vendor, thus encumbering a larger number of library employees.

Cataloging Expertise

One of the major drawbacks of outsourcing is loss of in-house expertise. Gaining or losing expertise is a matter of degree and depends on whether the library engages in selective or total outsourcing. It is clear that the library loses expertise when it eliminates its cataloging department. Catalogers do not catalog out of context or just to describe specific items. The greater aim of catalogers is to provide access to their own collections for their specific patrons.

Losing the Spirit of National Cooperation

One of the benefits of the current system, where thousands of academic, research, public, and special libraries contribute cataloging to cooperative union catalogs, is breadth and depth of cataloging.[21] In the past quarter-century, catalogers have built huge bibliographic and authority databases. Both are labor-intensive and both are costly, but they have greatly benefited the cataloging community. Since the advent of the online union catalogs developed by the bibliographic utilities, the number of cooperative programs has increased.

In order to maintain an acceptable level of quality in the national databases, the library profession, with leadership from the Library of Congress, is addressing the issue of quality. The Program for Cooperative Cataloging (PCC) is raising the standard by training librarians across the country, hoping this will result in better and more usable records, thus eliminating the need for local libraries to enhance or change those records. Under the umbrella of PCC, NACO (Name Authority Cooperative Program) and SACO (Subject Authority Cooperative Program) contribute authority records to the national databases. BIBCO (Bibliographic Record Cooperative Program) allows select libraries to contribute bibliographic records of recognized LC quality to the Library of Congress MUMS system and to the national online databases; CONSER (Cooperative Online Serials Program) allows selected libraries to contribute and enhance serial records; OCLC's Enhance and Upgrade capabilities enable member institutions to make permanent corrections or additions to bibliographic records in the OCLC database. All these efforts are designed to improve the quality of the records and the databases.

The users of bibliographic utilities have reaped tremendous benefits from these national programs. They provide high-quality records on a timely basis, reduce duplication of effort, promote standardization of cataloging, and have led to significant reductions in cataloging costs.[22] Reporting on a NACO survey, Jacqueline Byrd and Kathryn Sorury noted that contributors to NACO indicated that quality review was an integral part of the NACO process.[23] These cooperative efforts cannot be duplicated by outsource vendors, since the primary goal of a commercial operation is profit rather than benefit to the cataloging community. Over the years, catalogers have been to countless meetings to make those agreements workable. Catalogers feel responsible for the quality of national databases and question whether the outsourcing of cataloging will undermine this rich cooperative tradition.

Quality of Records

Outsourcing creates quality-control issues, a prime concern for catalogers.[24] The downside of increased efficiency, from the catalogers' point of view, is a decrease in quality because libraries will be forced to accept somebody else's cataloging without revision. Title by title, in-house catalogers review and edit records found in national databases as a form of quality control. Even though some services—TECHPRO, for example—perform some editing,[25] most, in the name of expediency, bypass editing altogether. The question about national standards—AACR2, LC rules interpretations, LC subject headings, and so on—and how they are applied comes up. Will outsourced cataloging conform to national cataloging standards? This leads some to argue that catalog records supplied by outsource vendors will result in lower-quality cataloging and will give patrons a mediocre bank of information.[26]

Fairness

Catalogers have a professional obligation to catalog all types of materials regardless of content or difficulty level. Such an obligation does not exist in the commercial world, where suppliers are able to discriminate among, and negotiate independently with, individual clients.

The decision to add to the collection is made by selectors and is seldom questioned by catalogers. When a library outsources, a second level of checking may occur. Some materials—such as ephemera or rare books—may not get added to the collection because the price of cataloging them does not justify it. For example, a small academic library in Colorado that cannot afford an in-house cataloging department has outsourced its cataloging to the Bibliographic Center for Research (BCR). When original cataloging is required, usually for gift materials, the library often chooses not to spend the additional money and does not add the book to the collection.[27]

WHY LIBRARIES CONSIDER OUTSOURCING CATALOGING

There is a set of circumstances that leads every library to evaluate its in-house cataloging operation. Usually this involves the continued erosion of the budget, reductions in staff, backlogs, the perceived high cost of cataloging, a reemphasis on public services, and inefficient cataloging departments. In the face of these adversities, cataloging managers have to devise methods to reduce backlogs, decrease turnaround time, and cut costs. Reevaluations often result in changed and simplified workflows and can also lead to outsourcing.

Libraries see outsourcing of cataloging in different lights: Some see it as a way to increase productivity, some as a way to lower costs; others want it all and expect the outsourcer to lower the costs of their cataloging and to add value to their records. Outsourcing can be used to support contradictory arguments. Routine cataloging can be outsourced in order to free experienced in-house catalogers for complex cataloging. Complex and original cataloging can be outsourced to supplement the library's expertise. Cataloging is also a good target for outsourcing because, unlike other library departments, it is a production department; it is easy to quantify output and to specify the number of records that can be outsourced or purchased from a vendor.

As in the case of approval plans, libraries can outsource cataloging when they have too much money or too little money. Typically, when a library receives extra funds, it goes to acquisitions. There is usually no corresponding funding increase for processing. Administrators are more willing to spend money on an outsourcing project than to hire extra staff. If a library is in dire financial straits, outsourcing may be the only option, because in contrast with staffing a department, outsourcing delivers a product and does not encumber the library with long-term obligations to employees. Outsourcing allows a library to predict its processing costs accurately and to budget accordingly.

Greater Efficiency

Academic libraries outsource their cataloging operations because they are unable to increase in-house productivity. Studies show that original catalogers spend only 40 percent of their time cataloging.[28] Vendor catalogers are less encumbered with nonproduction activities than professional catalogers working in libraries. The highest productivity thus can be achieved by outside vendors, whose catalogers devote minimal time to meetings and do not engage in research and other academic activities.

Timely Cataloging

Vendors provide a shorter turnaround time for cataloging than libraries can provide in-house. A materials jobber typically delivers the cataloging record at the time the book is selected for the library. If the library acquires the book first, and then sends it to the vendor to be cataloged, the book is returned within a month. This prevents backlogs.

Increased Productivity

Libraries expect to achieve greater productivity from a vendor. Indeed, reports from the field support this assumption. For example, the outsourcing of cataloging at the Loyola University of Chicago resulted in an increase in productivity of 50 percent over the previous year and 151 percent over the previous five years. Its backlog was significantly reduced, and books were cataloged, processed, and on the shelves within 10 days.[29]

Outsourcing can also help improve productivity by forcing the library to synchronize its activities with that of the vendor. The library cannot fall behind in its share of the work. This fosters an urgency that does not exist otherwise and may be the single most important element in increasing productivity. For example, loading federal document records received on a monthly basis from a vendor into the online system cannot be postponed, since the next shipment will arrive within a month.

Lower Costs

Cataloging, in-house or outsourced, costs libraries money. The question is, Will outsourcing cost less or more than in-house cataloging for a similar level of quality? Eliminating a catalog department or outsourcing selectively enables libraries to save staff dollars. Outsourcing also cuts down on overhead costs, reduces searching and telecommunications charges and hardware and software costs, and diminishes the need for training and evaluation. Vendors can catalog titles less expensively for two main reasons: economies of scale and relatively lower wages.

Outsourcing reduces duplication of work at the macrolevel. Rather than cataloging the same book hundreds of times, vendors benefit from an economy of scale, selling the same record to many libraries. However, the extent of this cost reduction is debatable. Vendors' economies of scale are not "so obvious as they would seem at first glance."[30] Savings occur when libraries outsource mainstream materials. For example, a vendor may resell over and over cataloging for mainstream publications but may not be able to do so for esoteric materials held by a handful of libraries. Similarly, for older or foreign-language materials, it is unlikely that the vendor can find acceptable copy, or it may have to perform original cataloging. In that case, vendors do not realize economies of scale and charge a premium for this type of cataloging.[31]

Vendors often pay their catalogers less and provide fewer fringe benefits than libraries. Attempting to debunk the "sweatshop myth," Arnold Hirshon and Barbara Winters write that vendors must deal with the same job market as libraries and that "vendor wages are likely to be comparable to that of the library."[32] However, job advertisements for catalogers posted by vendors on the Internet in 1996 show that vendors' hiring requirements and salaries are often not indicated or are lower than those listed by libraries;

more often than not, an MLS is not required. Credentials of staff range from MLS-degreed librarians to paraprofessionals with varying degrees of experience. Often, vendor catalogers are part-timers or retired catalogers. For example, OCLC's TECHPRO service requires an MLS or equivalent experience, offers an average salary, and provides benefits.[33] WLN does not require an MLS or cataloging experience and offers a rather low salary.[34] Library Associates's FastCat service does not require an MLS for its contract catalogers, provides no benefits, and does not post a salary.[35] Job postings in the fall of 1997 indicated that vendor hiring requirements and salaries are moving closer to those of libraries. Ultimately, for the library, what matters is that it can obtain the product cheaper than producing it in-house.

Value-Added Services

Value-added services add another dimension to the debate. Each time in-house catalogers or vendors handle a record, what further value do they add to it? In his study, James E. Rush writes that "most local cataloging contributes nothing to the value of the bibliographic record."[36] In his opinion, the degree of repetitive cataloging is leading to unacceptably high costs, "especially when considered in light of the lack of added value the repetitive cataloging provides."[37] He sees outsourcing as a way to eliminate wasteful duplication of efforts.

Nonetheless, both sides stress the value they can add to bibliographic records. In-house catalogers add value through participating in various national programs to upgrade existing records and customizing records for local needs. Vendors provide services such as table of contents and physical processing. In all cases, the final product is improved, and in all cases there is a price associated with the added value. It takes in-house catalogers more time to enhance or upgrade a record than to simply produce and download an existing record. Similarly, vendors charge a premium price for adding table of contents to bibliographic records or for physically processing the books.

Maximizing Staff Resource Use

Outsourcing cataloging often results in moving staff from technical services to public services. Some go so far as to say that outsourcing cataloging enhances public services because emphasis is placed on those tasks that involve a direct interaction with patrons.[38] For example, according to Thomas Moore, dean of libraries at the Central Michigan University Libraries, outsourcing of cataloging allows libraries to move some of their limited resources to other areas of importance.[39] In spite of outsourcing, all Central Michigan library staff were retained by the university. On the downside, transferring nonqualified staff to service points may result in a lower quality of services, at least until they get up to speed.

Within cataloging departments—if staff are retained—some claim that outsourcing creates the opportunity for catalogers to devote more time to "more professional and more necessary work" such as organizing bibliographic files in more relevant ways or developing Web pages.[40] This expectation may be unrealistic though, since most library administrators expect to reduce the number of catalogers as a result of outsourcing either through transfer to public services, as mentioned, or by not filling future vacancies.

STEPS TO OUTSOURCING CATALOGING

Outsourcing cataloging is a complex process that involves numerous steps. These steps are discussed in great detail in two recent how-to books. The first, published by ALA in 1995, titled *Outsourcing Cataloging, Authority Work, and Physical Processing: A Checklist of Considerations* and edited by Marie A. Kascus and Dawn Hale, consists primarily of lists of questions that the library needs to ask at every step. The second, written in 1996 by Arnold Hirshon and Barbara A. Winters, *Outsourcing Library Technical Services*, provides good RFP specifications for outsourcing cataloging. Any cataloging department that considers outsourcing needs to assess its operations in terms of cost and workflow, to make decisions regarding types of cataloging to be outsourced and methods and means of record delivery, to choose a vendor, and write a profile.

Evaluating the Cataloging Department

Costs

As discussed in chapter 3, evaluating costs is time-consuming and is particularly difficult because there are no off-the-shelf methods that are universally accepted by the profession. This leads many libraries either to not evaluate costs or to guess their costs. For this reason, it is not always possible to ascertain how much money libraries really save when they outsource. Karen A. Wilson, reporting about the outsourcing project at J. Hugh Jackson Library at Stanford University indicates that due to the number of variables involved, the savings "resulting solely from outsourcing are unknown."[41] Yet, the savings achieved from reducing the staff by half more than offset the fees paid to the outsourcing agencies.

However, in order for the decision to outsource to be sound, it is imperative for the library to conduct cost studies of its in-house operations. There are basically two ways to evaluate the cost of cataloging in a library: total output measure and microanalysis. Wright State University Library, which measured total output, figured out that it would save approximately $10 per title if it outsourced its cataloging operation. The library decided to outsource all copy and original cataloging and make students responsible for in-house processing.[42] The library literature reports that the savings ranged from $100,000[43] to $250,000 a year.[44]

Applying the microanalysis method, Dilys Morris of Iowa State University Library identified the cost of cataloging at her institution. She reports that, without outsourcing, her library has lowered its cataloging costs over time and that, surprisingly, the cost of acquisitions exceeds the cost of cataloging.[45] Morris reports that the reduction of cataloging costs occurred at her institution through reengineering, that is, "flattening the organization structure, reducing meetings, and allocating more staff time to products and services."[46] In comparing cataloging to acquisitions, she concludes that cataloging is an area that is more easily defined and thus would be easier to outsource.

Workflow

Evaluating workflow is equally important but easier to achieve. Cataloging does not function in a vacuum: Cataloging goals are set by collection development policy and the needs of public services. In this environment, the cataloging department balances national cataloging standards with local needs. These needs are incorporated into the internal workflow. Similarly, the outsourcing of cataloging does not function in a vacuum. Critical outsourcing issues include interactions between cataloging and other technical services departments and the library and its vendors.[47]

What Can Be Outsourced

All types of cataloging can be outsourced: copy and original, specialized and mainstream materials in all languages and all formats. No vendor is inclusive, and libraries may have to contract with several vendors for specific formats or languages. For example, OCLC's TECHPRO cannot catalog all non-Roman alphabet languages, and other vendors have similar limitations. The majority of outsource cataloging services rely primarily on copy cataloging available from the bibliographic utilities (OCLC, RLIN, WLN). Some outsourcing services also provide original cataloging, which in turn is added to the bibliographic utilities. This is the exception rather than the rule, as most needs for outsourced cataloging can be met by existing copy. The outsourcing of serials cataloging is seldom mentioned. Issues pertaining to serials need to be considered. Will both bibliographic and check-in records be created by the vendor? Who will process title changes?[48] Timeliness of serials information, a great concern for library patrons and public services, has not yet been addressed by vendors.

Methods of Outsourcing

Depending on the library's needs and the vendor's capabilities, outsourcing of cataloging can take four different forms: 1) The vendor can provide cataloging records at the time a book is ordered and sent to the library. This method, by far the most efficient, is gaining ground because it cuts down on red tape. 2) The library receives the books and then packs and sends them to the vendor to be cataloged. This method is not as efficient, since it involves shipping the books between library and vendors twice. It is a good option for cataloging backlogs and gift books. 3) To avoid sending books, the library can send photocopies of the title page, verso, and other chief sources of information to the vendor. 4) Finally, the library can send brief MARC records to the vendor, which then provides full catalog records to be overlaid or imported into the library's online catalog.

Not all vendors provide all options. The method of supplying cataloging also depends on the type of materials that need to be cataloged and on the capabilities of the library's online catalog. The marketplace provides enough variety to make it possible for any library to find a vendor that can deliver the product it needs.

Means of Delivery

Vendors can supply cataloging records in a variety of formats: cards and/or MARC records on disk, on tape, or through FTP. Catalogers have ample experience in selective outsourcing, as most have dealt with acquiring cataloging records for federal documents, authority control, and retrospective conversion. Accepting cataloging records from a cataloging vendor raises the same issues. Most libraries have already ironed out problems associated with incorporating vendor records into their database and have experience dealing with duplicate records, incomplete records, or missing records.

Choosing a Vendor

Choosing a vendor for cataloging should follow the same general principles as all other outsourcing arrangements: the RFP process, the bid, and the contract. The RFP should include a detailed description of what the library wants to purchase, including the quantity and type of material to be cataloged, and requirements concerning the quality of cataloging, turnaround time, and other special concerns such as foreign languages or different physical formats. In addition, if cataloging is outsourced to an approval vendor, which is increasingly common, the decision has to be made jointly between collection development and cataloging.

The Profile

Just as in the case of collection development, cataloging vendors require the library to fill out a profile defining the project requirements. The profile for cataloging specifies the type of records the library will accept, the origin of the record (Library of Congress or member copy), the amount and type of editing and local data to be added to the record, the method of identifying matches, the types of reports the vendor can prepare to explain what was found in the database and why a record was or was not sent, and other value-added services such as adding table of contents, customizing the call number, and physical processing. The profile also spells out costs for each option and the method of delivery. Profiles can be changed during the life of the contract to allow for corrections and improvements.

IMPACT ON LIBRARY OPERATIONS

The decision to outsource cataloging has to be made in conjunction with other departments because the effects can be far-reaching. Depending on the methods and services used, outsourcing cataloging could affect the acquisitions, collection development, systems, interlibrary loan, and reference departments.

Cataloging

With total outsourcing of cataloging, most staff positions may be eliminated, and internal cataloging routines discontinued. In most cases a skeleton cataloging crew remains, but this department performs vastly different tasks than traditional cataloging departments. Outsourcing requires that the department change its emphasis from cataloging to 1) managing the outsourcing operation and 2) bibliographic record management. The staff manage the outsourcing contract, oversee the downloading of records, export the records when they need to go to an authority vendor, and maintain the online catalog. Libraries report encountering difficulties in managing the workflow when cataloging records and their corresponding book shipments arrive at different times.[49] In-house staff also concentrate on record maintenance—volume and copy numbers; location changes; deletion of records when items are lost or withdrawn; and the processing of rush and reserve items, gift plates, and other local information that needs to appear in records.

Both total and selective outsourcing involve retraining and a general redesign of policies and procedures. In both cases, in the best scenario there is no manipulation of the outsourced bibliographic records by catalogers. Nonetheless, some editing of the record may still be necessary depending on the library's level of tolerance. Local notes, duplicate call numbers, shelflisting problems, series treatment, and local subject headings all may need to be corrected or added to fit properly within the library's collections. For approval plans, the percentage of CIP records remains high and is reported to range from 25 percent[50] to 60 percent[51] of all records. Upgrading CIPs could be done in-house, by the vendor, or by the bibliographic utility retroactively. OCLC, well aware of the CIP problem, began a program to work with book vendors, publishers, and the Library of Congress to accelerate the enhancement of CIP records.[52]

When selective outsourcing is chosen, in-house staff manage the contract but need to handle a split workflow because contract cataloging materials are processed differently by the department than materials processed in-house. The staff needs to devote considerable time to integrating "book-receiving and bibliographic-record-loading processes into their mainstream operations."[53]

Acquisitions

Besides the cataloging department, the acquisitions department is most affected by the outsourcing of cataloging. In an integrated online environment, acquisitions depends on electronic order records generated either in-house or by the vendor. Acquisitions needs this order information from the time an order is originated. These order records, used for invoicing, are typically linked to temporary or brief bibliographic records. Fully cataloged outsourced records should replace these temporary records. But depending on the capabilities of the local online system, this is not always feasible, and the cataloging record and the brief vendor-supplied or locally created record may coexist. When this is the case, it is necessary to merge these records. Indeed, merging can be problematic and time-consuming because there may not be a common control number like the OCLC number present in both records. The lack of such a number makes it difficult to match the bibliographic record with its corresponding order record without human intervention, and the possible savings achieved in cataloging may be offset—or even negated—by the extra work in acquisitions.

Collection Development

Outsourcing cataloging directly influences collection development. Collection development needs to maintain control over which books are bought. In this context, collection development's main concern is not to create a situation that in the name of expediency forces the library to accept unacceptable books. This situation can arise if the library decides to purchase shelf-ready, fully cataloged nonreturnable books from an approval plan.[54] Because no profile can be perfect, a library may choose to accept a certain number of books it may not otherwise buy or choose to outsource the cataloging of firm orders only. Wholesale cataloging of approval titles should not be done if the return rate is too high. In this case, the library and the vendor need to refine the profile to achieve an acceptable rate of returns. When the library outsources both cataloging and approval plans to the same vendor, collection development has to select the vendor and cataloging has to decide what records to accept.

Systems

In an outsourced environment, the systems department has to get more involved in the support of both cataloging and acquisitions. The degree of involvement depends on the method of record delivery. For example, FTP transactions and tape-loading require a steady commitment from systems. The level of involvement can be minimal, though, if data delivery occurs in more traditional ways such as card production. The main issue for the systems department is incompatibility among the various systems—the library's, the bibliographic utility's, the outsource vendor's—and the fact that systems personnel may need to become conversant with the protocols of the vendors' systems.

Interlibrary Loan

Outsourcing cataloging also affects interlibrary loan. The holdings code in the bibliographic utility needs to be updated to reflect ownership and availability of the book. This can be done by the library after the outsourced cataloging records have been received, or it can be done by the bibliographic utility itself at the time of cataloging. In most cases there is a discrepancy between the time the holdings are updated and the time the book is actually available for lending. The holdings statement can appear either too early— before the book is in the library—or too late, days or weeks after the book is actually on the shelves. For example, OCLC's PromptCat service can set holdings at the time the outsourced record is delivered or three weeks later. Problems also arise when the holdings have been set and the book has been rejected and returned to the approval vendor. Interlibrary loan has to be cognizant of these problems and evaluate holdings statements critically.

Reference

Rick Block writes that "good cataloging is fundamental to good reference service."[55] Regardless of the method of cataloging, it is crucial that the online catalog indicate the correct status of each book: ordered, received, in process, or cataloged and on the shelves. Reference librarians should not accept a decrease in the level of access provided in the system. As in the case of interlibrary loan, the premature or incorrect downloading of records in the online catalog can mislead reference librarians and patrons into assuming that a book is on the shelf when in fact it is not.

SOURCE OF CATALOGING RECORD

Most vendors use a bibliographic utility as the source for their cataloging records. In a few cases, vendors have built their own databases of records. Vendors also employ catalogers who can provide original cataloging.

Daniel CannCasciato points out that outsourcing services can function to the extent that a substantial bank of bibliographic records exists on which the vendors can draw. Currently, cataloging departments in thousands of libraries around the country contribute continuously to the growth of this rich resource. The contributing libraries receive little in return (in the case of OCLC, a credit for original cataloging). Approximately 77 percent of the records on OCLC are input by OCLC member libraries; for serials, the percentage is higher, 85 percent.

As nearly all outsourcing of cataloging services relies on the bibliographic utilities, it is important to maintain a critical mass of original cataloging contributions to the utilities' databases. Some feel that libraries that contribute original records need to get some leverage vis-à-vis the utilities that charge others for the records created by individual libraries.[56] One could argue that rather than receiving credit for contributing original records, individual libraries should charge OCLC. Vendors contribute few cataloging records; yet they sell them.

At the heart of the controversy is the question, To whom do the records belong? To the catalog department that created the record? To the bibliographic utility? To the cataloging community? Clearly, the utilities have successfully laid claim to the records. OCLC, for instance, has copyrighted its database, and a library needs to pay in order to access and download the records into its own database. Carmel C. Bush, Margo L. Sasse, and Patricia A. Smith note that "contracting for cataloging could muddy the already murky area of who owns the MARC records and how a library may use them."[57] When a library contracts out for a catalog record, it pays a fee to the vendor. The vendor does not pay back the library that created the original record. This issue gets more complex when the library in turn shares the outsourced record within a consortial catalog. Some vendors add an extra fee when records are shared by several libraries. It is up to the cataloging community to decide on the future direction of bibliographic databases.[58]

The reliance of cataloging vendors on bibliographic utilities such as OCLC, RLIN, and WLN raises the question of the availability of cataloging records if major contributors to these utilities decide to pursue contract cataloging. If one takes this scenario to the extreme and imagines that most academic libraries' cataloging departments will outsource their cataloging and thus quit contributing to the bibliographic utilities, outsourcing services will not operate as they do today. They will have to return a high percentage of books to the library for cataloging, or they will need to create a vast number of original records rather than using existing ones. Both options seem unworkable. If a vendor cannot provide a high percentage of copy cataloging records, cataloging will become more expensive because more original cataloging will need to be created. In the second scenario, vendors could go into the business of creating original records. This most likely would entail the hiring of full-fledged catalogers and would undoubtedly drive the per-record price much higher. CannCasciato argues that if the OLUC, for example, becomes moribund from lack of member contributions, it will not be able to support outsourcing services.[59]

CATALOGING VENDORS

Vendors can be divided into three categories: 1) bibliographic utilities and their network brokers, 2) materials jobbers providing cataloging services, 3) and companies supplying contract cataloging. Whereas their original purpose was not contract cataloging, bibliographic utilities and their networks entered the business of cataloging in the mid-1980s. Similarly, materials jobbers have been dramatically expanding their services to include contract cataloging. Many are still primarily in the business of serving public libraries rather than academic libraries. Some provide cataloging only for the books they supply to the library; others can catalog all library materials regardless of how they were acquired. Outsourcing services come and go. Only the major players are described here, but print and online directories list a multitude of other outsourcing services.[60]

Bibliographic Utilities As Vendors of Cataloging Records

The major bibliographic utilities, OCLC and RLG, offer cataloging services to academic libraries. Bibliographic utilities either work directly with libraries or have joint ventures with book or systems vendors. For example, OCLC now works with ten vendors, including BNA and Yankee Book Peddler, through its PromptCat service and, in 1996, RLG introduced its cataloging service, Diogenes (renamed Marcadia in 1997), a joint venture with Retro Link, a division of Ameritech. These services primarily provide contract copy cataloging with original cataloging as a sideline.

Each bibliographic utility calculates costs differently. OCLC includes the OCLC costs in the estimate for its contract cataloging. When dealing with materials jobbers, the library must pay the jobber for its services and pay the OCLC charges separately. OCLC's TECHPRO service costs are based on format, language, amount of editing, and the type of collection; PromptCat costs are based on the number of records processed and the method of delivery. RLG's Marcadia service costs are based on the number of searches and records delivered.

The OCLC TECHPRO Service

OCLC, which has been and still is an important player in the retrospective conversion business, expanded into the cataloging business. In 1985, it introduced its TECHPRO cataloging service as an offshoot of RETROCON, its retrospective conversion service. TECHPRO's goal is to provide current cataloging for libraries and to offer project-based and ongoing cataloging and physical processing tailored to the needs of any library off-site. For 10 years, libraries have been using this service to supplement current cataloging, to reduce backlogs, or to catalog materials in formats that require special expertise. At first, most of TECHPRO work was done for corporate libraries and special libraries, which traditionally have few, if any, catalogers. The second market was for large academic and public libraries' special projects such as foreign-language or nonbook formats. A third market is emerging as some larger academic and public libraries switch to total outsourcing.[61]

The TECHPRO service offers cataloging in all subjects and formats—music, law, medicine, non-English titles, computer files, scores, and audiovisual materials—but has had difficulty in the past cataloging unusual languages. TECHPRO staff do both copy and original cataloging for titles new to a library's collection. TECHPRO will receive materials directly from book vendors serving the library or from the library itself. Libraries either box their books and send them to Dublin, Ohio, or send photocopies of title pages. This service requires a minimum of 50 items per year or 10 titles per shipment. When TECHPRO receives the items or photocopies, OCLC staff members catalog them and perform customized local editing requested by the individual library. TECHPRO then supplies the library with MARC records on tape, diskettes, catalog cards, or, if the library is an OCLC member, records placed in the "save" file for local export.

Initially, academic libraries constituted a small percentage of TECHPRO libraries. By 1993, 22 academic libraries had used TECHPRO and more than 38,000 records had been processed.[62] Academic libraries have contracted with TECHPRO for the cataloging of finite special collections such as scores, sound recordings, and foreign-language publications. For example, Yeshiva University sent to TECHPRO its Thai-language books and compact discs; the Library of Congress, its Hungarian- and Rumanian-language materials; the Massachusetts Institute of Technology, its Arabic books; Florida Atlantic University, its music scores; and California State University–San Marcos, its Spanish language children's books.

All that changed when Wright State University signed a contract with TECHPRO to outsource its entire cataloging operation. Wright State was joined in 1995 by Central Michigan University, the second academic institution to outsource its entire cataloging operation, with the exception of serials, to TECHPRO. Currently, TECHPRO serves 70 libraries and its staff has grown from 8 to 35 in a few short years with plans for continuing growth.[63]

The OCLC PromptCat Service

TECHPRO primarily involves a one-to-one relationship between a library and OCLC; PromptCat always involves a third party, namely a book vendor. In addition, since most of the transactions are electronic, oftentimes the library's automation vendor needs to be included. The participants—the library, the materials vendor, the bibliographic utility, and the automation vendor—must coordinate and communicate carefully and extensively. Internal library communication among cataloging, acquisitions, collection development, and systems is equally important.

PromptCat, introduced in 1995, provides cataloging records for items shipped by the vendor on approval. First, the library fills out a profile with a participating vendor. According to the profile, the vendor supplies OCLC with an electronic file listing the titles that have been shipped to the library. Based on this file, called the manifest, OCLC delivers matching bibliographic records to the library. Records are delivered through any of the regular OCLC methods: cards, tape, electronic data exchange (EDX), and the PRISM save file. A library's options are limited by the capabilities of its online catalog, as illustrated by PromptCat testing at Michigan State University [64] and the University of New Mexico.[65] OCLC has been working with automation vendors to ensure that they support OCLC EDX capabilities.

Unlike TECHPRO, PromptCat supports only limited automatic editing, primarily in the call-number field. PromptCat provides detailed cataloging reports for each day of activity. These reports contain information—records matched, no records found, and so on—that facilitates the sorting and routing of materials in the general cataloging workflow. PromptCat vendors can also ship books in shelf-ready condition. Several options are available: binding, ownership stamping, barcoding, and security stripping. If the library wants the books in shelf-ready condition, an extra charge is added by the vendor. The extent of processing affects the final cost. The shelf-ready option will provide electronic files of labels for the physical processing of books. Libraries can choose either to have "the vendor pick up the label file and process the library's materials or to pick up an electronic label file themselves so they can process the materials in-house."[66]

RLG's Marcadia Service

Lagging behind OCLC, the Research Library Group (RLG), the academic library's database par excellence, did not offer contract cataloging services for its members until recently. In spring 1996, it began to offer the cataloging service Diogenes (renamed Marcadia in 1997), a joint service with Retro Link. RLG makes accessible its RLIN bibliographic files; Retro Link provides the search engine and the report-writing software. Marcadia is a copy cataloging service and is vendor neutral. Libraries do not need to be RLG members to sign up. It can be used to reduce backlogs, to keep up with current receipts, to upgrade minimal-level or Library of Congress CIP records, or for large reclassification projects. All formats and nearly all languages are available.

Marcadia requires that libraries transmit brief temporary machine records extracted from their library local catalogs to Marcadia through FTP. Marcadia accepts all brief records regardless of the library's online catalog as long they are in the MARC format. Marcadia runs these records against the RLIN database and delivers fully cataloged records to the library's own FTP server within a week. The library can also get records from the RLG FTP server. The cataloged records will then overlay the brief records in the local catalog. Marcadia will deliver records in USMARC, RLINMARC, or OCLCMARC format. Records for which an RLIN hit is not found are placed in a file of nonhit records, and RLIN hits that fail to meet the library's selection criteria are listed as "unacceptable hits." Marcadia will return nonhit and nonmatch records and a variety of electronic reports to help the library analyze results. The major difference between Marcadia and other cataloging services is that Marcadia is completely automated and requires no human intervention for the cataloging portion.

As with similar cataloging services, libraries can pick what type of RLIN records they want: records with LC call numbers, records cataloged by specific institutions, specific levels of cataloging, and so on. Marcadia provides sophisticated profiles reflecting the complexity of academic libraries' collections. The initial profile becomes the default; alternate profiles are used with batches of records for certain collections or libraries. Local fields such as local notes or holdings from the library's brief records can be merged into matched records if desired.

Retro Link offers supplemental services at an additional cost. Retro Link will verify LC call numbers against the latest edition of the LC classification outline; program format changes, for example, from non-MARC to USMARC; review and edit nonmatches; catalog unmatched records working from a photocopy of the title page, verso, and other chief sources of information; upgrade pre-AACR2 records to current AACR2 standards; and apply barcodes and spine labels.

Materials Jobbers

Materials jobbers have also entered the market of providing cataloging services. The availability of LC MARC tapes allows the jobbers to offer the same bibliographic records to a library as the utilities. Most jobbers supply copy cataloging, but some now also supply original records. Most materials jobbers can supply catalog cards and MARC records on disk. Fewer offer tape-load or FTP options. Most of the vendors customize cataloging records. A few offer enhancements such as tables of contents, summaries, author's affiliation, award, or approval profile information. Most jobbers that offer these value-added services allow libraries to share the enhancement with consortia for an additional cost. Materials jobbers also provide shelf-ready books. The examples given below represent only a sample of outsourcing vendors. Many had representatives who made presentations at the 1996 spring Southern California Online Users Group (SCOUG) conference.

Ingram defines outsourcing as a value-added service. Ingram, which has been selling books for more than 20 years, takes care of the title selection, shipping, cataloging, processing, and prebinding of paperbacks. Processing services include Mylar jackets, theft-detection systems, property stamps, and barcodes. Similarly, Brodart offers selection services and "custom contract technical services." Its cataloging service, called Compleat Book-Serv, which started in 1986, serves mostly public libraries. It offers cataloging for materials supplied by Brodart or shipped to Brodart by libraries. Brodart catalogers catalog with the book in hand and do copy and original cataloging. Brodart also provides physical processing for each item, including the application of barcodes, spine labels, security strips, and property stamping. Brodart loads a copy of the library's database into its own bibliographic database, IAS, to be used as a resource for cataloging and authority processing. This allows Brodart to use the records in the library's database as "guides," enabling Brodart catalogers to follow local cataloging and classification. IAS contains more than 17 million MARC records, including the Library of Congress MARC file. Brodart will upgrade CIP records and will check the LC name and subject authority files. The bibliographic records correspond to each shipment and are transmitted on tape, floppy disks, or electronically. Cost is variable depending on the service provided. Baker & Taylor also offers cataloging and processing services. It uses two sources of cataloging records: the Library of Congress MARC file and a file created by Baker & Taylor catalogers representing 15 percent of the total number of records. All these companies provide detailed reports to libraries, listing nonmatched records or nonacceptable records and providing statistical information.

Cataloging Companies

The third category of companies providing contract cataloging does not engage in the sale of materials. These companies provide a wide array of services ranging from cataloging to acquisitions, automation, circulation, collection development, document retrieval, loose-leaf filing, interlibrary loan, serials and technical processing, online searching, reference, shelving, and weeding. Most entered the business by offering their services to law and corporate libraries and by providing temporary or permanent catalogers to libraries. These small companies initially served small to medium-sized libraries, but in the 1990s, some expanded their services and began to serve some academic libraries, often managing projects. Some companies provide on-site catalogers, and others offer off-site cataloging. Advanced Information Management, Library Management Systems, and Library Associates sent representatives to the 1996 spring SCOUG conference. These companies have different price structures: some bill the libraries as a subscription, some as a fixed fee, and some as an hourly or unit-based fee. Library Associates, for example, which began as a temp company in 1986, started to offer contract cataloging in 1989. Initially, law firm libraries were its mainstay. The company offers cataloging, processing, and retrospective conversion services under its FastCat label. It is project oriented and supplements a library's cataloging. Library Associates catalogers work off-site, do copy and original cataloging, and access OCLC and RLIN using the library's password.

CONCLUSION

As the process of contracting out gains in scope, more companies are offering cataloging for libraries. In the early 1990s, libraries could select from a number of vendors if they purchased mainstream materials and if they had few needs for customization including classification, subject headings, and notes. It was more difficult to find a vendor who could supply cataloging for non-English materials or for specialized classification systems. Customization and specialization were limited, and there was a heavy reliance on bibliographic utilities for source records.

But this picture is changing. Outsourcing of cataloging is not static. It is evolving as vendors gain experience in the actual needs of cataloging departments and as libraries adopt total outsourcing. New services and improvements are constantly being introduced. The changes are incremental rather than radical. Today vendors hire catalogers, offer original cataloging, and work directly with bibliographic utilities to provide better services. Every library needs to be on top of the new developments, watch them carefully, and ensure that its vendor provides the latest innovations.

Vendors often advertise services that promise quick and accurate cataloging of materials for a price that library cataloging departments cannot possibly match. In theory, this service should save libraries substantial amounts of money by making cataloging departments obsolete. Evidently, outsourcing cataloging reduces or eliminates the number of catalogers in a library and will reduce the number of cataloging departments in the library world. This situation raises the following questions. Will catalogers go the way of full-time bibliographers? Will only the largest academic libraries keep their catalogers while small to medium-sized libraries rely on vendors to manage their cataloging activities? Some believe that large cataloging centers will catalog for discrete regions and that the job of the academic cataloger is doomed. Others think that "few of the tasks which can be outsourced threaten the job security of professional librarians."[67] Some reflect that outsourcing does not involve the "death of the catalog or the demise of catalogers" but should be seen as a more rational way to use scarce resources.[68] Many believe that catalogers have faced this kind of challenge before, have survived, and will be able to weather this latest round of change.

These questions cannot be answered unequivocally. Outsourcing of cataloging is not widespread enough to warrant predictions of doom even though the potential is there. Arnold Hirshon, Barbara A. Winters, and Karen Wilhoit summarize the situation by stating that "outsourcing is not right for every situation, but ignoring the issues that outsourcing raises is also not right."[69] Catalogers need to be aware of all the implications of outsourcing and take an active role in its shape and content. This will ensure that catalogers have a voice in the future of their profession. Otherwise, vendors and administrators will make the decisions for them and they may not like the results.

NOTES

1. Ellen J. Waite, "Reinvent Catalogers!" *Library Journal* 120 (November 1, 1995): 36.

2. Karen A. Wilson, "Outsourcing Copy Cataloging and Physical Processing: A Review of Blackwell's Outsourcing Services for the J. Hugh Jackson Library at Stanford University," *Library Resources & Technical Services* 39 (October 1995): 378.

3. "OCLC, Academic Book Center, SOLINET to Provide Automated Collection and Technical Services to New Florida University," *OCLC Newsletter* no. 225 (January/February 1997): 10.

4. Michael Gorman, "The Corruption of Cataloging: Outsourcing Erodes the 'Bedrock' of Library Service," *Library Journal* 120 (September 15, 1995): 33.

5. Sheila S. Intner, "Outsourcing—What Does It Mean for Technical Services?" *Technicalities* 14, no. 3 (March 1994): 3.

6. Brian Alley, "Reengineering, Outsourcing, Downsizing, and Perfect Timing," *Technicalities* 13 (November 1993): 8.

7. Wilson, "Outsourcing Copy Cataloging," 361.

8. Roxanne Sellberg, "The Teaching of Cataloging in U.S. Library Schools," *Library Resources & Technical Services* 32, no. 1 (January 1988): 33.

9. Wilson, "Outsourcing Copy Cataloging," 362.

10. Sellberg, "The Teaching of Cataloging," 33.

11. Ibid., 30.

12. Paul Strassman as quoted in Ann C. Davidson, " 'Obedience to the Unenforceable': The Ethics of Outsourcing," a reprint from *Searcher* (April 1996): 13.

13. Arnold Hirshon, "The Lobster Quadrille: The Future of Technical Services in a Re-engineering World," in *The Future Is Now: The Changing Face of Technical Services: Proceedings of the OCLC Symposium, ALA Midwinter Conference, February 4, 1994* (Dublin, OH: OCLC, 1994), 16.

←——

14.   Clare B. Dunkle, "Outsourcing the Catalog Department: A Meditation Inspired by the Business and Library Literature," *Journal of Academic Librarianship* 22, no. 1 (January 1996): 40.

15.   Michael Gorman, "Innocent Pleasures," in *The Future Is Now: The Changing Face of Technical Services: Proceedings of the OCLC Symposium, ALA Midwinter Conference, February 4, 1994* (Dublin, OH: OCLC, 1994), 40.

16.   Alley, "Reengineering," 1.

17.   "Outsourcing: By You, for You, or in Spite of You?" Conference of Southern California Online Users Group, City of Industry, CA, May 3, 1996.

18.   William Miller, "Outsourcing: Academic Libraries Pioneer Contracting Out Services," *Library Issues* 16, no. 2 (November 1995): [3].

19.   George Ritzer, *The McDonaldization of Society* (Thousand Oaks, CA: Pine Forge Press, 1996).

20.   Rick J. Block, "Cataloging Outsourcing: Issues and Options," *Serials Review* 20, no. 3 (1994): 74.

21.   Daniel CannCasciato, "Tepid Water for Everyone? The Future OLUC, Catalogers, and Outsourcing," *OCLC Systems & Services* 10 (spring 1994): 7.

22.   Dilys E. Morris, "Technical Services Costs and Resource Allocation," paper presented at "In or Out—In-House Innovation and Outsourcing: Technical Services Alternatives for the 90's." ALA Annual Conference, ALCTS Preconference, New York, July 5, 1996.

23.   Jacqueline Byrd and Kathryn Sorury, "Cost Analysis of NACO Participation at Indiana University," *Cataloging & Classification Quarterly* 16, no. 2 (1993): 120.

24.   Glen E. Holt, "Catalog Outsourcing: No Clear-Cut Choice," *Library Journal* 120 (September 15, 1995): 34.

25.   Karen Wilhoit, "Outsourcing Cataloging at Wright State University," *Serials Review* 20, no. 3 (1994): 70.

26.   CannCasciato, "Tepid Water," 5.

27.   Karen Dornseif, "Outsourcing Cataloging: An Alternative for Small Libraries," *Colorado Libraries* 21 (spring 1995): 49.

28.   Nancy J. Gibbs, "ALCTS/Role of the Professional in Academic Research Technical Services Department's Discussion Group," *Library Acquisitions* 18, no. 3 (1994): 322.

29.   Waite, "Reinvent Catalogers!" 37.

30.   Dunkle, "Outsourcing the Catalog Department," 34–35.

31.   Colleen F. Hyslop, "PromptCat Prototype: Accelerating Progress in Technical Services," in *The Future Is Now: The Changing Face of Technical Services: Proceedings of the OCLC Symposium, ALA Midwinter Conference, February 4, 1994* (Dublin, OH: OCLC, 1994), 35.

32.   Arnold Hirshon and Barbara A. Winters, *Outsourcing Technical Services: A How-to-Do-It Manual for Librarians* (New York: Neal-Schuman, 1996), 17.

33. Job Openings: OCLC TECHPRO. Listserv LIBJOBS @INFOSERV.NLC-BNC.CA. Wed., 6 Nov 1996 09:52:42.

34. Library Technician 3, Job announcement, WLN, Lacey, WA. Listserv LIBJOBS @INFOSERV.NLC-BNC.CA. Thurs., 28 Nov 1996 13:21:00.

35. Position announcements. Listserv AUTOCAT@UBVM.CC.BUFFALO.EDU. Thurs., 12 Sep 1996 13:58:44; and Outsourcing position—Contract Catalogers. Listserv LIBJOBS @INFOSERV.NLC-BNC.CA. Fri., 13 Sep 1996 12:25:41.

36. James E. Rush, "A Case for Eliminating Cataloging in the Individual Library," in *The Future Is Now: The Changing Face of Technical Services: Proceedings of the OCLC Symposium, ALA Midwinter Conference, February 4, 1994* (Dublin, OH: OCLC, 1994), 9–10.

37. Ibid., 11.

38. Bart Kane, "Taxpayers & Customers Win: Outsourcing," paper presented at "Outsourcing: By You, for You, or in Spite of You?" Conference of Southern California Online Users Group, City of Industry, CA, May 3, 1996.

39. "Central Michigan University Libraries Use TECHPRO," *OCLC Newsletter* (July/August 1995): 30.

40. Waite, "Reinvent Catalogers!" 37.

41. Wilson, "Outsourcing Copy Cataloging," 378.

42. Barbara A. Winters, paper presented at "In or Out—In-House Innovation and Outsourcing: Technical Services Alternatives for the 90's," ALA Annual Conference, ALCTS Preconference, New York, July 5, 1996.

43. CannCasciato, "Tepid Water," 6.

44. Alley, "Reengineering," 1.

45. Dilys E. Morris, "Technical Services Costs and Resource Allocation," paper presented at "In or Out—In-House Innovation and Outsourcing: Technical Services Alternatives for the 90's," ALA Annual Conference, ALCTS Preconference, New York, July 5, 1996.

46. Ibid.

47. Nancy J. Gibbs, "ALCTS/Role of the Professional in Academic Research Technical Services Department's Discussion Group," *Library Acquisitions* 18, no. 3 (1994): 322.

48. Block, "Cataloging Outsourcing," 76.

49. Wilson, "Outsourcing Copy Cataloging," 361.

50. Ibid., 374.

51. Barry Fast, "Outsourcing and PromptCat," *Against the Grain* 7 (April 1995): 50.

52. "OCLC to Accelerate Upgrading of CIP Data in Online Union Catalog," *AMIGOS Agenda & OCLC Connection* 95–10 (1995): 6.

53. Wilson, "Outsourcing Copy Cataloging," 361.

54.   Jim Dwyer, "Does Outsourcing Mean 'You're Out'?" *Technicalities* 14 (June 1994): 4.

55.   Block, "Cataloging Outsourcing," 75.

56.   CannCasciato, "Tepid Water," 8.

57.   Carmel C. Bush, Margo L. Sasse, and Patricia A. Smith, "Toward a New World Order: A Survey of Outsourcing Capabilities of Vendors for Acquisitions, Cataloging and Collection Development Services," *Library Acquisitions* 18, no. 4 (1994): 403.

58.   CannCasciato, "Tepid Water," 8.

59.   Ibid., 6.

60.   Joseph C. Tardiff, ed., *Information Industry Directory*, 17th edition (Detroit: Gale, 1997).

61.   Cynthia M. Whitacre, "OCLC's TECHPRO Service," *Serials Review* 20, no. 3 (1994): 77.

62.   "Conversion and Contract Cataloging Services," *OCLC Newsletter*, no. 205 (September/October 1993): 18.

63.   Cynthia M. Whitacre, TECHPRO manager, telephone conversation with authors, December 19, 1996.

64.   Kay Granskog, "PromptCat Testing at Michigan State University," *Library Acquisitions* 18, no. 4 (1994): 419–25.

65.   Claire-Lise Bénaud and Sever Bordeianu, "PromptCat: An Early Assessment," in *Advances in Collection Development and Resources Management*, ed. Thomas W. Leonhardt (Greenwich, CT: JAI Press, 1996), 223–38.

66.   "Pilot Projects to Produce Shelf-Ready Materials," *OCLC Newsletter*, no. 224 (November/December 1996): 25.

67.   Janifer Meldrum, "Outsourcing Issues Stir Conference Attendees," *MARCIVE Newsletter* 23 (September 1995): 1.

68.   Murray S. Martin and Ernie Ingles, "Outsourcing in Alberta," *Bottom Line* 8, no. 4 (1995): 34.

69.   Arnold Hirshon, Barbara A. Winters, and Karen Wilhoit, "A Response to 'Outsourcing Cataloging: The Wright State Experience,'" *ALCTS Newsletter* 6 (1995): 28.

8 *Retrospective Conversion*

Retrospective conversion, also called recon or retrocon, represented a major step in library automation. Whereas the definition of retrospective conversion—the conversion of paper records to machine-readable form—is straightforward, conversion issues and processes were complex and could "undermine, overwhelm, or otherwise affect the entire automation project."[1] Given the labor-intensive nature of conversion and the emergence of new priorities, segments of many academic libraries' collections remain unconverted. With most of their monographic and serial conversion completed by the late 1980s, libraries are now engaging in the conversion of government documents, microforms, manuscripts, and special formats such as scores or maps. Although the issues of cost, quality control, and turnaround time are the same, the parameters today are different from those of the early days. The depth of the bibliographic databases today is much greater, automated systems are well established, and librarians know their systems' requirements and limitations. Librarians today also benefit from more than 25 years of experience in dealing with conversion.

Outsourcing of conversion was not as contentious as outsourcing of cataloging is today even though conversion is considerably more complicated because it requires historical as well as current knowledge of cataloging.[2] The circumstances in which retrospective conversion took place in the 1980s differ greatly from today's context for outsourcing cataloging. Unlike in cataloging, the outsourcing of conversion was limited in time and was done on a project basis. The library's purpose for outsourcing was not to downsize or to save money, but to automate its collections as fast as possible. Also, unlike in cataloging, the outsourcing of retrospective conversion was an added responsibility for cataloging departments. Conversion activities did not result in staff transfers or layoffs. On the contrary, oftentimes they resulted in the hiring of additional staff, at least for the duration of the conversion project.

Even though the climates for outsourcing of conversion and cataloging are radically different, the goals of libraries were similar: to obtain bibliographic records at an affordable price. Many conversion issues, such as in-house conversion versus vendor conversion or the quality of converted records, were the same ones that are debated today in the context of outsourcing cataloging.

HISTORICAL BACKGROUND

The change in the cataloging environment from manual to electronic in the mid-1970s compelled libraries to convert their records, typically catalog cards, to machine-readable form. Retrospective conversion changed the way libraries use the catalog record. Once computerized, the record served the entire library—circulation, acquisitions, collection development, and interlibrary loan—and was no longer the sole purview of the cataloging department. When libraries began to plan for the future library catalog, there was a sense of urgency because librarians were eager to create a database to support circulation systems and serial lists with the long-term aim of supporting a public-access catalog.

Because retrospective conversion was inherently costly and time-consuming, libraries had to resort to vendors. The two critical factors were time and money: time because retrospective conversion could not be achieved quickly with existing staff, and money because libraries could not afford to hire and train the necessary staff to do retrospective conversion. The term *outsourcing* was not used in the library literature during the heyday of retrospective conversion. It was referred to as "out-of-house" conversion, and vendors were simply referred to as "conversion vendors."

Major conversion efforts were undertaken in the 1980s and occurred on two distinct levels, local and national. On one hand, individual libraries decided to convert their holdings to prepare for computerized catalogs. Within the library, catalogers, section heads, and the library administration had countless meetings to devise the best way to convert their collection. Meanwhile, nationally an enormous effort took place to ensure that research collections across the country were converted. The Association of Research Libraries (ARL) launched the Program for Coordinated Retrospective Conversion of Bibliographic Records for Monographs in North American Research Libraries (called the ARL Recon Project), which coordinated the conversion of monographic titles into machine-readable form. The struggle to obtain funding for conversion projects often overshadowed outsourcing issues. Starting in 1978, many research libraries were awarded grants, often federal grants under Title II-C of the Higher Education Act, to convert part of their collections. Some grants were used to convert libraries' individual holdings. Others were joint efforts among libraries to convert certain types of materials. These efforts resulted in several large databases from which all libraries could draw for their own conversion projects.

Libraries outsourcing their conversion had various vendor options: batch conversion; a stand-alone online cataloging database; or the contracting out of all the work associated with retrospective conversion.

Using a batch process, vendors such as OCLC, WLN, UTLAS, Brodart, and the Computer Company provided access to their databases. The library entered a "search argument," typically a Library of Congress catalog card number, an ISBN, part of the author's name, part of the title, or the publisher and the year of publication, on floppy disk. These entries were periodically sent to the vendor. The vendor used this information to search its database, created a magnetic tape of matching MARC records, and sent machine-readable records back to the library.

Other vendors provided stand-alone databases to be searched locally to retrieve machine-readable records such as GRC's LaserQuest, the Library Corporation's Bibliofile, the Library Systems & Services' MiniMarc, and UTLAS's ReMARC.

Last, vendors could perform the conversion of the library's titles using the library's shelflist cards or a substitute. Often, the first sweep through the card catalog was for the conversion of monographs, followed by more difficult materials. This was determined to be the fastest and most cost-effective method for putting the major portion of a collection in machine-readable form.

IN-HOUSE VERSUS OUTSOURCED RETROSPECTIVE CONVERSION

Libraries have two options when they convert from cards to machine-readable form: They can convert in-house or outsource conversion to a vendor. Whether performed in-house or outsourced, conversion involves "the use of a bibliographic source database against which the library matches its manual records and . . . creates a database of the local records of that library."[3] Each option has "advantages and disadvantages related to cost, staffing, time, and record quality."[4] Over the years, libraries have chosen both options by outsourcing part of their conversion project to a vendor in order to get a lot of records converted as quickly as possible and by performing some conversion in-house. Librarians have adapted "the best features of each option to meet local needs and budget constraints."[5] Although some librarians have been reluctant to "consider specific options, such as employment of contracted service,"[6] Ilene Rockman reported in 1990 that the majority of libraries preferred the "combined efforts of an outside vendor, in conjunction with work performed by in-house library staff."[7]

Still, libraries hold divergent views on how to achieve conversion. The University of Iowa libraries "were inclined to follow conventional wisdom and didn't seriously consider using an outside-vendor option;"[8]

George Washington University's Library concluded that the "use of a vendor is the most efficient way to complete a large conversion project within a reasonable time."[9] These views exemplify the two ends of the spectrum.

Some librarians made broad recommendations, suggesting that in-house conversion was usually the best option for small collections and vendor conversion was best for large collections,[10] but all acknowledged that the preferred option depended upon the particular local conditions and the availability of staff and space. In the following sections we will look at the issues of concern in retrospective conversion while also expanding on the in-house–versus–outsourcing consideration and on the experiences of libraries during the massive conversions of the 1980s. These issues continue to be equally valid today even though their magnitude is diminished.

RETROSPECTIVE CONVERSION ISSUES

Types of Records Converted

Libraries used vendors for different and sometimes opposing reasons. Some used vendors to convert monographs and did in-house conversion when having the piece in hand would facilitate the process, for example, for serials, music, maps, or non-Roman materials. Others chose to have vendors convert skeletal records even though it was more difficult to find corresponding matches. They felt that well-maintained local records should be converted in-house because they had more information than many of the records in an outside database and contended that outsourcing the conversion of these complete local records would create a potential for losing valuable information.[11]

Checking Holdings Before a Conversion Project

Prior to any retrospective conversion project, the library should do an inventory and make sure the items it plans to convert are still on the shelves and still important to the library in order not to convert items in poor condition or materials that should be discarded. This means checking the shelflist against the actual items. In practice, many libraries that outsourced conversion did not have the staff or time to check their holdings and converted entire portions of the shelflist, including items they no longer held. Some libraries limited themselves to inventorying "areas of suspected high loss."[12]

Problem Records

Serials records, often the last ones to be converted, presented the largest category of problem records. The change from the "latest entry" rule to the "successive entry" rule created a whole set of difficulties, as the conversion vendor had to split serials records in order to deliver only successive-entry records. The problem of "dash-on" entries, in which supplements were added to the catalog card with a different call number, also needed to be corrected. This practice was not done in the machine-readable environment, and conversion vendors either had to catalog "dash-ons" separately or add the information to a note in the main bibliographic record. The problem of music records was unique not only because of the editing but also because of the difficulty of online searching for uniform titles and generic titles, when there was no editor, LCCN, or other numeric key to search; and when the dates were uncertain dates.[13] As a result, conversion vendors had a difficult time retrieving the correct records.

Conversion Versus Recataloging

In-house conversion projects often entailed some recataloging, which slowed down the process. Vendor conversion did not allow for such recataloging. In the early days of conversion projects, some libraries aspired to use the same standards for conversion as for cataloging and wanted conversion to be used to improve cataloging, in effect recataloging the titles being converted. Few librarians undertook the task of simply converting their catalogs. Instead they tried to "correct cumulated, historical cataloging problems."[14] Such hopes were short-lived, and most determined that the MARC record should "only" match the cataloging card, clarifying what was conversion and what was recataloging. The line between what is considered conversion and what is considered recataloging still remains blurry in many cataloging departments, especially for the conversion of original records. Disagreements have arisen about inputting original records: Some consider it conversion; others want the original piece recataloged with the book in hand.

Standards

Local cataloging standards and local data greatly influenced the cost of a conversion project. Every library handles local data differently, and in some cases a library may have adopted specific cataloging practices to best fit local needs. These local practices usually proved to be costly. Many conversion projects happened just at the time AACR2 was implemented. Authority-control problems increased, since AACR2 headings conflicted with previous headings. Each institution had to decide whether to update headings to the AACR2 form and what to do when no AACR2 heading was present in the LC authority files. This created a difficult situation, and many converted headings had to be cleaned up later by an authority control vendor.

Maintaining Control

Not surprisingly, libraries who opted for in-house conversion found that they had more control over the project and the content of the records,[15] were aware of problem areas and could fix them immediately, and had an accurate day-by-day account of their progress.[16] Most agreed that out-of-house conversion could suffer from lack of local control and the inaccessibility of local materials, and recognized that in-house conversion would result in a "high quality project as the existing staff will be experts in their area of cataloging."[17] Proponents of outsourcing stressed that contracted retrospective conversion offered "the advantages of speed, experienced staffs, proper facilities, adherence to standards, and results of predictable quality."[18] Some observed that vendors had much "greater experience with retrospective conversion processes than their customers" and thus had more expertise than individual libraries.[19] Rather than each library having to reinvent the wheel, vendors could provide checklists of activities to be accomplished and practices to avoid, could offer "background information, guidelines for making decisions, and explanations of lessons learned by the vendors' staff through its experience."[20]

Staffing

Undertaking in-house conversion required a close look at staffing. During past conversion projects, many libraries contended that in-house conversion could be "impeded by insufficient experienced staff and inadequate space"[21] and estimated that it would be difficult for existing staff to absorb new duties, opinions that favored the use of a vendor. Many libraries that undertook conversion projects in-house reported staffing difficulties and acknowledged that it was often difficult to maintain current operations while staff were diverted to conversion activities.[22] Conversely, others noted staff's frustration over the "intrusion of other duties into time set aside for the project."[23] Staff felt overwhelmed by the sheer number of records, a feeling exacerbated by the lack of access to OCLC terminals at some institutions. Staff turnover, local hiring freezes, and changes in administrative priorities could modify costs and allow the conversion project to drag on, or worse, to prevent it from being completed.

Vendor conversion could be undertaken without hiring extra staff even though in-house catalogers were required to solve problems returned by the vendor, but libraries often hired a coordinator to prepare for and implement conversion. And vendors could also have staffing problems. For example, one vendor is reported to occasionally have had problems consisting of "unfilled positions or lots of turnover, which made it hard at times to finish conversion, especially when particular expertise was required."[24]

Timeliness

Many consider the time factor the main advantage in deciding to use a conversion vendor because collections could be "converted and loaded in the local database within a short amount of time, more quickly than if the local staff had to search OCLC and input information themselves."[25] Because of the magnitude of conversion projects in academic libraries, libraries that calculated how long it would take them to do the conversion in-house came up with astronomical numbers. Rice University estimated in 1980 that conversion would take 10 years in-house[26] compared to the average 2 years needed by vendors. Some resorted to conversion done on a part-time basis by regular staff, but projects appeared to "drag on interminably with little visible progress."[27] However, some questioned the amount of time actually saved "by contracting OCLC to convert the records considering the time it took to prepare, send, and receive records from OCLC and the number of times it was necessary to access the OCLC-converted records."[28]

QUALITY CONTROL ISSUES

A number of factors such as completeness of shelflist cards, the level of editing and authority control, and postconversion cleanup compounded the difficulties of undertaking retrospective conversion. Conversion projects were also saddled with the additional demands of weeding, recataloging, or reclassifying. Quality control issues are still valid in conversion projects undertaken in the 1990s.

Procedures for quality control were a crucial part of conversion projects and generated the most discussions within cataloging departments. The issue of acceptable error rates was often a source of disagreement between the library and the vendor. For example, Texas A&M reported that A&M and OCLC used a different formula and OCLC did "not fully agree with the sampling technique" used by A&M.[29] Monitoring quality was by far the stickiest point in vendor conversion. In-house catalogers had to check MARC records for accuracy against the shelflist cards and verify the accuracy of call numbers, holding codes, access points, and notes.

The quality of vendor records, a persistent concern in conversion projects, created a rift between catalogers and administrators. On one hand, libraries wanted to create a database of bibliographic records of high quality, fully realizing that quality would be the key element in their database, and on the other, they were aware that there were "considerable risks if standards and expectations" were too high because that would jeopardize the entire conversion project.[30] Jutta Reed–Scott warned that it was "tempting but dangerous to settle for sloppy conversion."[31] Librarians argued that vendors would not do as good a job of creating original records as in-house staff. The were also concerns about record cleanup. If conversion was performed in-house, a balance had to be reached between the desire to clean up and the need to complete the project expeditiously. Vendor conversion, for better or for worse, eliminated that concern.[32]

Incomplete Data

Typically, libraries sent their shelflist cards to a conversion vendor. In some instances, shelflist cards did not contain complete information. For example, in the past, some libraries filed only the first card of a multiple card set in the shelflist, and some did not file analytics. Information on shelfcards was often erroneous, especially on older ones. In large academic libraries, cards could be more than 100 years old and contained handwritten corrections, additional locations, specific copy information, and "information so old and outdated that current staff are no longer aware of what these notations mean."[33] To remedy the problem, some libraries shipped microfilm copies of main entry cards to the vendor, but vendors were still at a disadvantage because they had no access to the material itself.

Editing

The level of editing remained a highly debatable subject during the duration of conversion projects, and many reported that meetings about this topic ranged from "mild to stormy."[34] Conversion required some degree of editing in two areas: Records needed to reflect information on the card and needed to conform to local cataloging standards.

Historically, staff responsible for the overview of vendor conversion projects were willing to accept copy with less editing; in-house cataloging staff were more inclined to edit records. Because libraries realized that following a rigorous editing process would take them years, they often streamlined their specifications and decided to focus on certain fields in the MARC record, ignoring other fields considered less important. Often, they had to go through this process more than once, reducing their efforts to editing only access points and editing the fixed fields only minimally. As a result, libraries ended up with the same kind of problems they had with cards. Ultimately, the quality-versus-quantity debate was won by the proponents of quantity.

However, even the perfect match between the catalog card and the converted MARC record proved unwieldy to accomplish, so standards were cut and curtailed even more. Each library had to decide if it wanted to apply its local cataloging standards to the conversion project. For example, local series statements and local subject headings, which necessitated extra time while editing the record, added to the overall cost and length of the project and were often left out. Stephen H. Peters and Douglas J. Butler report that whether the "conversion is conducted in-house or contracted out to a vendor . . . the cost of verifying and subsequently editing records accounts for over half the total cost of the project."[35]

Authority Control

The level of authority control depended on the size and goal of the project. Some large libraries performed authority control according to strict guidelines. Others could not afford the extraordinary amount of time needed and required their conversion vendor to perform minimum authority control. Many libraries, especially in the early days, did not know how their future online catalog would report errors and conflicts and therefore did not ask their vendor to perform authority control. Most decided that the authority cleanup would be undertaken after the conversion was over and kept authority control efforts to a minimum.

Postconversion Cleanup

At the end of a conversion project, libraries were left with a sizable number of problems. Converted records continue to elicit negative comments from patrons and generate extra work nearly 20 years later. Regardless of how efficient the conversion vendor was, all conversion projects required cleanup. Cleanup typically entailed the following: going through the shelflist to find cards that were not converted, serials cataloged as monographs or vice versa, incorrect call numbers, holdings attached to the wrong record, and conflicts between authority records and bibliographic records. One library reported vendor conversion resulting in 124,000 unacceptable bibliographic records being added to the database. These records lacked such vital information as subtitles, physical description, and subject headings.[36]

MANAGING VENDOR CONVERSION

Before deciding whether the work will be accomplished in-house or by a vendor, three basic decisions have to be made: what will be converted, in what order will it be converted, and what will be the source of the cataloging information.[37] Other key factors in this analysis are quantity of work, type of materials and languages, local cataloging standards, and pertinent local data. Cost has never been the sole consideration, since libraries are not willing to spend years and years to complete a conversion project.

Proposal

In the early days, conversion proposals highlighted the benefits of closing the card catalog, converting the cards, and beginning a computerized catalog. First, the scope of the project had to be determined. Was the goal to convert the whole collection or particular subsets of the collection? Some libraries converted from A to Z. Others skipped the more difficult cards and concentrated on books. Others tried to anticipate circulation and began to convert first what would circulate most rather than stick to strict shelflist order. Often grant funding related to a particular subject area and thus defined the scope of the project.

The first task was to quantify the number of titles to be converted. In most instances, quantity was judged by measuring shelflist drawers and making a best guess. The second step involved sampling sections of the shelflist and searching the catalog cards against a bibliographic utility's database to determine what percentage of titles had copy and what percentage needed original inputting. Research on card-file sampling was available in the literature, but many libraries did not spend much time sampling. Librarians cautioned that sampling is a time-consuming and not always accurate endeavor and that it "might be used as a general guideline rather than as a basis for precise decision-making."[38] The size of the sampling was usually too small and led to very rough estimates. These less-than-scientific methods gave libraries an idea of the bulk of what needed to be converted but could not delineate the many problems associated with conversion. Because libraries had no choice but to convert, they went ahead even with approximate data.

Conversion Specifications

The contract needs to be specific and should tell the vendor exactly what to do. Even though the contract cannot take into account all situations, it stipulates the basic rules and is essential for quality control. Libraries need to prepare RFPs outlining the scope of conversion, the source of the cataloging data, how the matching will occur, what level of editing is required, the desired turnaround time, acceptable error rates, shipping methods, and quality-control requirements. Even though the Association of Research Libraries developed guidelines for record fullness for the conversion of monographic records published in 1985,[39] many academic libraries developed their own guidelines. Because of the length of these projects, libraries often reconsidered policies and procedures in an effort to speed up conversion. Over the length of conversion projects, specifications changed. Often the original specifications were detailed and called for editing the MARC record to match the library's card exactly. During the duration of the projects, a lot of editing went by the wayside, and libraries began to accept more records "as is." Some recognized that conversion vendors did not possess the same expertise as in-house staff and noted that even "when specific guidelines are drawn up for the utility, local practices in note fields and other areas will be missed."[40]

Cost

The professional literature of the 1980s reports that outsourcing conversion was cheaper than converting in-house and, conversely, that in-house conversion was very expensive.[41] Susan Baerg Epstein notes that if "you consider all costs, it is often less expensive to have a contractor perform the task."[42] Judy McQueen and Richard W. Boss report that vendor conversion prices were "particularly attractive"[43] but that "cost is extremely difficult to assess outside the specifics of a particular library's situation."[44] They conclude that "libraries, with their diverse collections, their distinct cataloging policy, their individual tolerance toward dirty records, could not come up with a conversion cost per record, the same way they are today grappling with the cost of vendor cataloging."[45]

As is the case today with outsourcing cataloging, libraries had difficulty taking into account costs such as equipment, space, supervision, training, and turnover and focused instead on direct costs. Complexity, size, and special requirements of conversion projects determine costs. The size and age of the collection, the language mix, whether the materials are unique, the amount of information desired in each record, and the completeness of existing bibliographic records all affect cost.[46] However, in a 1987 article, Marsha Ra noted that despite these variables, the actual cost of converting collections has not varied greatly.[47] To determine costs of vendor conversion is even more difficult than determining costs for outsourcing cataloging because the cataloging on shelfcards is older, reflecting decades of different cataloging practices, and is often incomplete. McQueen and Boss report accurately that "it is easier for a library to predict its costs for current cataloging because the universe of materials and cost factors are more clearly defined."[48]

Conversion-cost models are not readily available, and most "how we did it" articles describe how individual libraries prepared cost estimates in a fairly basic fashion (how many records could be converted per hour; records for LC cards, non-LC cards, serials, music titles, and non-English titles; the number of computers needed; the bibliographic utility costs; etc.) and compared their costs to the vendor's charges. Vendors charge different fees for conversion projects: a searching fee for searching each record against a database, an update fee to update holdings, an editing fee when the record needs editing to reflect the library's catalog card, and an original conversion fee when no record can be found. This complex fee system requires the library to submit a sample of its cards so that the vendor can estimate the total cost.

Choosing a Conversion Vendor

Libraries need an experienced vendor in order to reduce training and keep involvement of library staff to a minimum. Factors considered include cost, schedule, timeliness, number of records to be converted, experience of the agency, and training required.[49] The characteristics of each library's collections—size of the collection, types of subject headings, age and language mix of the collection, distinctiveness of the collection, classification schemes, amount of data to be included in each record, hit rate against the vendor's database—all were and continue to be contributing factors.

Managing vendor conversion projects still requires a substantial amount of staff time and cataloging expertise. Each library has unique procedures and each experiences its own problems depending on the quality of its shelflist. For example, the Music Library at the University of California–Berkeley reports that cards to be converted were pulled, photocopied, cut into card-sized slips, and mailed to OCLC. Upon return, the slips were separated into converted and not-converted categories when the vendor had found no match. The OCLC-converted records were then tape-loaded into the local system. The not-converted cards then had to be input by in-house staff.[50] Ongoing reconciliation of discrepancies lasted during conversion projects and typically lingered long after projects had ended.

CONVERSION VENDORS

At the height of conversion projects in the mid-1980s, there were more than 20 vendors including bibliographic utilities and their networks—especially AMIGOS and SOLINET—and commercial vendors. All competed with each other in offering services for retrospective conversion. Libraries were faced with an overwhelming array of options, each with varying costs and constraints. As is the case today, a majority of academic libraries used bibliographic utilities rather than commercial vendors for conversion. Size of the database favored the bibliographic utilities for large collections, but the smaller specialized vendors could fulfill a library's unique needs, particularly for nonbook formats. Over the span of the conversion activities, libraries often used more than one vendor to address their specific needs.

Bibliographic Utilities and Network Vendors

Today two bibliographic utilities, OCLC and WLN, offer conversion services. OCLC remains the larger player. RLG concentrates on seeking foundation funding to support conversion projects rather than offering conversion services per se.

OCLC

OCLC has been and continues to be the major vendor of retrospective conversion services. Along with its cataloging services, OCLC offers various conversion options: RETROCON, MICROCON, the Conversion Keying Service, TAPECON, and FULLMARC. RETROCON offers customized converted records; the batch conversion services, MICROCON, TAPECON, and FULLMARC, give libraries the opportunity to convert without the expense of a customized service. RETROCON and MICROCON have been used extensively by academic libraries, and TAPECON and FULLMARC have been used primarily by public libraries. Some contend that because OCLC's retrospective conversion business has been slowing down, OCLC has aggressively promoted outsourcing of cataloging to replenish its coffers.

RETROCON

RETROCON, OCLC's customized conversion operation, has been in the conversion business for more than two decades. Academic libraries are OCLC's largest RETROCON customer, representing 40 percent of all its library customers. By 1993, 217 academic or research libraries had used the RETROCON service and more than 26 million records had been converted.[51] For example, the University of California–Los Angeles, Columbia University, the University of Oregon, and Harvard University—OCLC's largest conversion project so far with the conversion of more than 5 million titles from Harvard University's card catalogs—all have outsourced their conversion projects through RETROCON. OCLC assigns a project specialist to guide the library through the conversion project and to write the technical specifications with a staff member designated by the library. These technical specifications then become part of a contract between OCLC and the library and include the project time frame, description of the materials to be converted, and quality-control guidelines. In 1993, OCLC had a staff of 175, organized into six teams assigned to various conversion projects.

Libraries send catalog cards to OCLC and RETROCON staff search for a matching bibliographic record in OCLC's Online Union Catalog (OLUC). Today, the matching record is found more than 90 percent of the time, and the RETROCON staff add the library's holding symbol and any local information the library has requested. When a matching record is not found in the OLUC, the RETROCON staff keys in a record based on the information on the catalog card. In 1993, RETROCON added around 300,000 new records and more than 3 million holdings to the OLUC.[52]

MICROCON

MICROCON, OCLC's batch conversion service, is more economical than the customized RETROCON service. Of all libraries having used MICRO-CON, 38 percent are academic libraries. By 1993, 294 academic libraries had used this service, and 15 million records had been converted. OCLC first sends the library software to be loaded into a personal computer that will be used for conversion. The library staff then enter unique identifiers when available (e.g., the OCLC control number, the Library of Congress Card Number, the ISBN, the ISSN) or derived search keys combining title, or author and title information, onto disks. All searches can be qualified by date, material type, and whether the record is in microform, to increase the chance of retrieving a unique match. The diskettes are then sent to OCLC to be processed. The search keys are compared to the OLUC, and all unique matches are transferred to the library's file. When 2 to 10 matches are found, they are printed out and sent to the library, where the staff can then select the correct records, input search keys on the diskette, and mail them back to OCLC. The MICROCON*PRO service uses MICROCON software and procedures, but the staff entering the search data are OCLC employees. Libraries with limited staff often choose this option.

Conversion Keying Service

The Conversion Keying Service is one of OCLC's newer conversion services. This service is used to convert rare or brief records. Often academic libraries use the Conversion Keying Service in combination with RETROCON. The keying service is useful for the conversion of rare-book collections when items are unlikely to match records in the OLUC. It is also used when a library's records lack information required by the OLUC, such as pagination or size. Rather than searching the OLUC and finding few matches, OCLC staff type the records into an ancillary database for the use of the contracting library. OCLC refers to the keying service as "Key What You See," meaning that it will enter whatever data the library provides into a MARC record. Conformance to AACR2 and the MARC record validation rules can be waived if the library desires, since this service is typically used when the data cannot meet minimum input standards. The library simply wants some brief bibliographic information in a MARC record to load into its online catalog. These conversion-keyed records are not added to the OLUC, and holdings are not set for this service.

TAPECON and FULLMARC

Existing library tapes with non–MARC records are formatted by the library or a tape vendor to offer one search key per record. The search keys are matched against the OLUC, and unique matches are transferred to tape and returned to the library. Multiple matches are identified and reported to the library for review. Only 18 academic libraries have used this service since 1993; 13 percent of those libraries have used TAPECON, which is primarily used by public libraries. Like TAPECON, FULLMARC is rarely used by academic libraries. Since 1993, two academic libraries have used this service. Libraries with existing tapes of records in a minimal MARC format can send those tapes to OCLC for matching against the OLUC. Because the records are in the MARC format, the system compares several fields to find a matching record. When unique matches are found, the library's institution symbol is set in the OLUC, and a full OCLC MARC record is returned. Records not converted are identified and reported to the library for review.

OCLC prices its MICROCON, TAPECON, and FULLMARC batch conversion services at the same levels. Libraries can decide which service is best for them rather than trying to fit their project into the least-expensive alternative.

WLN

WLN developed its retrospective conversion program in 1980. It is a regional utility serving mostly libraries in the western part of the United States and currently has a database of more than 8 million bibliographic records. Over the years, it has emphasized its commitment to quality control. Through its WLN MARC Record Service (MARS), WLN provides complete conversion services through various options: the Inputting Service, the Offline Batch Conversion service, and the *Laser*Cat service. MARS records are validated for missing or invalid data elements.

Inputting Service

Using photocopies of shelflist cards, original shelflist cards, or printed worksheets, WLN staff either search the WLN database for matches or create a MARC record. Regardless of the library's utility or local system, WLN can accommodate all types of MARC records (OCLC, RLIN, UTLAS) and takes into account local practices to ensure that the converted records are compatible with the remainder of the local database. This is the most customized of all conversion services.

Offline Batch Conversion

Batch conversion allows a library to send brief bibliographic data on diskettes. WLN runs the library's records against its database for selection of MARC records. Nonmatches are returned to the library or input by the WLN staff.

LaserCat

Libraries can search *Laser*Cat, WLN's CD-ROM catalog, to identify matches. Holdings information for matches is then keyed into diskettes, data from the diskettes is matched against the WLN database, and MARC records are generated for the library.

Commercial Vendors

At the peak of conversion activities in the mid-1980s, a variety of commercial vendors were active. Commercial vendors' services varied greatly from one to another. Some, such as Autographics, Brodart, and the Computer Company, offered services similar to those of the utilities. Others such as BNA, Inforonics, Marcive, and General Research Corporation offered only batch conversion services. Bibliofile used CD-ROM as the storage medium; Library Systems & Services Inc. used videodisc. Two companies specialized in keying services, EKI (Electronic Keyboarding Incorporated) and Saztec.[53] On the whole, commercial vendors' databases were not as comprehensive as the bibliographic utilities' and did not always include records for serials, scores, or audiovisual materials. Some offered MARC records, and others offered MARC-based records. Today many of these companies have shifted their emphasis away from conversion because there is less demand from libraries.

CONCLUSION

As in other outsourcing ventures, librarians responsible for conversion projects stress that "the communication between the library and the vendor is of extreme importance."[54] Communication with the staff outside the cataloging department is also considered crucial; other library departments have to understand the need not to change or pull cards from the shelflist, as this would cloud the conversion process. Expediency, speed, and tight budgets all contributed to vendor conversion, but large academic libraries acknowledged early on that no single approach could meet all of a library's retrospective conversion needs.[55] The literature is unanimous: Vendor conversion is the cheapest and fastest method of retrospective conversion.

Converting through a vendor allows for more predictable costs and deadlines, a plus for library administrators. Record charges, telecommunication costs, and other vendor fees can be determined in advance. The survey conducted for this book confirms the high occurrence of outsourcing of conversion. Sixty percent of the respondents indicated that they outsourced all or some of their conversion, often using more than one vendor.

Sue Fuller and Helen Palmer sum up the in-house and vendor conversion pros and cons. The in-house method, which they liken to the tortoise in the famous race, "has the advantage of better command of the project and quality control" and is "also convenient in terms of problem solving." Disadvantages encompass additional overhead, possible interruptions due to the demands of current workloads, and a slower pace. They equate vendor conversion with the hare. It has the "advantage of a speedier process unencumbered by the headaches of hiring, training, and eventual placement of temporary staff, not to mention the expense of additional equipment and space" and they add that the shortcomings of vendor conversion are less control over the project and uncertainty regarding quality.[56]

Despite the fact that many libraries are satisfied with the results of conversion and often report to be "generally very pleased with the quality of the work done,"[57] the quality of vendor conversion has been and still remains a concern. One of the main advantages of vendor conversion, speed, also causes the main disadvantage, which is decline in quality.[58] Most recognize that the conversion errors that plague the catalog are offset by the fact that the library collections converted to MARC bibliographic records at first laid the base for the online catalog and today continue to enrich national as well as libraries' databases. Nevertheless, outsourcing conversion projects has had a great impact on raising catalogers' awareness of the inadequacies of vendor-converted records in online catalogs. A decade after most full-scale conversion projects took place, catalogers are still cleaning up converted records. This may explain the caution with which catalogers approach the current trend of outsourcing cataloging.

NOTES

1. "Retrospective Conversion: Issues and Perspectives, a Forum Edited by Jon Drabenstott," *Library Hi Tech* 4, no. 2 (summer 1986): 106.

2. Amy Hart, "Operation Cleanup: The Problem Resolution Phase of a Retrospective Conversion Project," *Library Resources & Technical Services* 32, no. 4 (October 1988): 379.

3. Derry C. Juneja, "Quality Control in Data Conversion," *Library Resources & Technical Services* 31, no. 2 (April/June 1987): 148.

4. Brian Schottlaender, "Introduction," in *Retrospective Conversion: History, Approaches, Considerations* (New York: Haworth Press, 1992), 1.

5.   Joseph R. Matthews, "Retrospective Conversion: Issues and Perspectives," *Library Hi Tech* 4, no. 2 (summer 1986): 110.

6.   "Retrospective Conversion: Issues and Perspectives," 106.

7.   Ilene Rockman, "Retrospective Conversion: Reference Librarians Are Missing the Action," *Library Journal* 115, no. 7 (April 15, 1990): 41–42.

8.   Ruth Christ and Selina Lin, "Serials Retrospective Conversion: Project Design and In-House Implementation," in *Retrospective Conversion: History, Approaches, Considerations*, ed. Brian Schottlaender (New York: Haworth Press, 1992), 56.

9.   Andrew Lisawski, "Vendor-Based Retrospective Conversion at George Washington University," in *Retrospective Conversion: From Cards to Computers*, ed. Anne G. Adler and Elizabeth A. Baber (Ann Arbor, MI: Pierian Press, 1984), 219.

10.   James E. Rush, "Retrospective Conversion: Issues and Perspectives," *Library Hi Tech* 4, no. 2 (summer 1986): 112.

11.   Christ and Lin, "Serials Retrospective Conversion," 56.

12.   Michelle Koth and Laura Gayle Green, "Workflow Consideration in Retrospective Conversion Projects for Scores," in *Retrospective Conversion: History, Approaches, Considerations*, ed. Brian Schottlaender (New York: Haworth Press, 1992), 77.

13.   Donald T. Green and Dean W. Corwin, "Retrospective Conversion of Music Materials," in *Retrospective Conversion: From Cards to Computers*, ed. Anne G. Adler and Elizabeth A. Baber (Ann Arbor, MI: Pierian Press, 1984), 253.

14.   Rush, "Retrospective Conversion," 111.

15.   Koth and Green, "Workflow Consideration," 88.

16.   Elizabeth A. Baber, "Planning for Retrospective Conversion at Rice University: Vendor and In-House Alternatives," in *Retrospective Conversion: From Cards to Computers*, ed. Anne G. Adler and Elizabeth A. Baber (Ann Arbor, MI: Pierian Press, 1984), 17.

17.   Juneja, "Quality Control," 149.

18.   Rush, "Retrospective Conversion," 112.

19.   Matthews, "Retrospective Conversion," 110.

20.   Ibid.

21.   Ibid.

22.   Judy McQueen and Richard W. Boss, "Sources of Machine-Readable Cataloging and Retrospective Conversion," *Library Technology Reports* 21, no. 6 (November/December 1985): 631.

23.   Rita Broadway and Jane Qualls, "Retrospective Conversion of Periodicals: A Shoestring Experience," *Serials Librarian* 15, no. 1/2 (1988): 110.

24.   Mary K. Bolin and Harley B. Wright, "Retrospective Conversion of a Medium-Sized Academic Library," in *Retrospective Conversion: History, Approaches, Considerations*, ed. Brian Schottlaender (New York: Haworth Press, 1992), 43.

25. Koth and Green, "Workflow Consideration," 88.

26. Baber, "Planning for Retrospective Conversion," 12.

27. McQueen and Boss, "Sources of Machine-Readable Cataloging," 631.

28. Koth and Green, "Workflow Consideration," 90.

29. Nancy A. Douglas, "Retrospective Conversion Using OCLC at Texas A&M University Library," in *Retrospective Conversion: From Cards to Computers*, ed. Anne G. Adler and Elizabeth A. Barber (Ann Arbor, MI: Pierian Press, 1984), 5.

30. Matthews, "Retrospective Conversion," 106.

31. Jutta Reed-Scott, "Retrospective Conversion: Issues and Perspectives," *Library Hi Tech* 4, no. 2 (summer 1986): 114.

32. Susan Baerg Epstein, "Retrospective Conversion: Issues and Perspectives," *Library Hi Tech* 4, no. 2 (summer 1986): 106.

33. Juneja, "Quality Control," 154.

34. Sandra Card, "Problems and Solutions in a Retrospective Serials Conversion Project," in *Retrospective Conversion: From Cards to Computers*, ed. Anne G. Adler and Elizabeth A. Baber (Ann Arbor, MI. Pierlan Press, 1984), 241.

35. Stephen H. Peters and Douglas J. Butler, "A Cost Model for Retrospective Conversion Alternatives," *Library Resources & Technical Services* 28 (April/June 1984): 159–60.

36. Rick J. Block, "Cataloging Outsourcing: Issues and Options," *Serials Review* 20, no. 3 (1994): 74.

37. Koth and Green, "Workflow Consideration," 76.

38. Beth Sandore, "Streamlining a Conversion Project with a Staff PC Workstation and Shelf List Sampling," in *Restrospective Conversion: History, Approaches, Considerations*, ed. Brian Schottlaender (New York: Haworth Press, 1992), 125–26.

39. *LC Information Bulletin*, March 25, 1985.

40. Koth and Green, "Workflow Consideration," 98.

41. Matthews, "Retrospective Conversion," 107.

42. Susan Baerg Epstein, "Retrospective Conversion Revisited, Part 1," *Library Journal* 115, no. 9 (May 15, 1990): 58.

43. McQueen and Boss, "Sources of Machine-Readable Cataloging," 619.

44. Ibid., 632.

45. Ibid., 633.

46. Reed-Scott, "Retrospective Conversion," 116.

47. Marsha Ra, "The Need for Costing in a Cooperative Retrospective Conversion Project," *Technical Services Quarterly* 44, no.4 (summer 1987): 43.

48. McQueen and Boss, "Sources of Machine-Readable Cataloging," 633.

49.   Douglas, "Retrospective Conversion Using OCLC," 2.

50.   Koth and Green, "Workflow Consideration," 90.

51.   *OCLC Newsletter* (September/October 1993):13.

52.   Ibid., 12.

53.   McQueen and Boss, "Sources of Machine-Readable Cataloging," 614–15.

54.   Juneja, "Quality Control," 152.

55.   Kathleen L. Wells, "Retrospective Conversion: Through the Looking Glass," *RTSD Newsletter* 12, no. 1 (winter 1987): 11.

56.   Sue Fuller and Helen Palmer, "Back to the Future: Serials Conversion," *Serials Librarian* 19, no. 3/4 (1991): 232.

57.   Matthews, "Retrospective Conversion," 107.

58.   Laura Tull, "Contract Cataloging: Retrospective Conversion of a Technical Report Collection," *Technical Services Quarterly* 9, no. 1 (1991): 15.

9 *Authority Control*

Authority control "is about consistency."[1] It ensures that personal, corporate, conference and place names, series and uniform titles, and subject headings used in bibliographic records are correctly formulated. Authority control accomplishes this task by 1) distinguishing terms and defining the established terms with scope and usage notes; 2) making explicit the diverse relationships between terms; 3) formulating headings and references for these terms in accordance with established rules, thus multiplying access to a term through cross-references from variant forms; and 4) documenting this work by creating authority records. Various approaches have been followed to organize and manage authority work.

Vendor-supplied authority control often occurs at a critical juncture in technical services—after a retrospective conversion project or when the library migrates from one online catalog to another. In both cases libraries want to upgrade their bibliographic records and generate authority records before loading them into their databases. In these instances, vendor-supplied authority control happens as a by-product and only complements a larger project. More than in other outsourcing arrangements, numerous technological advances have dramatically increased the ease with which libraries can outsource authority work. This is one area where computer applications excel in both speed and accuracy. These factors also allow libraries to outsource their authority work to vendors on an ongoing basis. Over half of the libraries surveyed outsource or have outsourced authority control. Despite these developments, "the basic goals underlaying authority control have remained constant."[2]

The outsourcing of authority control has been eclipsed by a much broader issue, that is, the necessity for authority control. Some have advocated that with the computerization of library catalogs, authority control is no longer necessary; others have maintained that it remains essential.[3] Whether to perform authority control has dominated the debate. Nonetheless, a majority of librarians recognize that "new information technology in the form of computerized retrieval techniques" does not automatically mandate the end of authority control.[4] Once a decision is made by the individual library to implement authority control, vendor-performed authority control is a common strategy.

Performing authority control is labor-intensive, time-consuming, and costly. The demands to provide new services for patrons have been satisfied by transferring resources from cataloging to other library functions. The results have been fewer catalogers, with a corresponding neglect of authority work. Consequently, those libraries that choose to outsource authority control do so for mainly two reasons: They do not have enough staff to perform authority control in a satisfactory manner, and vendors offer attractive pricing.

HISTORICAL BACKGROUND

Since one of the goals of retrospective conversion was the creation of local automated databases, names, series, subject headings, and uniform titles had to be brought under control either during the conversion process or after the conversion was completed. For the duration of the majority of retrospective conversion projects, headings appeared in varied forms: AACR, AACR2, a combination of both, older forms, or unknown forms. Some libraries were overwhelmed with the magnitude of their conversion and chose to ignore authority control at the time. Kathleen Joyce Kruger notes that given the restrictions on staff and other resources, the "Pandora's box of authority control on the retrospectively converted records had to remain closed."[5] Some were cognizant of the difficulties encountered in controlling headings in current cataloging and the special problems in dealing with retrospective conversion and raised "the question of just how good a library's authority control can or should be."[6] Others foresaw the need for authority control, but automated catalogs in the 1980s often lacked storage and processing capacity, thus thwarting authority control efforts. Circulation systems, rather than the creation of authority files, remained the first priority.[7]

Some libraries decided to outsource authority control after the completion of their conversion and planned for the retrospective conversion of their local authority card catalogs. As online catalogs became a reality, the conversion of their manual authority card catalogs began. Many libraries relied on vendors during conversion projects because the capabilities of the local online catalogs did not compare with the capabilities offered by vendors. UCLA, for example, reported that it did an in-house authority project in conjunction with conversion, and low productivity was due partly to the limitations of its ORION system.[8]

The benefits of using an authority vendor for the conversion of large collections are evident. In 1992, Harvard signed a contract with OCLC for the retrospective conversion and authority control of one of its collections.

OCLC focused entirely on what could be done automatically and proved the automated process to be more cost-effective in the long run than the manual review process. This project showed that complex machine processing can correct vast numbers of headings with minimum human intervention. Robin K. Wendler reports that "OCLC's machine-intensive process performed as well as or better than the manual-intensive process."[9]

As local systems made uploading and downloading of records between the library and the vendor a relatively easy process, some libraries elected to contract out for authority work on an ongoing basis. Authority control is a dynamic process. New headings are added to the catalog, existing headings are updated or split into several headings, and conflicts between headings can occur. Ongoing authority work requires libraries to send their new cataloging records to the vendor, typically on a quarterly basis. Once the vendor has performed the work, both the corrected bibliographic records and the new authority records have to be reloaded into the library's online system.

IN-HOUSE VERSUS OUTSOURCED AUTHORITY CONTROL

Some libraries perform this function in-house, and others rely on "outside vendors to revise their headings and supply authority records for current cataloging."[10]

In-House Authority Control

Several major automation vendors rank high in providing sophisticated authority control modules. Such vendors (Dynix, Autographics, Atlas, Innovative, Geac, MSUS/PALS, Inlex, and CLSI) provide features most desired by librarians and are able to meet the authority control needs of most libraries.[11] There are two basic designs that support authority control: linked and unlinked authority systems. Some local systems are designed to link authority records to headings used in bibliographic records. Authority-controlled headings are not stored in bibliographic records, and links are created between the bibliographic heading field and the corresponding authority record. Searches for controlled headings are done in the authority file, and when a bibliographic record is displayed, the system reconstructs it from the linked authority data. In other systems, authority records and bibliographic records are stored in the local database, either in separate files or in a single file, but are not linked.[12] Libraries that perform authority control in-house have access to the most important sources, the LC name and subject authority files. In-house authority control allows greater flexibility than vendor-supplied authority control because it can be performed before or after a record is cataloged. Precataloging is defined as a review of authority-controlled access points before producing cataloging records, and postcataloging is defined as the detection of errors through systems checks.[13] Despite flexible workflow options and sophisticated capabilities (e.g., global changes, creation of exception lists, rapid update), authority work remains time-consuming, and libraries have contracted with vendors for this type of work.

Vendor-Supplied Authority Control

Vendor-supplied authority control is always done postcataloging. When working with an authority vendor, the library sends its bibliographic file to the vendor. The vendor matches the library's headings in bibliographic records against headings in authority files and either adds headings or replaces invalid headings with the authorized form. Most of the processes are computer-controlled and involve automatic comparisons and reconciliations of sets of records. Vendors benefit from proprietary software that can perform highly complex checking and updating of records. They also take advantage of their own authority databases. Vendor-supplied authority control is intimately linked with outsourcing cataloging. As more and more cataloging records bypass traditional cataloging channels and are loaded directly into the local catalog without the cataloger's review, the need for authority control increases.

Specifications need to be written for both authority and bibliographic records. For authority records, the library needs to make basic decisions: What happens to the database while the records are being cleaned up? Does it need all authority records or only authority records containing cross-references? Does it need authority records for names appearing only once in the local catalog? Once these decisions have been made, the library has to decide what types of authority records it will purchase (names, subjects, series, and uniform titles) and what new and updated records will be included. In the area of bibliographic records, the library needs to decide what fields or subfields should be validated, what fields will be automatically replaced, and which ones will not be automatically corrected and will be returned to the library.

In some instances, the headings in the bibliographic record do not match either the main heading or cross-references in an authority record and may not have been established by the Library of Congress. In other instances, the library may have created local headings. Nonmatches can be either returned to the library for review or handled by the vendor. Vendors emphasize batch machine processing, although manual inspection and editing of invalid headings are also available from some vendors.

GENERAL CONSIDERATIONS FOR OUTSOURCING

Extensive planning similar to the steps used in any outsourcing arrangement is required. Two scenarios are possible. A library can contract with a vendor for authority work on a onetime basis or for ongoing maintenance. A library already outsourcing its cataloging records to a vendor can additionally contract for authority work. For example, libraries buying GPO cataloging through Marcive may contract with Marcive for both bibliographic and authority records. Vendors either include authority control as part of their many offerings or solely specialize in this area. Both commercial vendors (e.g., BNA, Brodart, Baker & Taylor, Marcive, Libraries Technologies, Inc.) and bibliographic utilities and their networks offer such services. WLN, with its strong commitment to quality control, provides an exhaustive authority control program through its two modules: authority correction and authority matching. Recently, OCLC also began offering a new service that provides automated authority control to libraries.

Cost

It is generally agreed that vendor-supplied authority control is cheaper than performing it in-house. Angela Secrest writes that vendor authority control processing "is a cost effective way" to handle authority control.[14] However, cost estimates comparing in-house to vendor-supplied authority work are not readily available. Rather than focusing on costs, the literature stresses that vendor-supplied authority control allows the library to use its staff differently and more effectively.

The RFP

Authority vendors are quite flexible, and a library can expect a high level of customization. The RFP should include the following specifications: the source and currency of the vendor's authority files, the input and output specifications, the methodology for normalization and automatic correction of headings, the availability of manual review, the library's special needs, and the creation of printed reports and exception lists. The contract should also include a projected completion date for onetime projects or turnaround time for ongoing processing.

Source of the Vendor's Authority Files

There are numerous sources on which vendors can draw. The LC Name Authority File and the LC Subject Authority File, LC Children's Subject Authority File, National Library of Medicine MeSH Authority File, and, sometimes, the vendor's own authority files constitute the sources against which the bibliographic records are run. Some vendors maintain their own files of LCSH subdivisions for hierarchical checking of subject headings. Vendors can also build a customized file of a library's local authority records.

Input and Output

Input includes the type, number, and format of the bibliographic records being run against the authority file. Bibliographic records can be sent either on tape or via FTP to the vendor. Similarly, output consists of tapes or data sent via FTP. In the case of tapes, the tape format for the bibliographic and authority records and the number of records per tape need to be taken into account. The timetable for the receipt of both bibliographic records and their corresponding authority records needs to be specified, since the order of loading often affects the quality-control process at the local level.

Batch Processing

Typically, the vendor processes the subfield "a" of the heading of the bibliographic record if the entire heading with its subdivisions does not have an LC authority record. Thus, free-floating subdivisions in subject headings are ignored.

Normalization

Vendors normalize headings with regard to spacing, punctuation, diacritics, and capitalization to increase the likelihood of their matching a heading or reference in their authority file. The normalized form of a heading, where all letters are set in uppercase, MARC tags and subfields are removed, all punctuation and diacritics are deleted, and spacing between words is regularized, is run against the authority file. Matches are identified based on the comparison between the normalized form of the library heading and the normalized form of the authority record heading. In a second step, the same heading is matched against the heading in the bibliographic record, and if any differences appear, the heading in the bibliographic record is replaced with the heading from the authority file.[15]

Other normalization routines correct MARC coding, and some typographical errors, expand abbreviations to their full form (e.g., "U.S." to "United States"), delete canceled subfields (e.g., "Addresses, essays, lectures"), delete initial articles from uniform titles, and rearrange qualifying data for conference names in accordance with AACR2. A tagging error occurs when an incorrect tag is assigned to a bibliographic record field (e.g., a geographical subject heading is assigned a topical subject heading tag), and a subfield code error occurs when an incorrect subfield is assigned to text of that subfield or when the subfield code is missing. Typographical errors are defined when words differ minimally. The difference may be due to character omission, insertion, substitution, or transposition of characters (e.g., "Histroy" instead of "History"). Terms are sometimes abbreviated when they should not be or vice versa. Abbreviation errors also happen when records have the incorrect form of the abbreviation.[16]

Corrections and Deduping

Vendors update library headings to LC's latest headings and correct invalid forms of headings. If a library has used a heading that appears in a cross-reference, the heading will be flipped. Obsolete headings, which contain terms that are no longer valid, are replaced with the current headings. Incorrect qualifiers, incorrect order of headings, and inverted headings are corrected. Finally, peculiar headings are reported. Vendors will delete duplicate authority records if the library wishes. The vendor can also keep track of what authority records were sent to the library in order not to send duplicate records for ongoing authority processing.

Manual Review

Not all errors can be corrected through a batch process. Michele I. Dalehite notes that it is "premature to suppose that the results [of automated authority work] will replace all human intervention."[17] Not all headings used in bibliographic records have a corresponding authority record. The library can contract out manual review and have the vendor clear up problems.

Reports

Authority control reports typically include lists of unmatched headings, partially matched headings, headings that match multiple authority records, headings that have split, and headings that are incorrectly used (e.g., the heading is used as a subject heading but the authority record indicates that the heading cannot be used in that way).

CONCLUSION

As in other outsourcing activities, no one approach to managing authority work "is best for all libraries or for all situations."[18] Vendor-supplied authority control processing can be accomplished relatively cheaply and efficiently, but it cannot fully take care of all the snags. Of all the functions that can be outsourced, perhaps authority control benefits the most from the power of the computer. Unlike libraries, vendors can program computers to perform extremely complex authority processing for large numbers of records. Nonetheless, all those that have outsourced authority control stress that it cannot replace the "intellectual intervention involved in authority work"[19] and that although it serves as a tool to aid cataloging in maintaining authority data, "it does not eliminate authority work."[20]

NOTES

1. James Tilio Maccaferri, "Managing Authority Control in a Retrospective Conversion Project," in *Retrospective Conversion: History, Approaches, Considerations*, ed. Brian Schottlaender (New York: Haworth Press, 1992), 146.

2. Jennifer A. Younger, "Reframing the Authority Control Debate," in *The Future Is Now: Reconciling Change and Continuity in Authority Control: Proceedings of the OCLC Symposium*, *ALA Annual Conference, June 23, 1995* (Dublin, OH: OCLC, 1995), 1.

3. Jennifer A. Younger, "After Cutter: Authority Control in the Twenty-first Century," *Library Resources & Technical Services* 39, no. 2 (April 1995): 133.

4. Younger, "Reframing the Authority Control Debate," 2.

5. Kathleen Joyce Kruger, "MARC Tags and Retrospective Conversion: The Editing Process," *Information Technology and Libraries* 4, no. 1 (March 1995) : 56.

6. Maccaferri, "Managing Authority Control," 149.

7. Mary A. Madden, "Is This Somehow Connected? The Vendor Perspective," in *Authority Control: The Key to Tomorrow's Catalog*, ed. Mary W. Ghikas (Phoenix, AZ: Oryx Press, 1982), 90.

8. Maccaferri, "Managing Authority Control," 156.

9. Robin K. Wendler, "Automating Heading Correction in a Large File: Harvard's Experience," in *The Future is Now: Reconciling Change and Continuity in Authority Control: Proceedings of the OCLC Symposium*, *ALA Annual Conference, June 23, 1995* (Dublin, OH: OCLC, 1995), 6.

10. Stephen Hearn, "Authority Control," in *Guide to Technical Services Resources*, ed. Peggy Johnson (Chicago: American Library Association, 1994), 87.

11.   Sarah Hager Johnston, "Current Offerings in Automated Authority Control: A Survey of Vendors," *Information Technology and Libraries* 8, no. 3 (September 1989): 239.

12.   Stephen Hearn, "Authority Control," 87.

13.   Stefanie A. Wittenbach, *Automated Authority Control in ARL Libraries*. SPEC Flyer 156 (Washington, DC: Association of Research Libraries, Office of Management Studies, July/August 1989).

14.   Angela Secrest, "Automated Authority Control: Benefits and Pitfalls," *Iowa Library Quarterly* 26, no. 3 (1989): 8.

15.   Daniel Miller, "Authority Control in the Retrospective Conversion Process," *Information Technology and Libraries* 3, no. 3 (September 1984): 288.

16.   Edward T. O'Neill, "OCLC Authority Control," *OCLC Systems & Services* 10 (winter 1994): 42.

17.   Michele I. Dalehite, "Vendor-Supplied Automated Authority Control: What It Is and How to Get It," *Law Library Journal* 81 (1989): 120.

18.   Stephen Hearn, "Authority Control," 87.

19.   Secrest, "Automated Authority Control," 14.

20.   Dalehite, "Vendor-Supplied Automated Authority Control," 127.

10 Preservation

Preservation encompasses several activities designed to prolong indefinitely the usability of a library's collection.[1] These activities include binding, mending and repair, microfilming, photocopying, conservation, deacidification, digitization, and disaster recovery. The extent that each of these activities has been outsourced varies from nearly total outsourcing, as in the case of binding, to performing virtually all activities in-house, as in the case of digitization. The term outsourcing is not commonly used in the preservation literature. However, a specific search of the types of preservation methods used by libraries and the subsequent reading of the articles revealed that in the majority of cases, libraries use vendors for these activities, or, technically, outsource them. Seventy-nine percent of the libraries responding to the authors' survey indicated that they outsource some preservation function. The absence of the term *outsourcing* in the preservation literature underscores that outsourcing of preservation is not an issue of contention in librarianship.

Libraries have historically been involved in preserving their materials for future use. Prior to the 1960s, libraries focused on the preservation of individual items in their collections.[2] In the 1960s a greater awareness of preservation began to develop as librarians gained a better understanding of the global problem of material deterioration due to age, quality of materials, and environmental and use factors.[3] Since then, an increasing amount of money and effort has gone into preservation activities, and the practice has evolved from simply restoring physical materials to transferring information to a different format such as photocopy, microform, or digital records.

BINDING

For decades, binding has been the principal technique for preservation in libraries. Most experts agree that binding is one of the best preservation decisions a library can make.[4] One author even calls support for binding a decision to fund a preservation program.[5] Another author refers to binding as the only preservation treatment available to most libraries.[6] However, by the mid-1980s, binding no longer was the main preservation activity but one of many operations designed to preserve library materials.[7]

Brief History

Bookbinding as we know it goes back to the times of the Romans; during the early days of the printed word, it primarily served conservation and restoration functions.[8] It was a handcraft available only to collectors who could afford to have their priceless materials carefully and individually rebound or restored.[9] By the mid-eighteenth century, machinery was developed that reduced the cost of binding drastically, thus making it affordable to libraries. Oftentimes conservation is still incorrectly associated with the treatment of rare and unique materials, but it should be applied to all nonrare library materials as well in order to prolong their useful life.[10]

Function of Binding

Binding fulfills a dual function for libraries. On one hand it protects newly acquired materials from deterioration, as in the case of periodicals. Studies have shown that periodical collections that remained unbound over long periods of time suffered physical deterioration, mutilation, and theft and that later repairs were more expensive than initial binding.[11] Indeed, the most prevalent use of binding in libraries may be for journal collections. But binding can be used for a variety of other materials such as poorly bound paperbacks, books that receive heavy use, and virtually any other form of material printed on paper. In fact, most commercial binders are able to provide conservation and preservation services to libraries, and often a fine line divides routine binding activities from preservation.[12]

Outsourcing of Bindery Operations

With few exceptions—consisting of large libraries that have full-size binding operations in-house—binding has historically been contracted out. The nature of the operation itself dictates this necessity. Binding is an activity that requires specialized knowledge and skills, attention to detail, expensive machinery, and a large work area. It also benefits from economies of scale, since amortizing the cost of the expensive machinery and constant upgrades requires that the machines be used intensively. The specialized skills of the operators are also mastered over extended periods of time.

A 1989 survey of 100 academic libraries showed that those libraries that could afford to bind used a commercial binder. The study, conducted by a library that took its bindery operations back in-house, also revealed that the quality of the library's in-house binding was unsatisfactory to users and library staff and did not meet its preservation needs.[13]

Interviews with the heads of preservation units at two leading ARL libraries also indicate that outsourcing binding operations is the preferred method.[14] Furthermore, Carla J. Montori, head of the preservation unit at the University of Michigan Library, points out that even those libraries that have an in-house conservation lab use commercial binding for the bulk of their circulating collections.[15]

Binding is a well-developed, mature business with a long tradition of high standards and quality service. The relationship between libraries and binders has been called a partnership by some[16] and even a "symbiotic relationship"[17] that underscores the interdependence that exists between the two establishments. Libraries certainly need a vendor they can trust with handling important portions of their collections. For vendors, libraries provide an important market that is vital to their continued survival. By 1985 libraries were spending $39 million a year on preservation activities;[18] in 1990 libraries spent up to 10 percent of their materials budget and in some cases up to 50 percent on preservation.[19] As a result, a large number of companies can offer a variety of binding and preservation services to libraries at reasonable prices. Commercial binders also benefit from the standards developed by the Library Binding Institute (LBI). Adherence to the LBI standards by the binder ensures that a library receives quality binding designed to protect the materials for the long run. All these factors have made binding a good candidate for outsourcing.

The current challenge for commercial library binders is a decrease in the traditional binding of periodicals due to cancellations of serials. Binders see an opportunity to replace this lost income by providing binding for the growing number of paperback books that libraries are purchasing.[20]

MENDING

The mending and repair of damaged items has been the other aspect of libraries' efforts to preserve their collections in original form. Although few libraries perform all their binding in-house, most do some mending and repair. Most binders offer mending as an option and can perform this function on request.

PRESERVATION MICROFILMING

Next to binding, microfilming is probably the most common and most widely accepted method of preservation. Some of the large libraries began microfilming for preservation purposes in the 1930s.[21] Over time, film and camera quality and preparation of the originals improved to the point that microfilm is of excellent quality. Archival-quality microfilm has a predicted lifespan of more than 500 years, which rivals the best-quality paper and far surpasses the electronic media in use today. Equally important is the existence of standards for preservation microfilming. Thus a library that engages in preservation microfilming or that outsources this function has clear guidelines by which to judge the results.

Although initially high effort and cost are involved in converting to microform, duplication is easy and inexpensive. Copies are made from a working master to protect the archival master. Given the prevalence of this preservation method, libraries have engaged in cooperative programs that benefit the entire library community. For example, the masters can be stored at a national facility in environmentally ideal conditions. Availability of a preservation copy is indicated in national databases such as RLIN.[22] Thus a library contemplating the microfilming of a book can easily find out if another library has already done so.

Libraries routinely outsource preservation microfilming to commercial vendors.[23] As in the case of binding, the specialization required to produce high-quality, error-free work, and the use of specialized equipment favor using vendors. Expertise and equipment needs, the application of archival standards, production cost, bibliographic control, and long-term maintenance have been cited as reasons that in-house preservation microfilming is beyond the reach of most libraries.[24] Commercial vendors can perform a host of activities designed to save libraries time and money, such as preparing materials, filming, processing, and even setting up bibliographic records.[25] Although some studies indicate that libraries generally have access to microfilming facilities, paradoxically, the findings also show that little microfilming is done at the local level.[26] The existence of reliable, well-known vendors with a lot of expertise in this area probably discourages most libraries from developing or keeping these operations in-house.

PRESERVATION PHOTOCOPYING

The goal of preservation photocopying is to produce a "usable preservation replacement copy of an entire printed volume."[27] It is one of the less prevalent methods of preservation used by libraries. Photocopying is more a convenience to patrons than a long-term solution for overall library preservation concerns and is generally used for materials likely to circulate. Reports from the field that describe preservation photocopy projects indicate that they tend to be conducted in-house. Nevertheless, "Guidelines for Preservation Photocopying" by ALCTS refers to the agent that actually produces the photocopy as the vendor regardless of whether this entity is a commercial vendor, "another department in the institution, or even the staff in the department initiating the copying."[28] This observation is interesting because it shows the bias in the profession that preservation is generally outsourced even in cases where circumstantial evidence seems to indicate the contrary.[29]

Developments in photocopying technology and materials, especially the high quality of paper and toners available today, make photocopying a viable preservation method if a book or periodical needs to be preserved in its paper form. However, there are some disadvantages to this method that hamper its wide use. First, a photocopy is not a master record that can be cheaply reproduced. Subsequent copies cost essentially the same as the first copy.[30] Second, no space savings are realized by the library, as in the case of microfilming. Photocopying can be performed relatively cheaply in-house by libraries because of the easy availability of the equipment, but the cost stays low only as long as the amount to be preserved stays low. Although some vendors supply photocopying services, the fact that libraries can perform the function in-house and the fact that this kind of preservation benefits less from economies of scale make outsourcing photocopying a less attractive option. After photocopying, some libraries send the materials to be bound by their commercial binder.

In some instances, libraries participate in preservation photocopying ventures with other libraries. Recently, a cooperative project to photocopy brittle books for preservation purposes was begun at the University of Kansas. A list of titles to be copied is posted on a listserv—the Brittle Books List. Libraries can buy photocopies of brittle books and also recommend books to be copied by the operation. The actual photocopying is performed by a commercial vendor.

The most important reason libraries engage less in preservation photocopying than in other types of preservation is the lack of established standards for this method. The ALCTS guidelines are a good start but fall short of setting standards for the entire photocopying operation. And although users certainly prefer a paper copy of a book or journal, from the preservation point of view the photocopy does not offer the same advantages, especially in the area of sharing and duplication, that other forms do.

BOOK PRESERVATION BOXES

Another common method of preserving materials is to store them in boxes. Box technology enables materials to be preserved in their original form and prevents any further damage or alteration, as is the case with most other preservation techniques. The technology for developing the box materials and box design are also quite developed; vendors are able to provide alkaline boxes for books of any size and shape.[31] Generally, libraries buy the material for making boxes from library supply vendors and the actual encapsulation is performed in-house. Some libraries outsource the entire operation to a binder.

DEACIDIFICATION

Changes in the materials used to manufacture paper after the middle of the nineteenth century, when acids were unwittingly introduced into the manufacturing process, have created immense preservation problems for libraries.[32] Virtually all paper used after 1850 is acidic, and the effect of the acid on the paper became acute by the middle of the twentieth century. Large portions of libraries' valuable collections began deteriorating with a large percentage of books becoming increasingly brittle every year.

Beginning in the 1960s, deacidification was studied as a preservation method and was considered one of the most promising methods for book preservation until the mid-1980s. Several different deacidification processes were developed, and two were prominent during this period: the WEI T'O method, developed by a private company, and the diethyl zinc (DEZ) vapor phase mass deacidification process, developed by the Library of Congress. Regardless of the method chosen, a library that decided to implement a deacidification program had to use an outside vendor.[33]

However, there were problems associated with deacidification and this method of preservation fell out of favor in the 1990s.[34] Even the literature in support of mass deacidification included strong caveats. Deacidification does not reverse the effects of deterioration; it only stops further deterioration. The fact that deacidification is essentially a chemical engineering process with which libraries do not feel comfortable; the strong chemicals used; and the hazards posed to individuals, the environment, and the materials themselves made librarians cautious about deacidification.

Mass deacidification also required a large facility and specialized equipment and chemicals and thus was costly. Only a relatively low volume of materials were processed at one time because too many books in the batch could result in some getting uneven treatment or not being treated at all.[35] In the early 1990s, the premier deacidification company in the world, Akzo, had a capacity of 40,000 books annually, which given the needs of libraries was insignificant. In fact the deacidification industry to serve libraries did not develop into a strong one and deacidification never received the acceptance levels of other preservation methods.

A 1996 report on the state of mass deacidification worldwide warns that if libraries take a wait-and-see attitude, the commercial companies that would normally develop and refine the products and processes for mass deacidification would "withdraw and give up work on systems for the commercial market, which eventually might result in the undesirable situation that further development of promising techniques will no longer be possible at all."[36] It seems that this is already happening. By 1996 Akzo was no longer involved in deacidification activities. New methods, including digitization, have been found more practical and cost effective and environmentally more acceptable.

DIGITIZATION

Digitization, or the transfer of information to electronic form, developed rapidly in recent years. The advantages of digitization are numerous. Scanning a text into an electronic database makes its manipulation, reproduction, and dissemination extremely easy. In many cases it enhances the text by making it easier to search its contents. In some cases, such as large folios or maps, digitization may be the only way to preserve a document, since filming or photocopying such materials is difficult. Once a document is digitized, high quality-printers can be used to print it. But these reproductions are not always true to the originals; printers and scanners may alter colors and details.

The negatives of digitization outweigh the positives in regard to preservation, at least at the current writing. The lack of stability in the technology, which is advancing so rapidly as to make older systems obsolete every few years, is by far the least-appealing aspect of digitization.[37] There are already large numbers of files on magnetic tape that cannot be read with current machines. Thus older, obsolete machines must be maintained simply for the purpose of reading these files or information must be continuously transferred to new media. Either option is unacceptable. In addition, current storage media, whether magnetic or optical, have not proven stable for the long term; most estimates place their useful lifespan at 20 years. The data must be copied over and over to new media to make it last. Twenty years is certainly not an acceptable option compared with the 500-plus years offered by microfilm or alkaline paper. Data fatigue, deterioration, archiving, and storing are other issues that have to be solved.

Digitization is currently used as a stopgap measure for those materials that would disappear if they were not digitized. It can also be used to provide easy access to rare materials to a large number of users, as the Library of Congress is doing through its American Memory project. The University of Virginia indicated on the survey that digital scanning is done more to provide access than for preservation purposes. Some conservators also use the hybrid technique, in which an item is preserved both in digital and analog form.

Digitization is a new and expensive technology, and to date, most efforts in this area have been experimental. A recent survey of ARL libraries conducted by the Office of Management Studies (OMS) reveals that of 78 respondents, only 29, or 37 percent, have experimented with digitization.[38] The survey also shows that libraries that have engaged in this activity have purchased both the hardware and software necessary for digitization and are performing the pilot projects in-house. The factors mentioned previously, such as the instability of the medium, problems with archiving, technological changes, and obsolescence, have prevented it from being adopted on a large scale by either libraries or vendors. However, the abundance of high-technology companies in existence today certainly allows any library to find a vendor that can provide expertise in digitization.

DISASTER PREPAREDNESS AND CONTROL

Disasters can occur in a library at any time and may be caused by water, fire, earthquakes, biological infestations, vandalism, and the breakdown of mechanical systems.[39] In order to ensure minimal damage to the collection, a library has to be prepared to deal with such events. In most cases, libraries outsource this aspect of their operation to companies that specialize in disaster preparedness. The first step is to have the vendor do an on-site assessment of the collection to note where the collections are housed, identify the different kinds of materials that will need to be retrieved and the kinds of treatments they will receive, and, based on the value and replaceability of segments of the collection, to specify salvage priorities.[40] When a disaster occurs, the vendor will move the materials from the library to its own facility in order to provide the necessary treatment. One of the most common forms of treatment is freeze-drying books after a flood. The large freezers needed for this kind of treatment make it ideal for outsourcing.

OUTSOURCING CONSIDERATIONS

The labor-intensive nature of binding and preservation and the specialized skills involved has made them candidates for outsourcing from the time they appeared on the library scene. In fact, these services have been purchased from vendors by the majority of libraries, and constitute a significant expenditure on their part.

As with all other outsourcing operations, the cost to the library consists of more than just vendors' charges. The library still needs to engage in a labor-intensive process of preparing the materials to be sent to a vendor. In the case of routine bindery preparation, an entire library department with several staff members and a well-developed workflow may be engaged in this operation. In the case of preparation for preservation, a variety of departments may be involved. Collection development librarians first identify the items that should be sent out for treatment. Staff in the preservation department advise the selectors as to the options.

Regarding the treatment of materials, there are two models: Either staff in the library make the decision about the kind of treatment the materials will receive or the library delegates that decision to the vendor. Once the items and their method of treatment have been chosen, staff in the preservation department have to prepare, pack, and send the items to the vendor. Upon return, preservation staff have to quality-check the materials to make sure there are no errors. This is the level at which each item is dealt with separately, thus constituting a time-consuming and expensive step in the preservation of materials. This is also a step that has to be performed by in-house staff.

CONCLUSION

Preservation projects are expensive and are often funded by grants. Libraries cannot as a rule afford to support large-scale preservation projects out of their operating budgets even when these functions are outsourced, the notable exception being binding. The importance of preservation to a library's collection makes it imperative that libraries choose vendors that operate according to accepted preservation standards for library materials. The excellent relationships that have developed between libraries and vendors in this area provide a good example of how libraries can benefit from outsourcing.

NOTES

1. Murray S. Martin, "Binding, Mending, and Preservation: Value Maintenance Tools," *Technicalities* 15, no. 12 (December 1995): 8.

2. Margaret P. Trader, "Preservation Technologies: Photocopies, Microforms, and Digital Imaging—Pros and Cons," *Microform Review* 22, no. 3 (summer 1993): 127.

3. Margaret M. Byrnes, "Preservation of the Biomedical Literature: An Overview," *Bulletin of the Medical Library Association* 77, no. 3 (July 1989): 270.

4. Elizabeth H. Smith, "Library Binding Is a Service," *New Library Scene* 14, no. 6 (December 1995): 14.

5. Gregor R. Campbell, "Preservation," *New Library Scene* 13, no. 5 (October 1994): 5.

6. Carla J. Montori, "Managing the Library's Commercial Library Binding Program," *Technical Services Quarterly* 5, no. 3 (1988): 21.

7. Don Lanier, *Binding Operations in ARL Libraries*. SPEC Flyer 114 (Washington, DC: Systems and Procedures Exchange Center, 1985).

8. Lawrence S. Thomson, "Binding," *Encyclopedia of Library and Information Science* 2 (1969): 493.

9. Paul A. Parisi, "The Changing World of Library Binding," *Technicalities* 15, no. 12 (December 1995): 14.

10. *The Changing Role of Book Repair in ARL Libraries*. SPEC Flyer 190 (Washington, DC: Systems and Procedures Exchange Center, 1993).

11. Trudie A. Root, "Inhouse Binding in Academic Libraries," *Serials Review* 15, no. 3 (1989): 36.

12. Campbell, "Preservation," 6.

13. Root, "Inhouse Binding," 34.

14. Ellen Cunningham-Kruppa, head, Preservation Department, University of Texas at Austin, interview by authors, January 7, 1997. Frances C. Wilkinson, director, Acquisitions and Serials Department, and preservation officer, University of New Mexico General Library, interview by authors, January 24, 1997.

15. Carla J. Montori, "Managing the Library's Binding Program," 21.

16. Tim McAdam, "The Commercial Binding Agreement: Partners in Preservation," *Serials Librarian* 17, no. 3/4 (1990): 153.

17.   Smith, "Library Binding,"13.

18.   *Preservation Guidelines in ARL Libraries*. SPEC Flyer 137 (Washington, DC: Systems and Procedures Exchange Center, 1987).

19.   *Preservation Organizations and Staffing*. SPEC Flyer 160 (Washington, DC: Association of Research Libraries, Office of Management Studies, 1990).

20.   Jay Fairfield, "Our Challenge as Library Binders: Overcoming the Trends in Our Industry's Economics," *New Library Scene* 14, no. 4 (August 1995): 15.

21.   Byrnes, "Preservation," 269.

22.   Jan Merrill-Oldham, *Brittle Books Program*. SPEC Flyer 152 (Washington, DC: Association of Research Libraries, Office of Management Studies, March 1989).

23.   *Preservation Organizations and Staffing*. SPEC Flyer 160.

24.   Trader, "Preservation Technologies," 130.

25.   *Preservation Organizations and Staffing*. SPEC Flyer 160.

26.   Byrnes, "Preservation," 272.

27.   "Guidelines for Preservation Photocopying," *Library Resources & Technical Services* 38, no. 3 (July 1994): 288.

28.   Ibid., 289.

29.   Gay Walker, "Preservation Decision-Making and Archival Photocopying," *Restaurator* 8 (1987): 48.

30.   Trader, "Preservation Technologies," 129.

31.   Alan Keely, "Book Preservation Boxes," *North Carolina Libraries* 44 (summer 1986): 98.

32.   Carolyn Clark Morrow et al., "Mass Deacidification and the DEZ Vapor Phase Process," *Encyclopedia of Library and Information Science* 55 (1995): 200.

33.   Richard Frieder, "Mass Deacidification: Now That It Is Reality, What Next?" *IFLA Journal* 17, no. 2 (1991): 142.

34.   Frances C. Wilkinson, director, Acquisitions and Serials Department, and preservation officer, University of New Mexico General Library, interview by authors, February 19, 1997.

35.   Jacques Grimard, "Mass Deacidification: Universal Cure or Limited Solution?" *American Archivist* 57, no. 4 (fall 1994): 678.

36.   Henk J. Porck, *Mass Deacidification: An Update on Possibilities and Limitations*. (Amsterdam and Washington, DC: European Commission on Preservation and Access and Commission on Preservation and Access, 1996), 44.

37.   Clifford A. Lynch and Edwin B. Brownrigg, "Conservation, Preservation, and Digitization," *College & Research Libraries* 47, no. 4 (July 1986): 379.

38.   *Digitization Technologies for Preservation*. SPEC Flyer 214 (Washington, DC: Association of Research Libraries, Office of Management Studies, March 1996).

39.   *Preparing for Emergencies and Disasters*. SPEC Flyer 69 (Washington, DC: Systems and Procedures Exchange Center, 1980).

40.   Ibid.

11 Public Services and Systems

Outsourcing in public services and systems is viewed differently by the profession than other outsourcing projects, and there is typically less outsourcing activity in these areas. Public services are the least affected by outsourcing and can be considered the last stronghold of operations to be kept in-house. Technological developments regarding the exchange and delivery of information are affecting the way in which libraries provide services to patrons, but the operations still remain solidly anchored in the library. Systems, which is a relative newcomer to the library scene, has with a few exceptions mostly relied on vendor products with technical support provided in-house. Even those libraries that developed homegrown systems in the early days are switching to turnkey, vendor-developed products as they move on to third- or fourth-generation systems. The provision and support of systems do not in most cases truly conform to the definition of outsourcing, since many of the products acquired were never produced in-house or considered core. Nevertheless, discussions with colleagues and perusal of the literature indicate that librarians are interested in the issue of outsourcing system functions.

PUBLIC SERVICES

Public services have been minimally outsourced, a fact reflected both in the literature and in the survey conducted for this book. No respondent indicated outsourcing reference, instruction, or desk hours, and overall, outsourcing activities were virtually nil. The nature of public services, which consists of reference, instruction, online searching, circulation, interlibrary loan, and to a certain extent document delivery, is such that they depend to a larger extent on the libraries' in-house collections and facilities for their performance and are therefore more difficult to outsource. These services give a library its identity, and even if it were feasible to outsource them, it would probably not be advisable to do so.

Reference

It is generally agreed that because of the nature of reference and its reliance on materials housed on-site, which are specially and expertly selected for the needs of the library's clientele, it is unacceptable to outsource reference.[1] This is especially true of academic and large public libraries, which serve broad clienteles with varied interests. Librarians take advantage of contacts with faculty and students and rely on this knowledge to develop reference collections and services that best serve these clienteles. In addition, outsourcing requires a steady and measurable flow of work, which does not apply to reference services. Murray S. Martin contends that reference services are less amenable to outsourcing because they are labor-intensive and unpredictable "in flow, number, and content."[2] Whereas some corporate and public libraries have outsourced their reference services, this practice has not been reported in academic libraries. Even in those cases where libraries outsource reference, the operation is invisible to patrons. The outsourcing agency hires the reference librarians, but they work in the library, using the library's reference collection during the times the library is open. Moving the operation to the vendor's site would mean moving the library.

Instruction

The purpose of library instruction is to familiarize patrons with the library's collections and services. This requires two things: The instructor must be thoroughly knowledgeable about the collection, and instruction must take place on the premises so that the collection can be seen. Reference librarians have too often witnessed tours provided by outsiders and heard misinformation being presented to users, as during student orientations, to be comfortable outsourcing this function. Thus it is imperative to keep instruction in-house, and there is no indication that libraries outsource in this area. There has been an increased emphasis on instruction as part of the general provision of public services.[3] A recent study conducted by the Office of Management Studies (OMS) indicates that due to the proliferation of new products in new formats, the need for training is increasing in libraries.[4] Instruction services are gaining prominence in libraries, often breaking away from their traditional place in reference as they become independent departments with a broader mission.

Online Searching

Online searching has changed drastically over the past few years due to the advent of full-text databases designed for searching by end users and increased use of the Internet. Online searching has become less centralized and less dependent on a physical location for its performance. With online searching, outsourcing takes on a different meaning. Libraries do not hire an outside firm to provide a service that used to be provided in-house. As with periodical indexes, which have always been purchased from commercial publishers, libraries have always paid an outside firm, typically an online database provider, for access to the content of databases. Traditionally, librarians have acted as intermediaries, conducting online searches for patrons. The costs either were passed on entirely to patrons or were subsidized by the library to varying degrees. New technologies enable the end user to conduct the search without the intermediation of a librarian. The costs still remain in the new environment, but the method of providing the service has changed. The library's role has shifted from actually providing the search to selecting the services that will be made available, and providing the infrastructure, the connections, password protection, and the training to patrons, who then conduct the search themselves, either in the library or from remote locations. Some even say that the entire operation has been "outsourced" to patrons.

Interlibrary Loan and Document Delivery

Whereas the literature indicates that many libraries resort to the use of vendors for obtaining documents for their patrons, these operations are often not perceived as genuine outsourcing because they are administered in-house.[5] As exemplified in the survey, libraries do not outsource the administration of these services to vendors; nor do they report resorting to large private-sector full-service information providers for obtaining documents. Over 90 percent of the libraries that responded to the survey indicated that they do not outsource interlibrary loan or document delivery.

Historically, there was a distinction between interlibrary loan (ILL), which was free to qualifying patrons, and document delivery, which was run as a fee service within libraries. Document delivery has also been defined as "every form of document procurement other than that from reciprocal libraries."[6] Today, as more ILL departments are charging for their services, it is not readily apparent how the library actually acquires a particular document. There is a strong interrelationship between interlibrary loan and document delivery, and in the majority of libraries, the two operations are administered jointly.[7] This interrelationship is highlighted by claims that the current trend is to refer to all ILL as document delivery[8] and that the ILL unit of yesterday is being reorganized into the document delivery services of today.[9]

Traditionally, ILL materials were exchanged among libraries that developed close cooperative networks allowing them to lend books or provide photocopied articles to each other's patrons. If no library owned the needed item, the patron could not have access to it. As more libraries are canceling journal subscriptions, the pool of potential libraries as suppliers is diminishing, thus placing increased emphasis on commercial document suppliers.[10] Six types of document suppliers have been identified: libraries, document clearinghouses, database producers with their own collections, tables-of-contents vendors, commercial information brokers, and vendors of CD-ROMs that contain full text.[11]

The use of commercial services for acquiring documents has risen dramatically since the mid-1980s. In 1982, 27 percent of libraries surveyed by ARL used commercial vendors;[12] by 1992 the number was 74 percent, and by 1994, 87 percent.[13] This broad reliance of libraries on commercial document suppliers raises the question not of whether to use these services but how they affect libraries, their collections, and their services. Document supply centers draw from vast collections of documents that they own. These centers provide copies of materials from their collections for a fee to any library or user. Initially, the collections were large and made up of periodicals, but more and more they consist of full-text electronic databases. As library budgets have shrunk and the scope of library collections has diminished, ILL departments have been forced to resort to these commercial document centers for the fulfillment of requests, further obfuscating the lines between interlibrary loan and document delivery. The survey indicates that this form of outsourcing is not universally acknowledged by librarians as such even though services and products are obtained from document suppliers. Indeed, this perspective raises difficulties in interpreting answers to the survey.

Reasons for Using a Vendor

There are certain advantages to using a commercial vendor for document delivery. Some of these reasons are generic to outsourcing, such as avoiding development costs and taking advantage of economies of scale. Other elements are specific to document delivery. Vendors, due to their specialization, can supply documents faster and cheaper in most cases than libraries.[14] Document vendors, like their counterparts dealing with books and periodicals, also simplify the identification and ordering of materials. Perhaps one of the most important services that vendors provide to libraries is ensuring copyright compliance.[15] Vendors can also produce usage and financial reports, which libraries can use in their collection development decisions. In this context, vendors' collections have been called an extension of libraries' collections,[16] with one major difference: The library does not become the owner of the materials for which it pays. The use of vendors in document delivery is so prevalent that a white paper issued by the ARL Committee on Access to Research Resources and dealing with the future of information access advises that the commercial sector, not ARL, should devise the proper technical and systems enhancements to support document delivery.[17]

Criteria for Evaluating a Vendor

Libraries need to apply strict criteria in choosing among the large number of vendors that can provide documents for libraries. Some of the leading vendors that cover broad subject areas are the British Library Document Supply Centre, UMI Clearinghouse, Chemical Abstracts Services, UnCover, and ISI's Genuine Article.[18] In addition, a large number of vendors specializing in narrow subject areas or formats are listed in the standard industry directories.

Libraries need to evaluate vendors regarding turnaround time, accuracy, quality of the photocopies or electronic copies, record keeping, the types of usage reports they can generate, the ability to keep track of orders, and the ability to accept orders in a variety of ways such as fax, phone, E-mail, surface mail, and so on.[19] Vendors also need to be able to deliver the materials in a variety of ways convenient to patrons and to be able to accept payments in a variety of forms, such as deposit accounts or individual payments. Other criteria to consider when choosing a vendor include the number of titles in a vendor's collection and the subjects it covers.[20] Generally, libraries are advised to use two major vendors for mainstream materials and additional specialized vendors that focus on the library clientele's special needs, such as patents or technical reports.[21] In terms of ongoing evaluations of vendor performance, the feedback is almost constant. Patrons either receive the desired material in a good-quality, usable copy, or they don't. Libraries need to keep track of vendor performance and patron satisfaction in order to ensure that the product conforms to the quality of the library's overall services.

Effects on Collections and Public Services

The decision to switch from ownership to access has to be evaluated carefully because canceling subscriptions and replacing them with document delivery has quick, visible, and long-lasting effects on library collections. Libraries will also be shifting their emphasis from building collections to providing a service. This cumulative change will diminish the role of libraries over time, since library resources will be spent on acquiring materials for patrons as needed rather than building solid collections that will be used for generations. These all-important decisions need to be made by collection development librarians.

For public services, the impact lies in the area of information identification and delivery. The traditional methods of requesting a document and paying for it at a public service desk in the library are still common, but public service departments are training end users to conduct their own searches and place their own orders. Libraries offer a variety of payment options varying from the patron paying the full price of the document to the library paying the full cost. Here again, the service is "outsourced" directly to the users. The materials can be delivered to patrons through library channels, such as the ILL department, or they can be delivered directly to patrons' desktops.

SYSTEMS

Historical Background

Most industrial applications for computing operations were developed by computer companies, but the early automated library systems were developed by libraries in-house. Libraries saw themselves as unique in their automation needs and did not consider commercial options as viable. Large libraries with ample staff and technological resources and strong budgets embarked on ambitious projects of designing and implementing library automation systems. Few of these were willing to market their system to other libraries.

With the arrival of turnkey systems on the market, smaller libraries that did not have the means to develop systems in-house purchased automated systems from vendors. Once the automation vendors became established, the variety of products they offered grew and an increasing number of libraries were able to afford these off-the-shelf systems. Upgrades to the systems, which are an intrinsic characteristic of all computerized systems, were provided by vendors based on libraries' feedback.

Outsourcing Systems

There are several levels at which a library can outsource its systems operation. The spectrum ranges from a complete outsourcing of systems functions to partial outsourcing. A small number of libraries still carry out this operation in-house. A library can contract with a vendor to provide all computing functions, such as ownership and maintenance of the hardware, software maintenance, telecommunications lines, and troubleshooting. In this case, a library leases both the computer system and the service from the vendor. Essentially, all the library has to do is turn on the terminals in the morning. Variations on this scenario include different levels of owner-ship and responsibility. For example, the library may decide to purchase the public-access terminals but lease the servers from the vendor. The vendor would then be responsible for upgrades to the system and the software. A library can outsource individual system modules, such as the cataloging, circulation, or online public access catalog, or the entire range of modules that constitute a modern integrated online system. The example of the Chicago Library System (CLS) is a case in point. CLS serves over 300 libraries including 52 academic libraries in the Chicago area. CLS's central library automation operation is outsourced to Ameritech, which offers the various libraries a choice of different platforms such as Dynix, Scholar, or Horizon.[22] Within that system, libraries outsource to varying degrees. In all cases, the systems vendor provides only systems capabilities. Functional operations such as acquisitions, cataloging, and database maintenance are performed in-house by each library.

A library needs to determine which level of outsourcing meets its individual needs. Because this kind of outsourcing is not commonplace, vendors do not have a standardized pricing schedule. Rather, each case is priced individually depending on the size of the library, the number of branches a library system has, the number of terminals that need to be supported, the size of the database, and the equipment necessary to support the operation. Vendors have indicated a willingness to work with libraries in order to assess the feasibility and cost of such operations.

Even though academic libraries typically buy off-the-shelf systems, they generally have systems departments that maintain the organization's online system and the library's computer network. The systems department's functions include a variety of responsibilities ranging from purchase, installation, and maintenance of hardware and software, to teaching, applications support, and troubleshooting. Outsourcing activities take place in the areas of hardware and software support. Of the respondents to the survey that outsource, the greatest number outsource with their campus computing center.

In this area, libraries find themselves in an incongruous situation vis-à-vis industry. Contracting out information processing (IP) operations was one of the earliest and most successful outsourcing activities adopted by industry. Indeed, it has created some of the most successful and fastest-growing companies in modern times. An example is Ross Perot's former company, EDS, which has been providing data processing for such giants as the U.S. Postal Service and General Motors. Academic libraries have tended to maintain systems operations in-house because they have local resources such as campus computing centers or consortia from which to draw expertise and resources. Public libraries do not typically have access to a parent organization's computer facility and have traditionally relied more on vendors' expertise, though on a limited scale.

CONCLUSION

Despite the differences in definition as to what constitutes outsourcing in public services and systems, there are companies that can provide any level of service or product a library may require. Although these services are primarily marketed to corporate and special libraries, they are developing to serve other types of libraries. As the services become broader, the scope of outsourcing may increase to include academic libraries. Ultimately, the market offers enough choices for virtually any library to consider outsourcing.

NOTES

1. Sheila S. Intner, "Outsourcing—What Does It Mean for Technical Services?" *Technicalities* 14, no. 3 (March 1994): 4.

2. Murray S. Martin, "Outsourcing," *Bottom Line* 8, no. 3 (1995): 30.

3. Ibid.

4. Anna L. DeMiller, *Reference Service Policies in ARL Libraries.* SPEC Flyer 203 (Washington, DC: Association of Research Libraries, Office of Management Studies, August 1994).

5. Martin, "Outsourcing," 29.

6. Eleanor Mitchell and Sheila A. Walters, *Document Delivery Services: Issues and Answers* (Medford, NJ: Learned Information, 1995), 90.

7. Mary E. Jackson and Karen Croneis, *Use of Document Delivery Services.* SPEC Flyer 204 (Washington, DC: Association of Research Libraries, Office of Management Studies, November 1994).

8. Melissa Stockton and Martha Whittaker, "The Future of Document Delivery: A Vendor's Perspective," *Journal of Library Administration* 21, no. 1/2 (1995): 170.

9. Mitchell and Walters, *Document Delivery Services*, 85.

10. Mary E. Jackson, "The Future of Resource Sharing: The Role of the Association of Research Libraries," *Journal of Library Administration* 21, no. 1/2 (1995): 200.

11. Lee Anne George, "Document Delivery in the 1990s: An Overview," in *Managing Resource Sharing in the Electronic Age*, ed. Amy Chang and Mary E. Jackson (New York: AMS Press, 1996), 28.

12. *Document Delivery Systems in ARL Libraries.* SPEC Flyer 82 (Washington, DC: Association of Research Libraries, Office of Management Studies, March 1982).

13. Jackson and Croneis, *Use of Document Delivery Services.* SPEC Flyer 204.

14. Stockton and Whittaker, "The Future of Document Delivery," 171.

15. Ibid.

16. Jackson, "The Future of Resource Sharing," 200.

17. Ibid., 194.

18. Jackson and Croneis, *Use of Document Delivery Services.* SPEC Flyer 204.

19. Nancy S. Hewison, Vicki J. Killion, and Suzanne M. Ward, "Commercial Document Delivery: The Academic Library's Perspective," *Journal of Library Administration* 21, no.1/2 (1995): 137.

20. Alice Duhon Mancini, "Evaluating Commercial Document Suppliers: Improving Access to Current Journal Literature," *College & Research Libraries* 57, no. 2 (March 1996): 124.

21. Hewison, Killion, and Ward, "Commercial Document Delivery," 136.

22. Alice Calabrese and Jay Wozny, "The CLS Bottom Line: It's More Than Money, It's Service," *Bottom Line* 8, no. 2 (1995): 19.

12  *Conclusion*

In reflecting on the importance of outsourcing in academic libraries, the inevitable question arises: Is outsourcing a fad, or is it here to stay? In 1995 Sheila S. Intner listed it as one of the buzzwords that may soon fall out of favor in both library jargon and practice. It is in the company of such other passé terms as *Total Quality Management*, *information superhighway*, and *ownership versus access*.[1] A fitting report on CNN on January 1, 1997, related that along with *whatever*, *la macarena*, *multi-tasking*, *down time*, and *bridge to the twenty-first century*, *outsourcing* made the "twenty-first annual list of misused, overused, and useless words and phrases" compiled by Lake Superior State University.[2] Industry is experiencing a backlash against outsourcing. The highly publicized strikes against GM and Chrysler in 1996 and 1997, which were triggered by the companies' plans to outsource, again brought the word and the topic to the front page.

This notoriety is equally evident in the world of librarianship. The controversy over the Hawaii State Library system's decision to outsource its entire technical services operations and the recent efforts to condemn this action at ALA have kept the issue in the limelight. By fall 1997, the ALA Executive Board had appointed an Outsourcing Task Force, charged with advising the association on outsourcing issues as they relate to professional values and the ALA Code of Ethics. The decision of the library of the newest campus in the University of Florida's system to begin operations with minimal level technical services adds another dimension to the debate. These cases follow in the footsteps of the Wright State controversy and indicate that outsourcing is here to stay. At least for the time being, these examples seem to be the exception rather than the rule. The survey clearly shows that libraries' adoption of outsourcing is deliberate, incremental, and cautious. Outsourcing increases the need for coordination between the library and an array of vendors. It has implications for workflow, organizational structure, and staffing and challenges the role of the traditional librarian. It forces libraries to reflect on the way they operate and compels them to become more efficient and to take full advantage of technology. It requires that they consider the alternatives offered by the marketplace.

The question still remains: To what extent is outsourcing a threat to professional librarianship and how is it affecting the profession? If the outsourcing trend continues, what will happen to professional standards and criteria? Librarianship has a rich foundation, and librarians are building on this fertile professional legacy. The ideals of librarianship, based on the "goals of equal service, knowledge conservation," and the provision of order in "an increasingly chaotic world of information," need to be maintained.[3] Will those ideals be preserved in an outsourcing environment? Libraries are looking at short-term implications—saving money and cutting payroll— but the long-term implications can rarely be fully anticipated. It is the obligation of the decision makers to ensure that the essence of the profession, its commitment to "equitable access to . . . rich and poor, young and old, connected and unconnected, and the geographically remote," endures.[4]

In contrast, vendors need to make a profit, and they view information as a commodity to be made available to those who can afford it. Commercial objectives and academic libraries' interests are often at odds. What remains of paramount importance is the quality of the products or services that libraries acquire from commercial vendors and the continual need for libraries to maintain control over the vendors that provide them.

Librarians have been outsourcing for years very effectively. In the process they have bought products and services from multiple vendors: book jobbers, subscription agents, cataloging and preservation vendors, bibliographic utilities, and library consortia. Most vendors are large, broad-scope companies; a handful are start-up companies. More than ever, librarians need to communicate their objectives clearly, since communication is no longer limited to that between the library and its materials vendors. The library's systems vendor and its bibliographic utility have entered the picture, and all players depend on each other and have to work together. New strategic alliances between suppliers and customers are replacing former cooperative roles between these two. This raises the question of agreements, relationships, qualification of suppliers, common practices, and training. The customer-supplier relationship has its own built-in conflict: The library may want top quality and customization but not want to pay for it, whereas the supplier may want to deliver the minimum and charge the maximum rate. Some library activities have been outsourced for so long that both libraries and vendors have developed mutually agreed-upon standards, which makes it possible for libraries to judge the degree of success of the outsourcing arrangement. This is the case with established preservation methods such as microfilming and binding. Such standards are conspicuously absent from newer areas in which libraries outsource, such as document delivery and cataloging. The profession has to develop standards to ensure that these areas meet libraries' operational requirements.

Conference talks, electronic mail interchanges, and other communications among librarians give a distorted picture of the reality of outsourcing in libraries. Although outsourcing is taking place in most areas of librarianship, there is no large-scale rush to close entire departments and outsource their functions to commercial vendors. There are still many administrators who see outsourcing as anathema to librarianship. Yet outsourcing is an undeniably positive alternative in certain situations. Librarians have to learn how to integrate these alternatives in such a way that they will be beneficial, not detrimental, to the profession.

NOTES

1.   Sheila S. Intner, "The Buzzword Phenomenon," *Technicalities* 15, no. 6 (June 1995): 3.

2.   *CNN Headline News*, January 1, 1997.

3.   Murray S. Martin, "Outsourcing," *Bottom Line* 8, no. 3 (1995): 28.

4.   Warren J. Haas, "America's Libraries, Distinguished Past, Difficult Future: A Supplement to ARL #172, January 1994," *ARL: A Bimonthly Newsletter of Research Library Issues and Actions* 172 (January 1994): 4.

Appendix

Survey Questions and Results

The survey was sent to the 109 members of the Association of Research Libraries (ARL) and to 110 medium-sized, non-ARL academic libraries. Sixty-nine ARL and 70 non-ARL libraries responded. Answers are tabulated in three parts: "Total" represents the number of both ARL and non-ARL libraries that provided a response to the given question and the percentage that this represents from the total number of responses; "ARL" shows the number of ARL libraries that engage in a specific activity and the percentage that this represents from the total number of ARL responses received; and "Non-ARL" represents the number of non-ARL libraries that engage in a specific activity and the percentage that this represents from the total number of non-ARL responses received. The calculations were rounded to the nearest full number except when the number was less than 1 percent, in which case the exact percentage point is given. Numbers do not always add up to 100 percent because some answers were left blank.

1. **Is your library outsourcing collection development operations?**

        __ no

Total:	41 (29%)
ARL:	10 (14%)
Non-ARL:	31 (44%)

	__ if yes	__ approval plans	__ blanket orders	__ bookstore	__ other
Total:	97 (70%)	96 (69%)	45 (32%)	4 (3%)	5 (4%)
ARL:	59 (86%)	58 (84%)	36 (52%)	3 (4%)	3 (4%)
Non-ARL:	38 (54%)	38 (54%)	9 (13%)	1 (1%)	2 (3%)

If not currently outsourcing, do you have plans to outsource in this area?

	__ no	__ yes (please explain)
Total:	43 (31%)	4 (3%)
ARL:	11 (16%)	2 (3%)
Non-ARL:	32 (46%)	2 (3%)

2. **Is your library outsourcing acquisitions?**

	__ no
Total:	57 (41%)
ARL:	24 (35%)
Non-ARL:	33 (47%)

	__ if yes	__ preorder searching	__ serials check-in
Total:	82 (59%)	1 (.7%)	1 (.7%)
ARL:	45 (65%)	1 (1%)	0
Non-ARL:	37 (53%)	0	1 (1%)

	__ subscription agents	__ claiming	__ other (please explain)
Total:	80 (58%)	9 (6%)	3 (2%)
ARL:	44 (64%)	4 (6%)	2 (3%)
Non-ARL:	36 (51%)	5 (7%)	1 (1%)

If not currently outsourcing, do you have plans to outsource in this area?

	__ no	__ yes (please explain)
Total:	45 (32%)	5 (3%)
ARL:	19 (28%)	2 (3%)
Non-ARL:	26 (37%)	3 (4%)

3. **Is your library outsourcing preservation functions?**

	__ no
Total:	29 (21%)
ARL:	12 (17%)
Non-ARL:	17 (24%)

	__ if yes	__ binding	__ mending	__ microfilming
Total:	110 (79%)	106 (76%)	6 (4%)	52 (37%)
ARL:	57 (83%)	56 (81%)	1 (1%)	33 (48%)
Non-ARL:	53 (76%)	50 (71%)	5 (7%)	19 (27%)

	__ photocopying	__ digital scanning	__ conservation	__ other (please explain)
Total:	21 (15%)	7 (5%)	24 (17%)	3 (2%)
ARL:	16 (23%)	7 (10%)	17 (25%)	1 (1%)
Non-ARL:	5 (7%)	0	7 (10%)	2 (3%)

If not currently outsourcing, do you have plans to outsource in this area?

	__ no	__ yes (please explain)
Total:	25 (18%)	8 (6%)
ARL:	10 (14%)	5 (7%)
Non-ARL:	15 (21%)	3 (4%)

4. **Is your library outsourcing reference functions?**

	__ no
Total:	137 (99%)
ARL:	68 (99%)
Non-ARL:	69 (99%)

	__ if yes	__ reference assistance	__ library instruction	__ online searching
Total:	1 (.7%)	0	0	1 (.7%)
ARL:	1 (1%)	0	0	1 (1%)
Non-ARL:	0	0	0	0

	__ weekend or evening desk hours	__ other (please explain)
Total:	0	0
ARL:	0	0
Non-ARL:	0	0

If not currently outsourcing, do you have plans to outsource in this area?

	__ no	__ yes (please explain)
Total:	108 (78%)	1 (.7%)
ARL:	56 (81%)	0
Non-ARL:	52 (74%)	1 (1%)

5. **Is your library outsourcing interlibrary loan functions?**

	__ no	__ yes (please explain)
Total:	132 (95%)	4 (3%)
ARL:	65 (94%)	2 (3%)
Non-ARL:	67 (96%)	2 (3%)

If not currently outsourcing, do you have plans to outsource in this area?

	___ no	___ yes (please explain)
Total:	94 (68%)	6 (4%)
ARL:	49 (71%)	3 (4%)
Non–ARL:	45 (64%)	3 (4%)

6. Is your library outsourcing document delivery? In this case we are not looking for use of FirstSearch, Uncover, and other similar services that provide documents to patrons. We are interested in whether your library contracts with an outside contractor to identify, locate, and provide articles to patrons.

	___ no	___ yes (please explain)
Total:	129 (93%)	9 (6%)
ARL:	65 (94%)	4 (6%)
Non–ARL:	64 (91%)	5 (7%)

If not currently outsourcing, do you have plans to outsource in this area?

	___ no	___ yes (please explain)
Total:	94 (68%)	8 (6%)
ARL:	50 (72%)	5 (7%)
Non–ARL:	44 (63%)	3 (4%)

7. Is your library outsourcing any of its systems functions?

	___ no
Total:	68 (49%)
ARL:	35 (51%)
Non–ARL:	33 (47%)

	___ if yes	___ campus computing center	___ consortia
Total:	71 (51%)	56 (40%)	20 (14%)
ARL:	34 (49%)	31 (45%)	5 (7%)
Non–ARL:	37 (53%)	25 (36%)	15 (21%)

	___ vendor automation center	___ others (please explain)
Total:	7 (5%)	3 (2%)
ARL:	2 (3%)	3 (4%)
Non–ARL:	5 (7%)	0

If not currently outsourcing, do you have plans to outsource in this area?

	___ no	___ yes (please explain)
Total:	48 (35%)	6 (4%)
ARL:	23 (33%)	6 (9%)
Non–ARL:	25 (36%)	0

8. Is your library outsourcing cataloging functions?

         __ no

Total:	50 (36%)
ARL:	20 (29%)
Non–ARL:	30 (43%)

         __ if yes,

Total:	88 (63%)
ARL:	49 (71%)
Non–ARL:	39 (56%)

a) Which cataloging vendor(s) are you using?

	__Diogenes	__Marcive	__ PromptCat	__ TECHPRO	__ other
Total:	2 (1%)	61 (44%)	11 (8%)	35 (25%)	29 (21%)
ARL:	2 (3%)	33 (48%)	8 (11%)	25 (36%)	21 (30%)
Non-ARL:	0	28 (40%)	3 (4%)	10 (14%)	8 (11%)

b) What type of records do you acquire?

	__ 050 records	__ unique languages	__ unique collections
Total:	16 (12%)	16 (12%)	19 (14%)
ARL:	8 (12%)	12 (17%)	16 (23%)
Non-ARL:	8 (11%)	4 (6%)	3 (4%)

	__ U.S. federal documents	__ other (please explain)
Total:	63 (45%)	21 (15%)
ARL:	35 (51%)	13 (19%)
Non-ARL:	28 (40%)	8 (11%)

c) Is your library buying value-added services?

         __ no

Total:	48 (35%)
ARL:	25 (36%)
Non-ARL:	23 (33%)

	__ if yes	__ labeling	__ table of contents	__ security taping	__ other
Total:	38 (27%)	23 (17%)	17 (12%)	21 (15%)	9 (6%)
ARL:	21 (30%)	11 (16%)	8 (12%)	13 (19%)	5 (7%)
Non-ARL:	17 (24%)	12 (17%)	9 (13%)	8 (11%)	4 (6%)

If not currently outsourcing, do you have plans to outsource in this area?

	___ no	___ yes (please explain)
Total:	41 (29%)	39 (28%)
ARL:	13 (19%)	23 (33%)
Non-ARL:	28 (40%)	16 (23%)

9. Is your library outsourcing—or has it outsourced in the past— authority control functions?

	___ no	___ yes (please explain)
Total:	59 (42%)	76 (55%)
ARL:	24 (35%)	42 (61%)
Non-ARL:	35 (50%)	34 (49%)

If not currently outsourcing, do you have plans to outsource in this area?

	___ no	___ yes (please explain)
Total:	29 (21%)	20 (14%)
ARL:	9 (13%)	8 (12%)
Non-ARL:	20 (29%)	12 (17%)

10. Is your library outsourcing—or has it outsourced in the past— retrospective conversion?

	___ no	___ yes (please explain)
Total:	57 (41%)	83 (60%)
ARL:	19 (28%)	52 (75%)
Non-ARL:	38 (54%)	31 (44%)

If not currently outsourcing, do you have plans to outsource in this area?

	___ no	___ yes (please explain)
Total:	33 (24%)	10 (7%)
ARL:	6 (9%)	6 (9%)
Non-ARL:	27 (39%)	4 (6%)

11. Are there any areas in which your library is outsourcing that are not covered in this questionnaire?

	___ no	___ yes (please explain)
Total:	96 (69%)	30 (22%)
ARL:	44 (64%)	20 (29%)
Non-ARL:	52 (74%)	10 (14%)

Suggested Readings

Abel, Richard. "The Return of the Native." *American Libraries* 29 (January 1998): 76–78.

"ACC and AMA Warning over CCT for Libraries." *LA Record* (March 1992): 154.

Adler, Anne G., and Elizabeth A. Baber, eds. *Retrospective Conversion: From Cards to Computers.* Ann Arbor, MI: Pierian Press, 1984.

Agnew, Grace J. "Contracting for Technical Services: Shelf-Ready Services for Books." In *Against All Odds: Case Studies on Library Financial Management,* edited by Linda F. Crismond. Fort Atkinson, WI: Highsmith Press, 1993.

Alessi, Dana L., and Kathleen Goforth. "Standing Orders and Approval Plans: Are They Compatible?" *Serials Librarian* 13 (October/November 1987): 21–41.

Alexander, Adrian W. "U.S. Periodicals Price Index." *American Libraries.* Annual column in May issue.

Alley, Brian. "Reengineering, Outsourcing, Downsizing, and Perfect Timing." *Technicalities* 13 (November 1993): 1, 8.

AMIGOS Preservation Service: Texas Circuit Ride 1996. Outsourcing Preservation: Using External Services. Flyer.

"Army Libraries for Grabs." *Library Journal* 111 (October 15, 1986): 22.

Ascher, Kate. *The Politics of Privatization: Contracting Out Public Services.* New York: St. Martin's Press, 1987.

Baker, John. "Blackwell's in a New Marketplace." *Serials Review* 20, no. 3 (1994): 78–81.

Barber, David. "Electronic Commerce in Library Acquisitions with a Survey of Bookseller and Subscription Agency Services." *Library Technology Reports* 31, no. 5 (September/October 1995): 493–610.

Barker, Joseph W. "Vendor Studies Redux: Evaluating the Approval Plan Option from Within." *Library Acquisitions* 13, no. 2 (1989): 133–41.

Bazirjian, Rosann. "ALCTS/Automated Acquisitions/In-Process Control Systems Discussion Group, American Library Association Conference, New Orleans, June 1993." *Technical Services Quarterly* 11, no. 4 (1994): 66–68.

———. "Integrating Vendor Products/Services into the Automated Acquisitions Environment: An Introduction." *Library Acquisitions* 18, no. 4 (1994): 417–18.

Bénaud, Claire-Lise, and Sever Bordeianu. "Outsourcing in American Libraries: An Overview." *Against the Grain* 9, no. 5 (November 1997): 1, 16, 18, 20.

———. "PromptCat: An Early Assessment." In *Advances in Collection Development and Resources Management*, edited by Thomas W. Leonhardt, 223–38. Greenwich, CT: JAI Press, 1996.

"Berger Testifies Against Contracting-Out." *Wilson Library Bulletin* 60 (January 1986): 10–11.

Bernstein, Aaron. "Outsourced—and Out of Luck." *Business Week* 3433 (July 17, 1995): 60–61.

Bielsky, Katherine. "An Experiment in Outsourcing at the College of Charleston Libraries." *Against the Grain* 9, no. 5 (November 1997): 24, 26.

Bigus, Pam. "Outsourcing—One Paraprofessional's Experience." ASSOC-L listserv. Fri., March 1996.

Bing, Stanley. "Outsource This, You Turkeys." *Fortune* 132 (December 11, 1995): 43–44.

Block, Rick J. "Cataloging Outsourcing: Issues and Options." *Serials Review* 20, no. 3 (1994): 73–77.

Boss, Richard W. "Technical Services Functionality in Integrated Library Systems." *Library Technology Reports* 28 (January/February 1992): 5–109.

Bostic, Mary J. "Approval Acquisitions and Vendor Relations: An Overview." In *Vendors and Library Acquisitions*, edited by William A. Katz. New York: Haworth Press, 1991.

Bradsher, Keith. "Skilled Workers Watch Their Job Migrate Overseas." *New York Times*, August 28, 1995.

Branin, Joseph J., ed. *Collection Management for the 1990s*. Chicago: American Library Association, 1992.

Broadway, Rita, and Jane Qualls. "Retrospective Conversion of Periodicals: A Shoestring Experience." *Serials Librarian* 15, no. 1/2 (1988): 99–111.

Brockhurst, Chris. "Contracting Public Services." *LA Record* (July 1992): 430.

———. "Surrey Staff Left Out in Tendering Move." *LA Record* (May 1993): 271.

Brown, Lynne C. Branche. "An Expert System for Predicting Approval Plan Receipts." *Library Acquisitions* 17, no. 2 (1993): 155–64.

Burger, Robert H. *Authority Work: The Creation, Use, Maintenance, and Evaluation of Authority Records and Files*. Littleton, CO: Libraries Unlimited, 1985.

Bush, Carmel C., Margo L. Sasse, and Patricia A. Smith. "Toward a New World Order: A Survey of Outsourcing Capabilities of Vendors for Acquisitions, Cataloging and Collection Development Services." *Library Acquisitions* 18, no. 4 (1994): 397–416.

Byrd, Jacqueline, and Kathryn Sorury. "Cost Analysis of NACO Participation at Indiana University." *Cataloging & Classification Quarterly* 16, no. 2 (1993): 107–21.

Byrne, Sherry. "Guidelines for Contracting Microfilming Services." *Microform Review* 15 (fall 1986): 253–64.

Byrnes, Margaret M. "Preservation of the Biomedical Literature: An Overview." *Bulletin of the Medical Library Association* 77, no. 3 (July 1989): 269–75.

Calabrese, Alice, and Jay Wozny. "The CLS Bottom Line: It's More Than Money, It's Service." *Bottom Line* 8, no. 2 (1995): 18–22.

Caldwell, Bruce. "The New Outsourcing Partnership." *InformationWeek* (June 1996): 50–64.

Calhoun, John C., James K. Bracken, and Kenneth L. Firestein. "Modeling an Academic Approval Program." *Library Resources & Technical Services* 34, no. 3 (July 1990): 367–79.

Calk, Jo, and Sally Smith. "Automated Authority Control." In *IOLS '92: Integrated Online Library Systems Proceedings*, compiled by Judy McQueen, 27–59. Medford, NJ: Learned Information, 1992.

Campbell, Gregor R. "Preservation." *New Library Scene* 13, no. 5 (October 1994): 5–6.

CannCasciato, Daniel. "Tepid Water for Everyone? The Future OLUC, Catalogers, and Outsourcing." *OCLC Systems & Services* 10 (spring 1994): 5–8.

Cargill, Jennifer. "A Report on the Fourth International Conference on Approval Plans." *Library Acquisitions* 4, no. 2 (1980): 109–11.

Carpenter, Eric J. "Collection Development Policies Based on Approval Plans." *Library Acquisitions* 13 (1989): 39–43.

Caston, Geoffrey. "Academic Tenure and Retrenchment: The U.S. Experience." *Oxford Review of Education* 8, no. 3 (1982): 299–307.

"Central Michigan University Libraries Use TECHPRO." *OCLC Newsletter* (July/August 1995): 30.

Chang, Amy, and Mary E. Jackson, eds. *Managing Resource Sharing in the Electronic Age*. New York: AMS Press, 1996.

"CIOs Are Uncomfortable Making Out-sourcing Predictions." *Quality Progress* 25, no. 9 (September 1992): 18.

"CO Feasible for Main Activities." *LA Record* (November 1994): 581–82.

"Contract Negotiations for the Commercial Microform Publishing of Library and Archival Materials: Guidelines for Librarians and Archivists." *Library Resources & Technical Services* 38 (January 1994): 72–85.

"Contracting Out and Public Libraries." *Public Library Journal* 8, no. 4 (July/August 1993): 97–99.

"Conversion and Contract Cataloging Services." *OCLC Newsletter*, no. 205 (September/October 1993): 9–24.

Corbin, John. "Technology and Organizational Change in Libraries." *Library Acquisitions* 16 (1992): 349–53.

Cramer, Michael D. "The Acquisitions Connection: Interfacing Library and Materials Vendors' Systems: Report of the Program Sponsored by the LAMA SASS Acquisitions Systems Committee and the ALCTS RS Acquisitions Committee." *Library Acquisitions* 16 (1992): 299–304.

Creative Outsourcing: Assessment and Evaluation. Chicago: American Library Association, ALA-644, 1996. 2 audiocassettes.

Crismond, Linda F. "Outsourcing from the A/V Vendor's Viewpoint: The Dynamics of a New Relationship." *Library Acquisitions* 18, no. 4 (1994): 375–81.

Daines, Guy. "CCT Recommendation Unlikely." *LA Record* (January 1995): 6.

Dalehite, Michele I. "Vendor-Supplied Automated Authority Control: What It Is and How to Get It." *Law Library Journal* 81 (1989): 117–29.

Davidson, Ann C. " 'Obedience to the Unenforceable': The Ethics of Outsourcing." *Searcher* (April 1996): 12–14. Reprint.

Deutsch, Claudia H. "Operational Chores Swinging Back to In-House: With a Renewed Quest for Quality Control, 'Outsourcing' Fades." *New York Times*, December 18, 1994.

"Dispatches from the Front Line: Reports from the Contracting Out Pilot Projects." *Public Library Journal* 9, no. 4 (July/August 1994): 95–98.

Dodge, John. "Fear, Loathing on the Outsource Trail." *PC Week* (July 15, 1996): 1.

Dornseif, Karen. "Outsourcing Cataloging: An Alternative for Small Libraries." *Colorado Libraries* 21 (spring 1995): 48–49.

Dubberly, Ronald A. "Why Outsourcing Is Our Friend." *American Libraries* 29 (January 1998): 72–74.

Dunkerley, Michael. *The Jobless Economy?: Computer Technology in the World of Work.* Cambridge, MA: Polity Press, 1996.

Dunkle, Clare B. "Outsourcing the Catalog Department: A Meditation Inspired by the Business and Library Literature." *Journal of Academic Librarianship* 22, no. 1 (January 1996): 33–44.

Duranceau, Ellen. "Vendors and Librarians Speak on Outsourcing, Cataloging, and Acquisitions." *Serials Review* 20, no. 3 (1994): 69–83.

Durbin, Tom. "Juggling Too Much While Walking the Tightrope? Outsourcing Can Keep Busy Executives from Falling into the Pit." *Colorado Business* 22 (March 1995): 25–28.

Dwyer, Jim. "Does Outsourcing Mean 'You're Out'?" *Technicalities* 14 (June 1994): 1–4.

——. "From PromptCat to Recat; or, You Only Catalog Twice." *Technicalities* 15 (May 1995): 4.

Eldredge, Mary. "United Kingdom Approval Plans and United States Academic Libraries: Are They Necessary and Cost Effective?" *Library Acquisitions* 18, no. 2 (1994): 165–78.

El-Sherbini, Magda. "Contract Cataloging: A Pilot Project for Outsourcing Slavic Books." *Cataloging & Classification Quarterly* 20, no. 3 (1995): 57–73.

El-Sherbini, Magda, and Mary Harris. "Cataloging Alternatives: An Investigation of Contract Cataloging, Cooperative Cataloging, and the Use of Temporary Help." *Cataloging & Classification Quarterly* 15, no. 4 (1992): 67–88.

Ender, Kenneth L., and Kathleen A. Mooney. "From Outsourcing to Alliances: Strategies for Sharing Leadership and Exploiting Resources at Metropolitan Universities." *Metropolitan Universities: An International Forum* 5, no. 3 (winter 1994): 51–60.

Epstein, Susan Baerg. "Retrospective Conversion: Issues and Perspectives." *Library Hi Tech* 4, no. 2 (summer 1986): 106.

———. "Retrospective Conversion Revisited, Part 1." *Library Journal* 115, no. 9 (May 15, 1990): 56–58.

Fairfield, Jay. "Our Challenge as Library Binders: Overcoming the Trends in Our Industry's Economics." *New Library Scene* 14, no. 4 (August 1995): 15–16.

Falconi, Robert R. "Don't Bother Me with Work; I'm Contemplating the Universe." *Financial Executive* 11 (September/October 1995): 13–14.

Fast, Barry. "Outsourcing and PromptCat." *Against the Grain* 7 (April 1995): 50.

"Five Bids Received for CCT Pilot Plans." *LA Record* (May 1993): 261.

Frieder, Richard. "Mass Deacidification: Now That It Is Reality, What Next?" *IFLA Journal* 17, no. 2 (1991): 142–46.

Fuller, Sue, and Helen Palmer. "Back to the Future: Serials Conversion." *Serials Librarian* 19, no. 3/4 (1991): 231–33.

The Future Is Now: Reconciling Change and Continuity in Authority Control: Proceedings of the OCLC Symposium, ALA Annual Conference, June 23, 1995. Dublin, OH: OCLC, 1995.

The Future Is Now: The Changing Face of Technical Services: Proceeding of the OCLC Symposium, ALA Midwinter Conference, February 4, 1994. Dublin, OH: OCLC, 1994.

Gammon, Julia A. "EDI and Acquisitions: The Future Is Now." *Library Acquisitions* 18, no. 1 (1994): 113–14.

Gershenfeld, Nancy. "Outsourcing Serials Activity at the Microsoft Corporation." *Serials Review* 20, no. 3 (1994): 81–83.

Ghikas, Mary W., ed. *Authority Control: The Key to Tomorrow's Catalog: Proceedings of the 1979 Library and Information Technology Association Institutes.* Phoenix, AZ: Oryx Press, 1982.

Gibbs, Nancy J. "ALCTS/Role of the Professional in Academic Research Technical Services Department's Discussion Group." *Library Acquisitions* 18, no. 3 (1994): 321–22.

Gorman, Michael. "Innocent Pleasures." In *The Future Is Now: The Changing Face of Technical Services: Proceedings of the OCLC Symposium, ALA Midwinter Conference, February 4, 1994,* 39–42 . Dublin, OH: OCLC, 1994.

———. "The Corruption of Cataloging: Outsourcing Erodes the 'Bedrock' of Library Service." *Library Journal* 120 (September 15, 1995): 32–34.

Grahame, Vicki. "Approval Plan Processing: Integrating Acquisitions and Cataloging." *Technical Services Quarterly* 10, no. 1 (1992): 31–41.

Granskog, Kay. "PromptCat Testing at Michigan State University." *Library Acquisitions* 18, no. 4 (1994): 419–25.

Grant, Alison. "Outsourcing 'Down Under'." *Against the Grain* 9, no. 5 (November 1997): 22, 26.

Grimard, Jacques. "Mass Deacidification: Universal Cure or Limited Solution?" *American Archivist* 57, no. 4 (fall 1994): 674–79.

"Guidelines for Preservation Photocopying." *Library Resources & Technical Services* 38, no. 3 (July 1994): 288–92.

Guy, Fred. "Cataloguers Face Up to CCT Threat." *LA Record* (June 1993): 366.

Haas, Warren J. "America's Libraries, Distinguished Past, Difficult Future: A Supplement to ARL #172, January 1994." *ARL: A Bimonthly Newsletter of Research Library Issues and Actions* 172 (January 1994): 1–4.

Hammer, Michael. *The Reengineering Revolution.* New York: HarperBusiness, 1995.

Hanson, Eugene R., and Jay E. Daily. "Catalogs and Cataloging." *Encyclopedia of Library and Information Science* 4 (1970): 243.

Harrar, George. "Outsource Tales." *Forbes* 151 (June 7, 1993, suppl. ASAP): 37–39.

Harri, Wilbert. "Implementing Electronic Data Interchange in the Library Acquisitions Environment." *Library Acquisitions* 18, no. 1 (1994): 115–17.

Harrison, Bennett. "The Dark Side of Flexible Production." *Technology Review* 97, no. 4 (May/June 1994): 38–46.

Hart, Amy. "Operation Cleanup: The Problem Resolution Phase of a Retrospective Conversion Project." *Library Resources & Technical Services* 32, no. 4 (October 1988): 378–86.

"Has the Outsourcing Wave Hit You?" *Training and Development* 49 (November 1995): 18.

Hatfield, Deborah. "Partnerships in Information Services: The Contract Library." *Special Libraries* 85 (spring 1994): 77–80.

"Hawaii PL Collection Selection Outsourced in 5-year B&T Deal." *Library Hotline* 25, no. 17 (April 29, 1996): 1.

Hawks, Carol Pitts. "EDI, the Audit Trail and Automated Acquisitions: Report of a Presentation." *Library Acquisitions* 18, no. 3 (1994): 351–53.

Heanue, Anne A. "Fed Librarians Meet As More Libraries Face Contracting." *American Libraries* 17 (December 1986): 822.

Hedges, Seven J., and Peter Cary. "The ValuJet Crash in the Everglades Raises New Questions About the FAA's Oversight of Start-Up Airlines." *U.S. News & World Report* 120, no. 21 (May 27, 1996): 36.

Hewison, Nancy S., Vicki J. Killion, and Suzanne M. Ward. "Commercial Document Delivery: The Academic Library's Perspective." *Journal of Library Administration* 21, no. 1/2 (1995): 133–43.

Hirshon, Arnold. "A Response to 'Outsourcing Cataloging: The Wright State Experience.' " *ALCTS Newsletter* 6, no. 2 (1995): 26–28.

———. "The Lobster Quadrille: The Future of Technical Services in a Re-engineering World." In *The Future Is Now: The Changing Face of Technical Services: Proceedings of the OCLC Symposium, ALA Midwinter Conference, February 4, 1994*, 14–20. Dublin, OH: OCLC, 1994.

Hirshon, Arnold, and Barbara A. Winters. *Outsourcing Technical Services: A How-to-Do-It Manual for Librarians.* New York: Neal-Schuman, 1996.

Hirshon, Arnold, Barbara A. Winters, and Karen Wilhoit, "A Response to 'Outsourcing Cataloging: The Wright State Experience.' " *ALCTS Newsletter* 6 (1995): 26–28.

Holt, Glen E. "Catalog Outsourcing: No Clear-Cut Choice." *Library Journal* 120 (September 15, 1995): 34.

———. "Economics: R.I.P. NOTIS; Preparing for Vendor Death and Transformations." *Bottom Line* 8, no. 1 (summer 1994): 54–55.

"Honolulu Is Talking." *Newsweek* (October 28, 1996): 8.

Hopkins, Judith. "The ALTCS Commercial Technical Services Cost Committee." *Cataloging & Classification Quarterly* 15, no. 1 (1992): 106–9.

"House Oversight Group Hears Berger and Owens Oppose Contracting Out." *American Libraries* 16 (December 1985): 758–59.

Hyslop, Colleen F. "PromptCat Prototype: Accelerating Progress in Technical Services." In *The Future Is Now: The Changing Face of Technical Services: Proceedings of the OCLC Symposium, ALA Midwinter Conference, February 4, 1994*, 33–38. Dublin, OH: OCLC, 1994.

"In or Out—In-House Innovation and Outsourcing: Technical Services Alternatives for the 90's." ALA Annual Conference, ALCTS Preconference, New York, July 5, 1996.

Intner, Sheila S. "Outsourcing—What Does It Mean for Technical Services?" *Technicalities* 14, no. 3 (March 1994): 3–5.

———. "The Buzzword Phenomenon." *Technicalities* 15, no. 6 (June 1995): 2–3.

Jackson, Mary E. "The Future of Resource Sharing: The Role of the Association of Research Libraries." *Journal of Library Administration*, 21, no. 1/2 (1995): 193–202.

Jasper, Richard P. "Academic Libraries and Firm Order Vendors: What They Want of Each Other." *Acquisitions Librarian* 3, no. 5 (1991): 83–95.

———. "Automating Acquisitions and Serials: Synthesis from Chaos." *Library Acquisitions* 17 (1993): 79–84.

Johnson, Kirk. "Workplace Evolution Alters Office Relationships." *New York Times* October 5, 1994.

Johnson, Marda. "PromptCat Development at OCLC." *Library Acquisitions* 18, no. 4 (1994): 427–30.

Johnson, Peggy. "Accessing Microfilm and Microfiche Collections." *LibraryLine* 7, no. 1 (January 1996): 1.

Johnson, Peggy, ed. *Guide to Technical Services Resources.* Chicago: American Library Association, 1994.

Johnson, Thomas L. "Cataloging Service Contracts: The Riverside Experience." *Technicalities* 6, no. 6 (June 1986): 13–15.

Johnston, Sarah Hager. "Current Offerings in Automated Authority Control: A Survey of Vendors." *Information Technology and Libraries* 8, no. 3 (September 1989): 236–64.

Juneja, Derry C. "Quality Control in Data Conversion." *Library Resources & Technical Services* 31, no. 2 (April/June 1987): 148–58.

Kaatrude, Peter B. "Approval Plan Versus Conventional Selection: Determining the Overlap." *Collection Management* 11, no. 1/2 (1989): 145–50.

Kaeter, Margaret. "An Outsourcing Primer." *Training and Development* 49 (November 1995): 20–25.

Kane, Bart. *Service First.* Honolulu: Hawaii State Public Library System, April 1996.

Kascus, Marie A., and Dawn Hale, eds. *Outsourcing Cataloging, Authority Work, and Physical Processing: A Checklist of Considerations.* Chicago: American Library Association, 1995.

Katz, William A., ed. *Vendors and Library Acquisitions.* New York: Haworth Press, 1991.

Keely, Alan. "Book Preservation Boxes." *North Carolina Libraries* 44 (summer 1986): 97–105.

Keeth, John Earl. "Approval Plan Rejects—To Keep or Not to Keep—Is That the Question?" *Library Acquisitions* 16 (1992): 167–69.

Kelly, Bill. "Before You Outsource." *Journal of Business Strategy* 16, no. 4 (July/August 1995): 41.

———. "Outsourcing Marches On." *Journal of Business Strategy* 16, no. 4 (July/August 1995): 38–42.

Kruger, Kathleen Joyce. "MARC Tags and Retrospective Conversion: The Editing Process." *Information Technology and Libraries* 4, no. 1 (March 1995): 53–59.

Lancaster, Hal. "Saving Your Career When Your Position Has Been Outsourced." *Wall Street Journal,* sec. B1, December 12, 1995, eastern edition.

"LC Responds to Deacidification Bids from Industry: All Offers Are Turned Down." *Library of Congress Information Bulletin* 50 (September 23, 1991): 347.

Lee, Sul H., ed. *Issues in Acquisitions: Programs & Evaluation.* Ann Arbor, MI: Pierian Press, 1984.

Levin, Marc A. "Government for Sale: The Privatization of Federal Information Services." *Special Libraries* 79 (summer 1988): 207–14.

Libby, Katherine A., and Dana M. Caudle. "A Survey on the Outsourcing of Cataloging in Academic Libraries." *College & Research Libraries* 58, no. 6 (November 1997): 556.

"Library Announces Book Preservation Plans: Status of the Mass Deacidification Program." *Library of Congress Information Bulletin* 50 (May 6, 1991): 162.

"Library of Congress and Mass Deacidification RFP." *ALCTS Newsletter* 2, no. 8 (1991): 89–90.

Livingston, Dennis. "Outsourcing: Look Beyond the Price Tag." *Datamation* 38, no. 23 (November 15, 1992): 93–97.

Lonnerblad, Bengt. "Contracting Out—An Alternative for Public Libraries?" *Scandinavian Public Library Quarterly* 8 (July/August 1993): 97–99.

Luther, Judy, and Dottie Marcinko. "How Can I Make You Happy? A Report of the ALCTS Acquisitions Librarians/Vendors of Library Materials Discussion Group Meeting, Midwinter Meeting, Denver, January 1993." *Technical Services Quarterly* 11, no. 2 (1993): 80–81.

Lynch, Clifford A., and Edwin B. Brownrigg. "Conservation, Preservation, and Digitization." *College & Research Libraries* 47, no. 4 (July 1986): 379–82.

Mancini, Alice Duhon. "Evaluating Commercial Document Suppliers: Improving Access to Current Journal Literature." *College & Research Libraries* 57, no. 2 (March 1996): 123–31.

Manley, Will. "The Fiasco Factor." *American Libraries* 28, no. 11 (December 1997): 96.

Mann, Sallie E. "Approval Plans As a Method of Collection Development." *North Carolina Libraries* 43 (spring 1985): 12–14.

Maher, William J. "Ensuring Continuity and Preservation Through Archival Service Agreements." *Archival Issues* 19, no. 1 (1994): 5–18.

Martin, Murray S. "Binding, Mending, and Preservation: Value Maintenance Tools." *Technicalities* 15, no. 12 (December 1995): 8–13.

———. "Outsourcing." *Bottom Line* 8, no. 3 (1995): 28–30.

Martin, Murray S., and Ernie Ingles. "Outsourcing in Alberta." *Bottom Line* 8, no. 4 (1995): 32–34.

McAdam, Tim. "The Commercial Binding Agreement: Partners in Preservation." *Serials Librarian* 17, no. 3/4 (1990): 153–54.

McQueen, Judy, and Richard W. Boss. "Sources of Machine-Readable Cataloging and Retrospective Conversion." *Library Technology Reports* 21, no. 6 (November/December 1985): 595–732.

Mechling, Jerry. "Reengineering: A Fad?" *Governing* 9 (April 1996): 70.

Meldrum, Janifer. "Outsourcing Issues Stir Conference Attendees." *MARCIVE Newsletter* 23 (September 1995): 1, 5.

Millar, Heather. "The Electronic Scriptorium." *Wired* (August 1996): 94–104.

Miller, Daniel. "Authority Control in the Retrospective Conversion Process." *Information Technology and Libraries* 3, no. 3 (September 1984): 286–92.

Miller, David P. "Outsourcing Cataloging: The Wright Experience." *ALCTS Newsletter* 6, no. 1 (1995): 7–8.

Miller, Heather Swan. "Ethics in Action: The Vendor's Perspective (Workshop Report from the 1994 NASIG Conference)." *Serials Librarian* 25, no. 3/4 (1995): 295–300.

———. "Reality in the Age of the Virtual: Experiences on the Threshold of the Electronic Library." *Against the Grain* 7, no. 2 (April 1995): 1, 7.

Miller, Rachel B. "The Impact of Automated Acquisitions on Collection Development: Report of the Program Sponsored by RASD Collection Development and Evaluation Section." *Library Acquisitions* 16, no. 3 (fall 1992): 300–301.

Miller, William. "Outsourcing: Academic Libraries Pioneer Contracting Out Services." *Library Issues* 16, no. 2 (November 1995): [1–4].

Minoli, Daniel. *Analyzing Outsourcing.* New York: McGraw-Hill, 1995.

Mitchell, Eleanor, and Sheila A. Walters. *Document Delivery Services: Issues and Answers.* Medford, NJ: Learned Information, 1995.

Montgomery, Jack G. "Outsourced Acquisitions? Let's Meet the Challenge." *Against the Grain* 7, no. 2 (April 1995): 66–68.

Montori, Carla J. "Managing the Library's Commercial Library Binding Program." *Technical Services Quarterly* 5, no. 3 (1988): 21–25.

Morley, P. "The Advantages to Outsourcing." *Networking Management Europe* (January/February 1993): 24.

Morris, Dilys E. "Staff Time and Costs for Cataloging (at Iowa State University)." *Library Resources & Technical Services* 36 (January 1992): 79–95.

"NAL (National Agricultural Library) Contracts Out Stack Retrieval." *Library Journal* 110 (January 1985): 24.

Nardini, Robert F. "Approval Plans: Politics and Performance." *College & Research Libraries* 54, no. 5 (September 1993): 417–25.

———. "The Approval Plan Profiling Session." *Library Acquisitions* 18 (fall 1994): 289–95.

Nissley, Meta. "Rave New World: Librarians and Electronic Acquisitions." *Library Acquisitions* 17 (1993): 165–73.

"NJ ILL in Three-Week Stranglehold (Infolink and State Library Blame Each Other for Lapse in Contract)." *Library Journal* 120 (February 15, 1995): 110.

" 'No Privatization' Claim." *LA Record* (August 1991): 489.

"NYPL Book Catalog Conversion Four-year Contract to OCLC." *Library Hotline* 25, no. 7 (February 19, 1996): 6.

"OCLC, Academic Book Center, SOLINET to Provide Automated Collection and Technical Services to New Florida University." *OCLC Newsletter* no. 225 (January/February 1997): 10–11.

"OCLC to Accelerate Upgrading of CIP Data in Online Union Catalog." *AMIGOS Agenda & OCLC Connection* 95–10 (1995): 6.

"OCLC Users, Contributors Increase in Global Scope." *Library Hotline* 25, no. 6 (January 12, 1996): 7–8.

Ogburn, Joyce L. "An Introduction to Outsourcing." *Library Acquisitions* 18, no. 4 (1994): 363–66.

"On Outsourcing (Six Poll Questions to Help Determine Readers' Views on the Importance of Outsourcing in Their Companies)." *Nation's Business* 84, no. 3 (March 1996): 68.

O'Neill, Ann L. "How the Richard Abel Co., Inc. Changed the Way We Work." *Library Acquisitions* 17 (1993): 41–46.

O'Neill, Edward T. "OCLC Authority Control." *OCLC Systems & Services* 10 (winter 1994): 40–48.

"The Outing of Outsourcing (Corporate America's Enthusiasm for Subcontracting Has Made This One of the More Enduring Management Fads of the 1990s)." *Economist* 337 (November 25, 1995): 57–58.

"Outsource Discourse: Sheila Intner and Sue Kamm Look for Common Ground on the Thorny Issue of Contracting Out Library Services." *American Libraries* 28, no. 9 (October 1997): 63–66.

"Outsourcing: By You, for You, or in Spite of You?" Conference of Southern California Online Users Group, City of Industry, CA, May 3, 1996.

"Outsourcing in Hawaii's PLs: Lessons, Unresolved Issues." *Library Hotline* 25, no. 44 (November 4, 1996): 1–2.

Palmer, R. E., ed. *Preserving the Word.* London: Library Association, 1986.

Parisi, Paul A. "The Changing World of Library Binding." *Technicalities* 15, no. 12 (December 1995): 14–15.

Pasterczyk, Catherine E. "A Quantitative Methodology for Evaluating Approval Plan Performance." *Collection Management* 10, no. 1/2 (1980): 25–38.

Peters, Stephen H., and Douglas J. Butler. "A Cost Model for Retrospective Conversion Alternatives." *Library Resources & Technical Services* 28 (April/June 1984): 159–60.

Porck, Henk J. *Mass Deacidification: An Update on Possibilities and Limitations.* Amsterdam and Washington, DC: European Commission on Preservation and Access and Commission on Preservation and Access, 1996.

Portugal, Frank. *Exploring Outsourcing: Case Studies of Corporate Libraries.* Washington, DC: Special Libraries Association, 1997.

Quinn, James Brian, and Frederick G. Hilmer. "Strategic Outsourcing." *McKinsey Quarterly* 1 (1995): 48–70.

Quinn, Judy. "The New Approval Plans: Surrendering to the Vendor . . . or in the Driver's Seat?" *Library Journal* 116, no. 15 (September 15, 1991): 38–41.

Quint, Barbara. "Disintermediation." *Searcher* (January 1996): 1–2. Reprint.

———. "Professional Associations React to the Challenge: Interviews with SLA's David Bender and AIIP's Jane Miller." *Searcher* (May 1996): 14–19. Reprint.

———. "Teltech: Tool or Rival?" *Searcher* (February 1996): 3–7. Reprint.

———. "Uncover: The People's Choice? Interview with Rebecca Lenzini." *Searcher* (March 1996): 7–12. Reprint.

Ra, Marsha. "The Need for Costing in a Cooperative Retrospective Conversion Project." *Technical Services Quarterly* 44, no. 4 (summer 1987): 39–48.

Rebarcak, Pamela A. Zager. "Closing the Loop: Reconceptualizing Acquisitions in the Electronic Age; An ALCTS Preconference Report." *Library Acquisitions* 19 (spring 1995): 111–13.

Reed-Scott, Jutta. "Retrospective Conversion: Issues and Perspectives." *Library Hi Tech* 4, no. 2 (summer 1986): 114.

Reid, Marion T. "Closing the Loop: How Did We Get Here and Where Are We Going?" *Library Resources & Technical Services* 39 (July 1995): 267–73.

Reidelback, John H. "Selecting an Approval Plan Vendor II: Comparative Vendor Data." *Library Acquisitions* 8, no. 3 (1984): 157–202.

Reidelback, John H., and Gary M. Shirk. "Selecting an Approval Plan Vendor III: Academic Librarians' Evaluations of Eight United States Approval Plans Vendors." *Library Acquisitions* 9, no. 3 (1985): 177–260.

"Retrospective Conversion: Issues and Perspectives, a Forum Edited by Jon Drabenstott."*Library Hi Tech* 4, no. 2 (summer 1986): 105–20.

Ritzer, George. *The McDonaldization of Society.* Thousand Oaks, CA: Pine Forge Press, 1996.

Rockman, Ilene. "Retrospective Conversion: Reference Librarians Are Missing the Action." *Library Journal* 115, no. 7 (April 15, 1990): 40–42.

Root, Trudie A. "Inhouse Binding in Academic Libraries." *Serials Review* 15, no. 3 (1989): 31–40.

Rossi, Gary J. "Library Approval Plans: A Selected Annotated Bibliography." *Library Acquisitions* 11, no. 1 (1987): 3–34.

Rothery, Brian, and Ian Robertson. *The Truth About Outsourcing.* Hampshire, England: Gower, 1995.

"Rule Out Privatisation–Labour." *LA Record* (August 1995): 414.

"Rumblings of Mutiny: Contracting Out." *Library Journal* 110 (July 1985): 14.

Rush, James E. "A Case for Eliminating Cataloging in the Individual Library." In *The Future Is Now: The Changing Face of Technical Services: Proceedings of the OCLC Symposium, ALA Midwinter Conference, February 4, 1994,* 1–13. Dublin, OH: OCLC, 1994.

Sasse, Margo. "Automated Acquisitions: The Future of Collection Development." *Library Acquisitions* 16, no. 2 (1992): 135–43.

Schneider, Karen G. "The McLibrary Syndrome." *American Libraries* 29 (January 1998): 66–70.

Schottlaender, Brian, ed. *Retrospective Conversion: History, Approaches, Considerations.* New York: Haworth Press, 1992.

Secrest, Angela. "Automated Authority Control: Benefits and Pitfalls." *Iowa Library Quarterly* 26, no. 3 (1989): 8–17.

Sellberg, Roxanne. "The Teaching of Cataloging in U.S. Library Schools." *Library Resources & Technical Services* 32, no. 1 (January 1988): 30–42.

Shirk, Gary M. "Contract Acquisitions: Change, Technology, and the New Library/Vendor Partnership." *Library Acquisitions* 17, no. 2 (1993): 145–53.

———. "Outsourced Library Technical Services: The Bookseller's Perspective." *Library Acquisitions* 18, no. 4 (1994): 383–95.

Sinderman, Martin. "Outsourcing Gains Speed in Corporate World." *National Real Estate Investor* 37 (August 1995): 42–53.

Smith, Elizabeth H. "Library Binding Is a Service." *New Library Scene* 14, no. 6 (December 1995): 13–16.

Smith, Linda C., and Ruth C. Carter, eds. *Technical Services Management, 1965–1990: A Quarter Century of Change and a Look to the Future.* New York: Haworth Press, 1996.

Spyers-Duran, Peter, ed. *Approval and Gathering Plans in Academic Libraries.* Littleton, CO: Western Michigan University Libraries, 1968.

Spyers-Duran, Peter, and Daniel Gore, eds. *Advances in Understanding Approval and Gathering Plans in Academic Libraries.* Kalamazoo: Western Michigan University, 1970.

———. *Economics of Approval Plans.* Westport, CT: Greenwood Press, 1971.

Spyers-Duran, Peter, and Thomas Mann Jr., eds. *Shaping Library Collections for the 1980s.* Phoenix, AZ: Oryx Press, 1980.

St. Clair, Gloriana, and Jane Treadwell. "Science and Technology Approval Plans Compared." *Library Resources & Technical Services* 33 (October 1989): 382–92.

Stockton, Melissa, and Martha Whittaker. "The Future of Document Delivery: A Vendor's Perspective." *Journal of Library Administration* 21, no. 1/2 (1995): 169–81.

Strauch, Katina. "Interview with Dan Halloran, President and CEO, Academic Book Center." *Against the Grain* 8, no. 1 (February 1996): 1–5.

"Tendering May Spread to All Library Activities." *LA Record* (July 1992): 432.

Thompson, Mary Beth, and Lisa German. "ALCTS Acquisitions Librarians/Vendors of Library Materials Discussion Group." *Library Acquisitions* 18 (fall 1994): 313–16.

Trader, Margaret P. "Preservation Technologies: Photocopies, Microforms, and Digital Imaging—Pros and Cons." *Microform Review* 22, no. 3 (summer 1993): 127–34.

Tull, Laura. "Contract Cataloging: Retrospective Conversion of a Technical Report Collection." *Technical Services Quarterly* 9, no. 1 (1991): 3–18.

Wagner, Jennifer L. "Issues in Outsourcing." In *Emerging Information Technologies for Competitive Advantage and Economic Development*, edited by Mehdi Khosrowpour. Harrisburg, PA: Idea Group, 1992.

Waite, Ellen J. "Reinvent Catalogers!" *Library Journal* 120 (November 1, 1995): 36–37.

Walker, Gay. "Preservation Decision-Making and Archival Photocopying." *Restaurator* 8 (1987): 40–51.

Warzala, Martin. "The Evolution of Approval Services." *Library Trends* 42 (winter 1994): 514–23.

Weaver, Barbara F. "Outsourcing—A Dirty Word or a Lifeline?" *Bottom Line* 7, no. 1 (summer 1993): 26–29.

Weisbrod, Elizabeth J., and Paula Dufy. "Keeping Your Online Catalog from Degenerating into a Finding Aid: Considerations for Loading Microformat Records into the Online Catalog." *Technical Services Quarterly* 11, no. 1 (1993): 29–41.

Wells, Kathleen L. "Retrospective Conversion: Through the Looking Glass." *RTSD Newsletter* 12, no. 1 (winter 1987): 10–11.

Weston, Rusty. "It's Hard to Buck Outsourcing Tide." *PC Week* (July 15, 1996): 1, 105.

Whitacre, Cynthia M. "OCLC's TECHPRO Service." *Serials Review* 20, no. 3 (1994): 77–78.

White, Herbert S. "What Price Salami? The Federal Process of Contracting Out Libraries." *Library Journal* 113 (January 1988): 58–59.

Wiegand, Wayne A. "The Politics of Cultural Identity." *American Libraries* 29 (January 1998): 80–82.

Wilhoit, Karen. "Outsourcing Cataloging at Wright State University." *Serials Review* 20, no. 3 (1994): 70–73.

Wilson, Karen A. "Outsourcing Copy Cataloging and Physical Processing: A Review of Blackwell's Outsourcing Services for the J. Hugh Jackson Library at Stanford University." *Library Resources & Technical Services* 39 (October 1995): 359–83.

Wilson, Karen A., and Marylou Colver, eds. *Outsourcing Library Technical Services Operations: Practices in Public, Academic, and Special Libraries.* Chicago, IL: American Library Association, 1997.

Winters, Barbara A. "Catalog Outsourcing at Wright State University: Implications for Acquisitions Managers." *Library Acquisitions* 18, no. 4 (1994): 367–73.

Wittenberg, Charles R. "The Approval Plan: An Idea Whose Time Has Gone? And Come Again?" *Library Acquisitions* 12, no. 2 (1988): 239–42.

Womack, Kay, et al. "An Approval Plan Vendor Review: The Organization and Process." *Library Acquisitions* 12, no. 3/4 (1988): 363–78.

Younger, Jennifer A. "After Cutter: Authority Control in the Twenty-first Century." *Library Resources & Technical Services* 39, no. 2 (April 1995): 133–41.

Index

◀━━━